THE ESSENTIAL GUIDE TO HIKING IN THE UNITED STATES

THE ESSENTIAL GUIDE TO
HIKING IN THE UNITED STATES

CHARLES COOK

MICHAEL KESEND PUBLISHING
NEW YORK

In memory of my mother and father

The Essential Guide to Hiking in the United States
Copyright © 1992 by Charles Cook

Cover Design: Kirschner Caroff Design Inc.
Book Design: Jackie Schuman
Map Preparation: Jackie Schuman & Charles Cook

Library of Congress Cataloging-in-Publication Data
Cook, Charles, 1945–
    The essential guide to hiking in the United States /
    Charles Cook p. cm.
    Includes bibliographical references (p.   ) and index.
    ISBN 0-935576-41-X
    1. Hiking – United States – Guide-books.   2. United States –
Description and travel – 1981 – Guide-books.
I. Title, II. Title: Hiking in the United States.
GV199.4.C66   1992   92-34801
917.3 – dc20   CIP

CONTENTS

*Map of the United States showing major
national trails appears on page 54*

PREFACE

This is a book for hikers, would-be hikers, and anyone else who has ever felt an inclination or desire to venture out into nature or the wilderness on foot. I hope it will contribute to your enjoyment of the outdoors, and perhaps help expand your horizons regarding the incredible range of hiking opportunities that exist throughout this country.

Ever since a friend introduced me to the activity over twenty years ago, hiking has had a marked effect on my own life. I'd have to say that hiking has positively affected my outlook, my awareness of nature and the earth, my level of health and fitness, and my life direction. For over a decade it's also been the center of my work life, as I take groups on hikes and wilderness trips throughout most of the year. The rewards have been immeasurable.

At the same time, as with other activities, hiking doesn't seem to be for everyone. It requires varying amounts of effort, a minimal level of fitness (or more), and can involve challenges and occasional discomforts. Those who enjoy exercise and who love walking will take to it most readily.

By a recent estimate over 41 million Americans hiked last year. Hiking continues to grow in popularity, and for good reason. The potential benefits and pleasures are many. If you're new to hiking and ready to give it a try, be prepared to find your life enriched in more ways than you might have imagined.

Part I of this book offers a complete look at the essentials of hiking. This section should be especially useful to beginners. The focus is on day hiking, and everything that's involved in this activity. Overnight trips involve a number of special considerations which are not addressed here. A number of books are currently available on the subject of backpacking and camping, and such sources should be consulted before embarking on an overnight trip.

Some of the information in Part I may be helpful to experienced hikers as well. Take a look at this section if you haven't hiked in all climates or areas of the country, or if time has passed since you've been on the trails. Some hiking resources presented in this part of the book might also be useful to you.

Part II comprises the bulk of the book. This section offers a guide to major trails and hiking areas in all fifty states, along with some resources for each state. Few of us have hiked in all of the states or are aware of the full range of possibilities, and this is the first time such a comprehensive listing has been available for the entire country in a single volume. I hope it will be of help to you in discovering new places to visit and explore.

My original intention was to present an exhaustive listing of hiking areas and trails in the United States, which soon proved to be an impossible task for a single volume. However, in this book you'll find a thorough listing of major trails and important hiking areas throughout the country, along with many smaller and lesser known locations which have substantial trail networks. A discussion of the criteria that were used in making selections is offered at the beginning of Part II.

Have I visited every one of these areas and hiked all the trails? The answer is no. That would probably take a lifetime or more to accomplish. Still, during the past two decades I've traveled in four-fifths of the states, and hiked many thousands of miles of trails. I've visited a substantial number of the areas listed here, including most of our major National Parks and a number of National Forests. My experience has been most extensive in the eastern United States, where I've walked the Appalachian Trail and some other major trails end-to-end, and explored a great many eastern parks and other wild areas.

Aside from my own personal experience, the primary sources of information for Part II came directly from the locations themselves. I am grateful for the often extremely detailed literature and maps sent by our National Parks, National Forests, countless state parks and forests, state information agencies, and trail organizations. Without these materials and other generous assistance this project would have been impossible. Additional information and perspectives were obtained from an assortment of sources, including some of the numerous trail guidebooks available for many parts of the country.

I wish you good reading. After you have the information you need, don't let anything stand in the way of getting out there and hiking! In spite of our planet's and country's current environmental problems, and the fact that some of our natural areas are in trouble, there remains a great deal of beautiful wild land in many parts of the United States for us to enjoy.

I believe our country and world would benefit greatly if nature became more a part of our lives, if we better knew the perspective and balance that the natural world can teach us. Certainly we have much to gain personally from spending time in nature and wilderness. Hiking is one superb means of doing so. I hope you'll have many rewarding days on the trails!

INTRODUCTION

Few activities are healthier or more natural for us than walking. Human beings are built to walk, and most of us are able to do so with relative ease and efficiency. Walking often plays such an integral part in our daily lives that the ability may be taken for granted, yet it can be a source of the greatest enjoyment, satisfaction, and fulfillment.

Walking is especially rewarding when you have ample time and space and attractive surroundings to walk in. While you may enjoy it anywhere, even in the most congested urban areas, some people think the best walking of all begins when you leave streets and sidewalks behind and venture out into the wilder places.

When you walk for an extended time or distance in the natural world, the realm of mountains and wilderness, the activity is usually referred to as hiking. It's a purposeful kind of walking. Your purpose in hiking might be exercise, exploration, recreation, contact with nature, pleasure.

On a hike you typically follow marked or unmarked trails for at least a few miles, and sometimes much farther. A hike can range from easy walking over nearly level land to strenuous trail-climbing in mountainous terrain. You may hike in a slow and leisurely fashion, stopping frequently, or keep a much brisker pace. If you maintain a steady stride for some distance it's likely to amount to quite an aerobic workout.

The easiest trails are usually found in lowland areas. An easy trail might be hilly, but changes in elevation will be minor and the footing relatively free of obstacles. Moderate (intermediate-level) mountain trails tend to be more rugged. You may have to pick your way among rocks and tree roots, and elevation changes will require some extra exertion. The most difficult trails can be quite steep and challenging. You might have to climb over boulders and perhaps engage in some "rock scrambling," which demands considerable agility and balance.

You may go hiking with a group, with a friend or two, or alone. By yourself you have the most freedom—to find your own pace, take rest breaks as you choose, and hike as far as you wish—but going alone does entail some greater risks. Sharing a hike with others can add richness to the experience. Something in the process seems to cement friendships, and it often adds up to a memorable day.

Like most other wilderness activities, hiking can offer a sense of adventure. Even though potential dangers are few and rarely encountered, the unknown and unexpected often await you up the trail. Most experiences will tend to be positive, to be sure—but no matter how well prepared you are or how familiar with an area, it's impossible to forecast just what you'll see or discover. You might encounter the fury of a sudden storm, or come upon a scene of almost astonishing beauty, or find yourself face to face with a moose. This unpredictability can lend an edge of excitement to the day.

Hiking "grounds" you and utterly immerses you in the natural environment. Few activities bring a person more intimately in contact with nature. Many who are caught up in the demands of civilized life find this aspect especially attractive. If you hike a good deal you're likely to find yourself developing a feeling of greater connectedness with the earth beneath your feet, a deeper sense of personal relationship to the planet.

Hiking provides a true feast for the senses. While exercising in the fresh mountain air and sunshine, in the midst of often splendid scenery, your pores and senses slowly open up to soak it all in. Not every place is spectacular, but a sublime beauty and an incredible array of life-forms can be found in virtually any natural area. And some regions are indeed stunning—with soaring peaks and plunging cliffs, wild rivers and roaring waterfalls, shimmering clear-water lakes and mountain meadows filled with wild-flowers. Photographs or words can never quite do it all justice. There's no substitute for going on foot and experiencing the wilderness firsthand.

Hiking offers you a way of unwinding, letting go. It's often a pleasure to rest when you reach an especially scenic spot. The quiet, the soothing sounds of wind and water, the beauty of the environment can draw you into a state of deep relaxation and serenity. It's not surprising that many foot travelers experience a "hiker's high" in the wilderness, inspired by the presence of such splendid surroundings, witnessing nature at her most magnificent. You're likely to return from such a trip feeling refreshed and renewed, more fully alive and complete. . . .

HOW TO USE THIS BOOK

If you're new to hiking or relatively inexperienced, or could use a brush-up, read Part I first. Here you'll find information about all the essentials of hiking, including how to get started, how to locate a group, and what equipment and clothing you'll need for a day hike. Also discussed are such matters as planning a trip, avoiding getting lost, and minimizing your impact on the environment.

When you're ready to plan a trip, the information in Part II will give you a huge number of options to choose from. First, look at your own state and perhaps nearby states. All are listed in alphabetical order. You'll find "Major Trails" (if there happen to be any in your state), "Best Hiking Areas," and in some cases "Other Recommended Locations."

If a particular trail or hiking area sounds interesting, you'll need to get additional information before preparing to visit. A trail guidebook or booklet should be obtained, if available, along with a detailed hiking map of the area or trails. Using the address or phone number provided, contact the appropriate park agency or trail association and request information.

The "Hiking Resources" section at the end of each chapter provides a listing of some currently available hiking guidebooks. These may be obtained from local bookstores or sporting goods stores, by mail from some trail associations, or from mail-order companies which specialize in such guidebooks (see *Some Hiking Resources* at the end of Part I for a listing of mail-order companies). Not all existing guidebooks will be found in the "Hiking Resources" sections. There are self-published and unpublicized trail books available for some parts of the country, commonly sold by hiking clubs or trail associations. When you contact such nonprofit groups, enclosing a self-addressed stamped envelope will be appreciated.

If you'd like to thoroughly explore all of the hiking possibilities in your state (or any other state) or locality, contact agencies and trail associations listed in the "Hiking Resources" section for each state. They may have information on trails or areas which were not included in this book. Some of the comprehensive hiking guidebooks available for certain states may also give you leads to other interesting places to visit. Finally, for each state there's an address and phone number to contact for a "State Highway Map and Travel Information," to aid you in getting to the places and trails you're interested in exploring.

PART I

HIKING ESSENTIALS

ONE

Getting Started

Taking up a new activity can be a pleasurable process. It's great to discover something you enjoy doing which adds something positive to your life. Yet some aspects of a wilderness-oriented activity like hiking can be a bit daunting at first when you're a beginner—and along with the potential rewards there are a few possible pitfalls to steer clear of. For maximum enjoyment and safety it's wise to learn some basics before plunging in.

Doing a little reading on the subject can be helpful. Aside from the present book, which should provide a good starting point, it's worth looking at other books which focus on hiking and related outdoor/wilderness topics. There are also several magazines available which include information about hiking (see *Some Hiking Resources* at the end of Part I).

In addition, a number of clubs and trail associations publish newsletters with useful hiking information. You'll find addresses for many of these organizations in Part II under "Hiking Resources" for each state.

Going With A Group

A useful step to take in getting started—and enjoyable in its own right—is to go hiking with a group. Throughout the country there are many organizations, formal and informal, which sponsor hikes. These include clubs and various non-profit groups, as well as some outfitters and other for-profit businesses. In certain areas there

are also independent professional guides who take individuals and groups hiking.

Going with others under the guidance of an experienced leader provides the opportunity to learn about hiking in a relatively risk-free fashion. You can find out whether the activity is right for you, and hopefully have a good time in the process.

It's important to avoid signing up for a hike which may be too ambitious for a beginner. Any activity can be spoiled by overdoing it to the point of exhaustion the first time. Even if you're in good shape it's wise to "ease into" hiking, allowing the body and muscles a chance to adjust to a somewhat different form of exercise.

If you're fortunate enough to have a friend or friends who are seasoned hikers, you probably have an ideal way to learn the ins and outs of hiking. The right friend—someone who hasn't forgotten what it's like to be a beginner—can be a wonderful help in teaching the essentials and getting you started on the right foot.

Finding A Group

The addresses of some organized hiking groups will be found in the state-by-state resource listings in Part II of this book. If no group is listed for your locality, it may be worth asking around a bit. Some hiking groups don't do much to publicize themselves. Check bulletin boards, especially at sporting goods or outdoor specialty stores. Also, many national outdoor and environmental organizations have local chapters which offer hikes. Try writing the headquarters of such organizations to inquire whether there are chapters near you.

Hiking Clubs

Many hiking groups are organized as clubs. Joining a club is an inexpensive and enjoyable way to get involved in hiking. Like all organizations, clubs vary a good deal. Some are quite serious about hiking, while others have primarily a social focus. There will probably be differences in the frequency and variety of trips, format and policies followed, leadership, and in the kinds of people attracted.

Most clubs charge an annual membership fee, and day hikes are usually available for free or at nominal cost. Participants must usually provide their own transportation or share expenses.

It's probably worth looking into more than one club, if that's an option in the area where you live. Request literature and ask questions. Enclose a self-addressed stamped envelope when writing, since clubs usually operate on small budgets.

Outdoor Businesses and Guides

In some parts of the country, outfitters and independent guides conduct hikes. Going with a guide or outdoor business means paying a fee for each trip, but transportation and additional services are usually provided. Sometimes memberships are offered, reducing the cost if you're a regular participant. The best of such businesses and guides will provide a thoroughly enjoyable and professionally-run trip.

As with clubs, the nature and quality of the experience could vary considerably. Investigate and ask questions before signing up.

Hiking Alone

Hiking alone is not for the inexperienced. There are too many things that could go wrong or blunders you could make with potentially dangerous consequences, such as getting lost and being forced to spend a night in the woods without adequate gear or clothing. The wilderness is a very different world from the one most of us have grown up in, a realm with different ways and rules, which on occasion can be merciless to the uninitiated or unprepared. It's foolhardy to go far into the wilderness alone until you have developed considerable skill and experience in following trails, using map and compass, and taking care of yourself in the wilds.

Many organizations advise against ever hiking alone, for reasons of safety. A lone hiker who has an accident could be in serious trouble indeed. Yet some of us do hike alone, taking the greatest care to avoid any possible mishap. There's risk involved, but it's much reduced when you have the necessary know-how. We can all benefit from some solitude at times, and solitude out in nature can be a truly special experience.

If and when you do go out alone, it's always advisable to let someone know exactly where you're going and when you'll be back (so if you didn't return as scheduled, others would have an idea of where to search for you).

Physical Preparation

Hiking makes some physical demands, of course. Even an easy hike can involve walking several miles over hilly terrain, requiring effort and exertion at times.

Anyone who is physically active and fit is not likely to find hiking difficult. Those who jog, run, cycle, swim, or engage in other vigorous aerobic activity should take to it especially quickly, and won't need any special preparation. It's to be expected that your muscles may be a bit sore after the first couple of hikes, since the body must move in some new ways.

If you are relatively sedentary or not in good condition but would still like to try hiking, it's advisable to first do a little physical preparation—to embark on walking or other exercise programs and work up to a distance of a few miles on ordinary ground before attempting a substantial hike. Going far into the wilderness is risky if you're not fit. Overextending yourself could mean exhaustion and difficulty in getting back out, plus a greater chance of injury.

In general the more walking you do, the easier hiking is likely to be. Participating in aerobic exercise on a regular basis can't be recommended too highly. This is certain to make a healthy contribution to your life and will undoubtedly increase your enjoyment of hiking.

On the hike itself, just before beginning it's good to do a little stretching to loosen up muscles and joints—especially in any areas where you might feel stiff. You'll then be able to move more freely and comfortably, reducing the likelihood of an injury.

What to Bring: Hiking Gear

Each of the following items is appropriate for a day hike, whether one is day hiking from home or from a wilderness campsite. It makes sense to be conscientious about bringing these things along for maximum safety and comfort while in the wilderness.

Additional items which pertain solely to camping and backpacking (sleeping bags, tents, etc.) are not discussed here. There are many books available about backpacking and camping, and these sources should be consulted for detailed information about overnight equipment, and how to camp safely in the wilds.

At the end of this chapter you'll find a checklist which summarizes what to bring.

Hiking Boots

The protection of your feet needs to be given top priority when hiking. Foot pain or discomfort can quickly take the fun out of the activity, and an injury could prevent you from walking at all. Hiking boots are designed to provide comfort and support for the feet and ankles while walking on rough ground. Wearing them will reduce the wear and tear on your feet and minimize the risk of an injury.

Typically five to seven inches high, hiking boots are usually amply padded and offer minimal flexibility at the ankles. Most have a rugged lug sole (somewhat like a tire tread) which will provide good traction on a variety of surfaces. The sole is rather rigid, which makes the process of maintaining balance while walking on rocks or stones much easier. Boots will also protect the feet from any mud or water on the trail.

A minority of hikers are known to "get away with" wearing sneakers or other soft shoes on even the most rugged hiking trails. Some resist wearing boots because of the belief that they're too heavy or uncomfortable (which at one time was more likely to be true than today), or because of a bad experience with poorly fitted boots. Some are unaware of the risks. Without boots it's much easier to twist an ankle or sustain a more serious injury by slipping or stumbling and falling. If the trail is wet, sneakers will be soaked almost instantly, and in cool or cold weather this will be uncomfortable and occasionally even dangerous.

While hiking boots are considered to be essential on the more rugged trails, they are less so on easier trails. If you're hiking strictly on soft earth or sand, they're not really necessary at all. Any rubber-soled shoe or boot will suffice. Some of us still choose to wear hiking boots on easy trails, since an occasional small stone or tree root could still cause us to stumble unexpectedly. Wearing boots is always the safest way to go.

Hiking boots are traditionally classified into three categories: lightweight, mediumweight, and heavyweight. Heavyweight boots are not designed for ordinary hiking (they're made for mountaineering, which requires the most rigid boot possible). Mediumweight boots provide substantial support with quite limited flexibility. These are especially appropriate for carrying heavier loads, as in backpacking, but are also suitable for day hiking.

The most attractive choice for day hikers is a lightweight boot, which is especially flexible. In recent years there's been quite a revolution in boot design, and some boots are now far lighter than those in the past. Previously, breaking in boots was a major task, and the weight of the boots as well as the difficulty of breaking them in were often intimidating to beginners. Many of today's lightweight boots fortunately require little or no breaking in, and are often supremely comfortable. However, a few of the very lightest now available are not much more than glorified sneakers, providing little if any ankle support. These are not adequate for most hiking. It's important to have boots which don't flex too easily at the ankles.

In buying boots the most important thing of all is finding a good fit. Some aspiring hikers decide on boots based on their appearance or the recommendations of a friend or salesperson, take only a few moments to try them on, and discover later while hiking that the boots don't fit properly. Spend as much time as necessary in the store walking around with the boots on. If you decide to buy, wear them at home a while before taking them on a hike (many stores will accept returns if the boots haven't been worn outside). If there's any doubt about the fit, don't buy them. Try different boots, another store, or return some other time. Comfortable boots can help make hiking a joy, while poorly fitted (blister-or-pain-producing) boots could very easily spoil the whole experience.

It's best to buy hiking boots from a store which specializes in top quality gear and has knowl-edgeable salespeople. A good salesperson can help a lot with the process. It's important to have plenty of space in front for the toes so that when you're walking steeply downhill, your toes won't bang against the (usually) hard inside front of the boot. Try kicking the floor to see if your toes hit the front. They shouldn't. At the same time, there mustn't be too much space around the ankles, or your foot may constantly slip up and down at the heel, leading to general discomfort and blisters. Be sure to wear heavy hiking socks when trying on boots (some stores will have "try-on socks" available).

Remember that no brand of boot will fit everyone. The shape of your foot may not conform to that of the boot, and your usual size might not provide a good fit. Keep trying different boots until you find the right one.

Most boots require some maintenance to sustain a long life. Leather will eventually dry out and usually requires the application of wax or oil to avoid cracking. Some boots are reasonably waterproof when purchased, while others will require an application of waterproofing (some boots are more waterproof than others, but none will keep the water out indefinitely if you spend an extended time in the rain). The procedures vary depending on the particular boots and the materials used in making them. A salesperson will usually have information about caring properly for the boots being purchased.

Other types of boots are sometimes used for hiking. These include "work boots," army boots, and various types of outdoor boots. Some are rather similar in construction to hiking boots, and may be perfectly adequate. Most, however, do not offer as much ankle support (there may only be thin leather around the ankle). Certain boots are insulated for cold weather, which means they're probably too hot for use during the warmer seasons. Boots that come up much higher than the ankles may not be comfortable for hiking. If you already own boots which you believe might suffice, there's certainly no harm in carefully venturing out on a hiking trail to see how well they do.

Good hiking boots will give years of service and hundreds or even thousands of miles of pleasure. The best boots are usually somewhat expensive, adding up to an investment, although some of the new nylon lightweights are quite reasonable in price. Top quality hiking boots generally run in the range of $100 to $200. Some of the lightweights are available for as little as $50 to $75 or less. It may be possible to find a bargain, but inexpensive boots are often on the flimsy side, and in most cases can't be expected to last very long.

In recent years there has been some concern about the environmental impact of hiking boots, especially on the more fragile high mountain trails. Lug soles may contribute to tearing up such trails, particularly when wet and muddy, leading to erosion and possibly irreversible damage. One alternative is to have "low impact" soles with a minimal tread put on your boots. These are not often found in stores at the present time, but are sometimes available by special order. Another responsible solution is to choose different footwear when you'll be walking on the most fragile trails. Probably more of us need to avoid such trails altogether in favor of those which can sustain human impact more successfully.

RAINWEAR

In much of the country rain must always be considered a possibility. Rain sometimes appears suddenly and unexpectedly, especially in mountain areas. Temperatures may drop dramatically during a storm, high winds often arise, and the rain itself can be quite cold. A hiker without rainwear during such conditions could be in trouble. In the worst possible case, getting soaked and badly chilled might mean life-threatening hypothermia.

Those of us who hike in a variety of mountain and wilderness settings generally get in the habit of *always* bringing raingear along. The exception, of course, is when you're hiking in the desert or other areas which have little or no precipitation. In all other places and circumstances it's best to carry rainwear, regardless of how positive the weather forecast or how beautiful the morning sky. Sooner or later you'll find yourself caught in an unpredicted storm, and having the rainwear along will make life a lot safer and more comfortable.

Many people place an unreasonable amount of trust in weather forecasts, and this is a habit well worth breaking. Accurate predictions are especially difficult to obtain for mountain areas, where the weather is often extremely changeable. It's good to pay attention to any warnings about severe weather, but otherwise it's best to have few expectations and be ready for all possible weather. There are many days when rain is predicted which turn out to be quite dry and sunny in the wilderness, and other days when rain materializes without a hint of warning in the forecast.

In choosing raingear you have a number of options. Among the most popular choices and very much recommended is the nylon poncho, with hood attached. This garment has the advantage of being loose fitting and "air-conditioned," protects the body down to the knees, and can double as an emergency tarp when opened up. The only minor disadvantage is that in high winds, which might be encountered on an open mountain ridge or other exposed area, a poncho may snap and capture the wind like a sail.

A good long-lasting poncho will generally run from $20 to $40. Inexpensive vinyl ponchos are available for as little as $5 or less. The latter are O.K. for emergency protection, and may last a few times, but could easily come apart in a strong wind or when snagged on a branch. It's worth buying a better quality poncho.

Nylon rain suits, which include a jacket with hood as well as pants, are also available. A rain suit provides more complete protection from the rain than a poncho, but has the disadvantage that it's less air-conditioned. If you're hiking in warm weather, a rain suit may feel hot. Prices run from $35 to $75 or more. There are also inexpensive vinyl rain suits, but these are undependable.

For those who prefer ponchos and want better

protection for their legs, rain chaps are a convenient item to own. Each chap is a separate nylon leg which attaches to one's belt. Chaps allow for more passage of air than rain pants. They're especially recommended when cold and wet weather is within the realm of possibility.

The age-old problem of rainwear breathability was supposedly solved back in the 1970s with the introduction of several new fabrics, the most popular of which is Gore-Tex. These "breathe-able but waterproof" materials permit moisture from perspiration to pass out through the fabric, but prevent rain from coming in. They may often work as advertised, but reports from the field over the years have been mixed. A number of enthusiastic supporters firmly endorse these products. Others question their worth, claiming that the garments often leak when they become dirty or a bit worn. In any case, such items are far from inexpensive, with rain jackets alone usu-ally running $100 to $200. The final word on the value of these products doesn't seem to be in yet.

Nylon is normally the fabric of choice for hiking rainwear, making for a sturdy, light-weight, and compact item when stuffed into a day pack. Be sure to avoid heavy rubberized rain garments and other products which are bulky and cumbersome to carry.

All rainwear eventually begins to leak when it has received a good deal of use, and needs to be periodically replaced. The life of the rainwear will be prolonged if you refrain from using it for other purposes, such as to sit on (having a separate nylon or plastic sheet or pad is a good solution for times when the ground is wet). Raingear also needs to be kept away from such possible hazards as thorn bushes, sharp objects, and sources of intense heat like hot radiators or campfires.

WATER BOTTLE OR CANTEEN

It's essential to drink water while hiking. Since any water encountered along the way may not be safe, it usually must be brought along. One can also boil, filter, or use tablets to purify water, but for day hiking the safest and simplest bet is to carry an adequate supply for the day.

Your need for water varies considerably, depending on previous intake of water, the air temperature and humidity, whether you're hiking in direct sunlight or shade, what condition you're in, and how strenuously you're exercising. Insufficient intake of water can have serious ramifications, especially in hot weather. It's wise to carry an ample supply, more than you think you'll require.

Individual needs naturally differ, but for most people one quart or liter may suffice for a day of easy to moderate hiking in cool or cold weather. In warmer temperatures and for more strenuous hiking, a minimum of two to three quarts or liters is highly recommended, and a gallon or more for difficult, long-distance, hot-weather hiking. However much you bring, it's still possible to become a bit dehydrated, and thirst alone won't always tell you how much your body needs. To avoid the potentially unhealthy consequences of dehydration, it's a good idea to drink plenty of water throughout the evening following a hike. Incidentally, most headaches which occur during or after hikes are due to dehydration.

A large assortment of water bottles, canteens, and other liquid carriers are available. Plastic water bottles are the lightest and most popular for that reason. Useful sizes for hiking include 1, 1½, and 2 liters. The better quality bottles are virtually leakproof and very sturdy. Some give off a slight taste, but there are now clear plastic bottles on the market which seem to have elim-inated that problem. Traditional metal canteens are also still available. These are often nearly indestructible, but somewhat heavier than the plastic variety.

In warm or hot weather you can put your water bottle or canteen in the freezer overnight, if you wish, in order to have ice water for the hike. When freezing water in advance, be sure to leave some air space in the container (water expands when freezing and may crack the bottle if it's full to the brim).

In cold weather some people prefer to bring a thermos along with tea or coffee or some other hot drink. The only drawback of a thermos is that it's rather bulky. Be sure that any thermos brought is completely unbreakable.

Some hikers carry other liquids such as juices along as well. It goes without saying that any juice or other liquid should be brought in an unbreakable container (a glass bottle inside a day pack could shatter if the pack is dropped or banged against a rock).

DAY PACK

A day pack is a small frameless backpack which has enough room for everything you need to bring on a day hike: lunch, liquid, rainwear, extra clothing, plus a few small items. A day pack is the most appropriate way to carry these things, as it leaves the arms and hands free and doesn't interfere with movement.

A shoulder bag might do for a short hike, but it will usually be less comfortable than a day pack. Attempting to carry anything in your hands tends to be tiring and cumbersome. Walking is easiest and most enjoyable with both hands free, and you may need to use your hands at times for support or balance.

Day packs come in assorted shapes and sizes. Many have multiple pockets or compartments, which provide a means of organizing the items you bring. Virtually all day packs are coated for waterproofness, but never trust that a pack will keep all water or moisture out. Any items such as

clothing which must be kept dry are best wrapped in plastic bags. If you use a poncho it will cover the day pack, providing better protection from the rain.

Day pack prices generally run from $20 to $45. Less expensive day packs are available, but these are typically of lower quality and less sturdy or durable. A good pack will give several years or more of service.

Any day pack that you're considering buying should be tried on. Most packs will be comfortable, but the particular positioning of the shoulder straps and other features of design may not be right for your back.

There are also many bigger packs on the market. Medium-size "weekender packs" are made for light overnight use, and full-size external or internal frame packs are designed for extended trips. These are unnecessarily large and inappropriate for day hiking.

OTHER ITEMS

Map and Compass

It's vital to carry a map and compass, especially when hiking alone. In a group, one or more persons must have these items and know how to use them. Entering the wilderness without map and compass is asking for trouble, as the potential for getting lost is greatly increased. Carrying a guidebook is also recommended, if one is available for the area visited.

First Aid Kit

Bringing a first aid kit should be considered mandatory. In a larger group one or more participants must have a kit. Serious injuries are rare while hiking, but minor cuts or scrapes may occur. Items to be brought should include bandages, adhesive tape, and antiseptic cream or liquid—plus an elastic Ace-type bandage in case of a twisted ankle or a knee problem. Moleskin and molefoam are also important for dealing with blister problems (see Chapter 6 for more about these items).

Insect Repellent

It makes sense to always bring bug repellent along in warm weather, preferably a small container of concentrated repellent. The presence of bugs is dependent on such factors as air temperature and recent rainfall, and can't necessarily be predicted. At times the repellent will prove essential for your comfort.

The effective ingredient in most commercial preparations is "Deet" (Diethyl-meta-toluamide). Those repellents with the highest concentrations of Deet may be the most effective, but some people who use it have allergic reactions to the chemical, and the overall safety of such repellents is open to question. There are now a number of all-natural bug repellents on the market which may provide a healthier alternative.

Sunscreen and Sun Hat

It's important to avoid extensive exposure of your skin to the sun. In forested areas you're likely to receive relatively little direct sunlight, so in such environments there's no need for concern. In sunny, open terrain (such as in the desert or above treeline in the mountains) you may need to use every means of protection possible, including sunscreen lotion and a wide-brimmed hat.

Regarding the need for sunglasses there's a difference of opinion. Except perhaps for snow hiking in the sunshine, some experts believe that sunglasses are unnecessary for healthy eyes, which have the capacity to adjust to widely varying amounts of sunlight without harm. Others feel that sunglasses should be worn. If you'll be hiking extensively in open areas and think you'll be in need of sunglasses, bring them along.

Whistle

A small whistle is recommended in case there is an emergency, such as getting lost. A series of three blasts is the normal signal for help. The whistle should be used only for emergencies and not for play (any use could be interpreted by others as a call for help).

Flashlight with Spare Batteries

This is an item which you usually bring on an overnight trip. A flashlight can occasionally prove important on a day trip as well. It's possible to be seriously delayed because of underestimating the distance to be hiked, having some

---

CHECKLIST OF GEAR FOR A DAY HIKE

(1) WHEN HIKING WITH AN ORGANIZED GROUP

Hiking boots
Day pack
Plastic water bottle or canteen (filled)
Waterproof poncho
Extra sweater or heavy shirt
Lunch & snack foods
Toilet paper
Plastic litter bag

In summer or warm weather:
Extra water
Bug repellent
Sunscreen or lotion
Sun hat

In cool or cold weather:
Plenty of additional warm clothing

(2) WHEN HIKING ALONE OR WITH FRIENDS:

Bring all of the above plus:
Map
Trail guidebook
Compass
First aid kit
Whistle
Flashlight (with spare batteries & bulb)
Pocket knife
Matches
Watch

(See Chapter 3 for complete clothing checklist)

---

difficulty following a trail, or perhaps discovering late in the day that a critical section of trail is closed or flooded—and that you have to return the long way. In other words, sooner or later you may find yourself on the trail after dark.

Without a flashlight you could end up spending a night in the woods, possibly unprepared, and in cold weather this would be a serious situation. If you're hiking alone it's essential to bring a flashlight on all trips, along with spare alkaline (long-lasting) batteries and also an extra bulb. A small lightweight flashlight is most appropriate.

Toilet Paper

It's sensible to carry a small amount of toilet paper or other tissue in case nature calls while you're in the wilderness. On occasion there will be an outhouse or other facility which can be utilized, but more often you'll need to use the woods.

Knife

Having some kind of knife for practical use is recommended, although it's not so necessary if you're with a group. Swiss Army Knives have been popular for years, and the fancier ones include practically a full toolkit of useful items (scissors, small screwdriver, can opener, etc.). A simple knife with folding blade is adequate.

Matches

It's a good idea to bring matches along, especially when hiking alone or with just a friend or two. Should you somehow manage to get lost or injured and be forced to spend a night out, being able to start a fire for warmth might be vital. The smoke from a fire could also help any rescuers to locate you. Bring waterproof matches, or keep them sealed in plastic bags or a waterproof container.

Walking Stick

Some hikers like to use a staff or walking stick, which can aid in balancing. Whether to carry a stick or not is a matter of personal preference. A minority of hikers have such items, but some swear by them. Others find they would rather have both hands free while walking.

A situation where a walking stick has particular proven value is for stream crossings. When it's necessary to cross on rocks or wade through water, balance can almost always be maintained better with a stick.

Attractive staffs and sticks are available for sale in some stores and by mail order. It's also easy to procure a makeshift stick on the trail when you need one by finding a fallen branch of suitable size.

FOOD

If you're just going out for the day, lunch will usually be the main meal on the trail. Presumably you'll have breakfast prior to leaving for the hike, and supper or dinner at the end of the day. A substantial breakfast is highly recommended, since you'll be making some energy demands on your body.

It's also important to have an adequate intake of food during the hike itself. A day of exercise is not the appropriate time to fast. Food is required to fuel the body, and on a long hike many calories are burned through exertion. If the day is cold, additional calories may be needed to keep

you sufficiently warm. Along with lunch it's good to have some other foods to snack on, especially if you'll be hiking for many hours.

While almost anything may be brought on a day trip, the most perishable foods (soft fresh fruit, for example) are best avoided in warm or hot weather. Aside from the ever popular sandwich, items such as cheese and crackers, small tins of sardines or other fish, and "gorp" (trail mix of nuts and dried fruit) are very suitable. In the proper container it's possible to bring things like salad or yogurt.

It's a good idea to pack all food in sturdy

double plastic bags and/or plastic containers, to avoid possible leakage inside the day pack. Self-sealing bags are especially popular for this purpose.

A few hikers bring a small stove for heating soup or other food for lunch, but most of us are reasonably content with a cold lunch (and while a stove is usually essential for an overnight camping trip, even a ministove will take up a good amount of space in a day pack).

ITEMS TO LEAVE AT HOME

Radios

Radios of all kinds have found their way into the woods, much to the chagrin of many of us who love the sounds of nature and who enjoy vacations from man-made noise. If you play a radio you'll obliterate all of the natural sounds around you, and probably annoy other hikers who are visiting the wilderness in search of peace and quiet. Those of us who love music can surely live without it for a few hours or more and benefit from the relative silence.

Walkman-type radios are obviously less intrusive to others. If you choose to bring such a radio, however, you'll still be cheating yourself of first-hand contact with nature. Some bring radios because of a fear of boredom. Yet with time, most of us discover there's really no reason to ever be truly bored when out in the wilderness, a place where the pleasures are simple but as rich as any in this world.

Pets

Domestic animals don't really belong in the wilds, and have the potential for getting into trouble there. Unleashed dogs sometimes harass or harm wildlife, and dogs that bark and present threatening behavior to passing hikers are obviously not appreciated. On the other hand, it's true that few people will raise objections to meeting a quiet, well-behaved pet on the trail.

Dogs and other pets are not permitted in some parks and wilderness areas, but are allowed in others (sometimes only on a leash). Where pets may be legally brought, it's still important for owners to realize their responsibility to make sure the pet doesn't damage vegetation, contaminate water sources (the animal's waste should always be buried), disrupt the peace and quiet sought by many hikers, or tangle with wildlife. If this isn't possible, it's best to leave your pet at home.

PURCHASING HIKING GEAR

Whenever possible it's recommended to buy hiking equipment from a specialty store which carries only the highest quality merchandise. Most regular sporting goods stores will also have at least a small selection of hiking gear, although quality may vary. Check local yellow pages for listings under hiking, camping, or sporting goods.

Be cautious about buying from some discount outlets which sell only low-priced gear. If a canteen springs a big leak or a poncho self-destructs in a storm, it could be inconvenient or worse. Purchasing well-made, dependable, first-rate gear is always advisable.

In addition to regular stores, there are several major mail order outfits which carry an excellent selection of hiking items. See *Some Hiking Resources* at the end of Part I for a listing of these companies.

THREE

What To Wear: Hiking Clothing

CLOTHING

At the end of this chapter you'll find a checklist which summarizes the clothing that's appropriate to bring on a day hike.

Clothing requirements vary a great deal depending on the season, which part of the country you're hiking in, and local weather and temperature. If it's warm or hot you obviously need little clothing, whereas in the cold your comfort and sometimes even survival are dependent on being adequately dressed.

In many mountain areas the weather is so changeable that it's necessary to be prepared for a wide range of possibilities. It's vital to *always* have extra clothing along, which will provide a safe margin of comfort should it be much cooler than expected. In some of the highest mountains even sleet or snow sometimes falls in summertime. When you're hiking in these areas, warm clothing should never be left at home, regardless of the forecast and how warm or hot it might be at the beginning of the day. Conditions can change rapidly, and without sufficient clothing you could be left dangerously vulnerable.

Layering is the recommended way to dress in cool or cold weather. Rather than bringing one heavy, warm garment, it's better to carry and wear several lighter layers. Each layer traps air and adds additional insulation. As you begin to feel cold or to overheat, you can put on or take off layers accordingly. Your body will let you know when you're overheated or underheated, and it's important to heed these messages. Failing to respond means inviting discomfort or worse.

The best time to put on additional clothing is at the *first sign* of being cold. If you wait till you're really chilled, it'll be much more difficult to warm up. Likewise, when you're starting to sweat and feel more than a hint of overheating, it's time to shed a layer or two. If you wait too long, clothing may get drenched with perspiration—and later on when resting you'll be more susceptible to chilling, especially if the day is windy and cool.

Cotton clothing is very comfortable and understandably favored by many people. Yet cotton has a serious drawback for hiking, namely, that it provides no insulation when wet. If there's any possibility of getting caught in the rain, especially when it's cold, wearing all-cotton clothing is extremely risky. Even in temperatures of 50°-60° F, getting soaked to the skin in cotton clothing could lead to a case of hypothermia. Raingear will normally provide some protection, but in heavy rain it's still difficult to keep the clothing underneath completely dry. If your clothing gets wet it may be impossible to stay warm enough. Even on a dry day, the moisture from perspiration will reduce the insulating ability of cotton clothing.

Wool and synthetics have the great advantage that they *will* provide insulation when wet. Thus, when hiking in most areas, it's wise to always carry or wear some clothing which is partly or entirely made of wool or synthetic materials (such as polypropylene or nylon). It's certainly all right to wear some items of cotton, especially in fair weather, but also having synthetic or wool clothing along is highly recommended—for safety and better protection in case of rain.

Carelessness about dressing for the outdoors is especially prevalent among those without extensive experience. Many of us grow up without paying much attention to the functional nature of clothing, and when we get cold, we're rarely far from a house or apartment or car or other warm place to duck into.

Some men, for instance, are raised to tough it out and ignore discomfort. This can be dangerous in the wilderness. There's no external source of warmth readily available when you're miles from the nearest highway, and you can't always count on your body to generate the necessary heat—especially if you're cold, wet, and tired. On occasion, carelessness about clothing could literally mean one's life.

Hiking Socks

Heavy wool ragg socks have long been the first choice of many hikers, and these socks still have much to recommend them. A heavy sock provides extra cushioning in the boot, giving some additional protection and reducing the impact of each step. Since wool provides warmth when wet, it's especially appropriate to wear in those parts of the country where rain is likely and cool or cold temperatures possible (such conditions are common in many mountain areas, even in the summer). Along with wool, synthetics will likewise furnish some insulation when wet, so these stand next in order of preference.

Since cotton will provide no warmth at all

when wet, many of us avoid cotton socks altogether for hiking. In warm or hot temperatures, cotton is certainly acceptable, but on occasion in the mountains the temperature may drop drastically even on a hot summer day. Aside from possible rain, socks get damp from perspiration while hiking. Having cold feet is never a pleasure, and getting chilled is a condition always worth avoiding.

Many hikers also wear *liner socks*—thinner inner socks which go next to the skin. Liner socks will help diminish any rubbing and friction on the feet—reducing the possibility of blisters or sore spots, and providing a bit of extra warmth in cold weather. These socks are generally available in wool, silk, and various synthetics. Liner socks are especially recommended when you're wearing new boots or hiking on unusually rough trails.

In warm or hot weather your feet may overheat. In such conditions you may want to remove socks and boots whenever you take a break.

Pants

For maximum comfort and freedom of movement it's best to wear pants which are loose-fitting. Although jeans have long been popular for outdoor activities, and will withstand lots of abuse, they have serious disadvantages for hiking. At times you'll need to stretch your legs when hiking uphill or downhill, and jeans are often too constrictive. They're also usually made of cotton, and will absorb a considerable amount of water, making for miserable walking when wet. Amply-cut pants which are at least part synthetic or wool are the recommended choice for hiking.

Shorts

Shorts will give your legs the most amount of freedom, of course. They're especially good for warm or hot weather—the air-conditioned way to go. A drawback of wearing shorts is that your legs are exposed to any available insects, as well as possible unfriendly plants (poison ivy, thorn bushes, etc.) which might lie along the path. Also, some trails are relatively overgrown and bare legs may get scratched as you push your way through the bushes. Shorts are best for wide and well-maintained trails which are not unusually rugged. When in doubt, bring shorts in your day pack and change into them if conditions are suitable.

Underwear

As with other clothing, it's best to avoid all-cotton underwear if you'll be hiking in potentially cool or cold temperatures. Underwear is especially likely to become damp from perspiration, and if it's cotton you'll get chilled much more easily.

Thermal underwear is usually unnecessary for day hiking, except when you are out in below-freezing temperatures. Wearing thermal underwear entails the inconvenience of having to remove other layers of clothing to get to it, which may be necessary if you overheat. It's easier to take off or put on outer layers or garments as needed.

Shirts

A T-shirt by itself may be enough for the upper body when walking in warm weather (although additional clothing should always be brought in case the temperature drops). A regular short-sleeved shirt is O.K., but it's good to bring at least one long-sleeved shirt along as well. At some point you might need to protect your arms from the sun, or perhaps from insects, or from the cold. A heavy wool shirt is appropriate in lower temperatures, and will usually be the equivalent of a sweater in warmth.

Sweaters

A sweater is a suitable item to wear in cooler weather, or to bring along on practically any trip for additional warmth when you need it. Two lighter sweaters are usually preferable to one heavy one, since with thinner layers you can better regulate the amount of insulation needed at any particular time.

Down Vest or Jacket

Down-filled garments are especially desirable because they're quite warm but compress into a small space, and will often fit into your day pack. Down, however, must be kept dry at all costs, so these items should never be worn in the rain. When wet, down will provide little or no insulation. It also takes forever to dry out.

A down vest is a popular alternative to a sweater. Also appropriate in cool or cold weather would be a light down jacket, sometimes called a down sweater, which is essentially a down vest with sleeves. You may not need these items while actually hiking, but if it's a cold day or the temperature drops they'll be useful or even necessary during rest breaks, when your body needs extra insulation. Then again, the temperature might be lower and the wind stronger than expected, and you might require several layers to keep comfortable even while moving.

A heavy down jacket will be too hot for hiking except in extreme cold, and too bulky for the day pack. If possible, avoid any garment which won't stuff or fit into the day pack, including down items which have a thick outer shell (those with a thin nylon shell compress much more easily).

There are also vests and jackets available with synthetic fill. These have the great advantage and safety factor that they'll provide some insulation when wet, but the disadvantage is that they're somewhat bulkier and will not fit so readily in the pack. It's possible to tie an extra item or two of clothing around your waist when walking, but carrying it in the pack is always preferable.

Shell Parka or Windbreaker

A shell parka or windbreaker is a thin garment made of nylon or other material, usually with a hood, and typically water repellent or waterproof. This item is recommended to go over other clothing, especially in cool, windy, or damp weather. A windbreaker or shell parka will provide a good barrier to the wind and limited protection from rain, with a surprising amount of additional warmth for relatively little weight and bulk. It may be worn over many layers or few.

Mittens or Gloves

Hands and other extremities may need some protection even in temperatures which are not very cold—particularly in the rain and wind. Packing at least light mittens or gloves is a good idea if you could encounter temperatures below 50° F or so. Mittens will usually be warmer than gloves. Avoid thin leather gloves, which provide minimal warmth and may wet through quickly.

Cap or Hat

A wool cap is highly recommended for cool or cold weather. A significant amount of heat is lost from an uncovered head. You may feel considerably warmer and more comfortable by covering your head when appropriate. Along with knitted caps, various other types of outdoor hats are also available.

Swimsuit

Swimming can be an appealing option in warm weather when you are hiking near water. If you know there may be a suitable lake or pond or river or stream, you may want to bring a swimsuit along. Otherwise, a pair of shorts and a T-shirt will usually do as a substitute. Skinny-dipping is possible in some areas, but it's not considered acceptable everywhere, and there isn't always privacy. Regulations regarding swimming vary from one locality to another. In many wilderness areas you can swim wherever you wish, but in other areas (smaller parks in particular) swimming may be forbidden or restricted to public beaches.

CHECKLIST OF CLOTHING FOR A DAY HIKE

Hiking socks
Liner socks (optional)
Long pants
Long-sleeved shirt
Extra sweater or heavy shirt
Shell parka or windbreaker

In summer or warm weather:
T-shirt
Shorts (optional)
Swimsuit

In cool or cold weather:
Down vest or jacket
Additional layers
Gloves or mittens
Cap or hat
Thermal underwear (in below-freezing temperatures)

Always bring extra clothing in case conditions are cooler than expected

---

FOUR

Planning a Trip

DECIDING WHERE TO GO

In this country we have an enormous range of possibilities when it comes to choosing where to hike. Part II of this book lists many of these areas. There are more options in some parts of the United States than others, of course. Some states have relatively few trails or wilderness areas, while others have major National Parks, National Forests, and/or other extensive parklands, often with thousands of miles of hiking trails.

If you're fortunate enough to have natural areas near where you live, hiking is something you'll probably do fairly close to home. When on vacation, however, some of us travel a considerable distance to hike, at times even to the far corners of the country.

The vast majority of hikers go to the best-known areas. There are guidebooks and maps which cover such places, and sometimes public transportation is available. Many of these locations are popular or famous for good reason, such as spectacular scenery. Geographic location and accessibility also enter in.

The disadvantage of going to a well-known area is that you may find yourself sharing the trails with many other hikers, perhaps more than you would like to rub elbows with in a day. Visiting a lesser-known location will usually mean much more quiet, an opportunity to enjoy nature without distractions. Some trails will be little used and offer solitude. It's also true that the most famous parks do not have a corner on all the beautiful scenery, even though they may be well worth visiting. Many of the smaller places are still quite interesting and attractive, and hiking can be just as rewarding in such areas.

Guidebooks and Maps

In deciding which trails in a particular area to explore, you should consult a hiking guidebook, when available. Such guidebooks are sold at outdoor specialty stores, some sporting goods stores, and larger bookstores—and occasionally at park information centers or gift shops. You should bring the guidebook along on your hike, as the information included is likely to be useful or even necessary in finding your way.

A good guidebook will give an overview of an area, an idea of what to expect in terms of scenery and terrain, and some detailed trail data. Many guidebooks include a map or maps, so it may not be necessary to purchase these separately. The quality and size of guidebook maps vary enormously, however. If superior maps are available elsewhere you may want to obtain these as well.

Whereas a guidebook can be a very useful item, having some kind of map is mandatory, an essential tool to obtain before setting out on a wilderness hike. Without one the risks of getting lost or disoriented are too high.

Special hiking maps (which indicate all the trails clearly) are available for many of the most popular parks and natural areas. While they're sometimes sold at park entrances or gift shops, in many cases they must be obtained in advance by mail or from a store. Many sporting goods stores stock maps, and special map stores are found in a few locations. Maps purchased should be as up-to-date as possible, since the trails in some areas undergo frequent changes.

If a standard hiking map isn't available for a particular place or region, and there's no guidebook which includes maps, your next best bet is to obtain U.S. Geological Survey topographic maps. These may be procured for virtually any location in the country. The maps are attractive and give a good overall picture of an area, but have the drawback that hiking trails are often absent or incorrectly shown. Topographic maps may be found at map stores, some sporting goods stores, or by writing to: U.S.G.S., 1200 S. Eads Saint, Arlington, VA 22202 (for states east of the Mississippi) or U.S.G.S., Box 25286, Denver, CO 80225 (for states west of the Mississippi). Request an index map, which will allow you to identify precisely the map or maps required.

Other Sources of Information

It's frequently possible to obtain a map or brochure for free or at nominal cost by contacting a park or the appropriate governmental agency which oversees an area you're interested in. The quality of free maps is not always high, so the professionally made maps found in sporting goods stores are usually preferable, when available. For lesser-known areas, however, these brochures and maps may be the only source of information conveniently obtainable, and thus are important to get hold of.

Some hiking clubs and trail associations also put out maps or booklets for particular trails or hiking areas. A number of these organizations will be found in the state-by-state resource listings in Part II, along with the addresses and phone numbers of relevant state agencies. When writing to a trail association or club, remember to enclose a self-addressed, stamped envelope with any request for information.

STAYING FOR THE NIGHT

If you really enjoy spending time in the wilderness, often a day just doesn't seem long enough. Sooner or later you'll probably find yourself pondering the idea of an overnight trip. There are quite a few options to consider. Among the most adventuresome choices would be wilderness camping or backpacking.

On a backpacking or wilderness camping trip one carries everything necessary to spend a night or more in the wilds. A full-size backpack is usually required, along with a sleeping bag and tent, plus food for the duration of the trip. With modern lightweight gear such a trip is less difficult than many imagine, but it does make some physical demands.

You can walk with the pack each day and camp in a different place each night, which will permit you to explore and penetrate far into a remote wilderness area. Or you can establish a base camp and take day hikes from that point each day. Either way you'll have the freedom to remain out in the wilds for as long as you wish.

Camping and backpacking trips require a good deal of additional preparation, and many other considerations are involved. The subject, however, is beyond the scope of this book.

Another option, popular with millions of Americans, is car camping at campgrounds. The advantage of car camping is that nothing has to be carried beyond a short distance from your car, and practically anything may be brought along, regardless of bulk or weight. The major disadvantage is that you are usually camping close to others (and sometimes near a highway), often meaning man-made noise including sounds of radios and TVs, and other possible intrusions.

For those who prefer not to camp out, some parks offer hotel-type lodging, or cabins for rent. Accommodations can vary from primitive to luxurious. Information about such facilities is usually available from park information centers or headquarters. If the park is popular you may have to book far in advance.

A final overnight option (and easiest as a last-minute choice) is to find a bed and breakfast, guest house, inn, motel, or hotel near the hiking area of your preference.

PERMITS

Permits are required in order to hike or camp in certain parks, forests, preserves, and wilderness areas. This requirement is common for back-country camping in some of our more popular National Parks and Forests, and especially for designated wilderness areas which receive heavy use.

Permits have come into use for day hiking as well in a small but growing number of areas, particularly for overused wilderness areas on public lands, and also for private preserves. A primary reason for permits is to control and often restrict the numbers of hikers entering, and sometimes to collect revenue. Permits are usually free when public lands are involved, with a fee frequently required when the lands are private.

A permit may sometimes be obtained in advance by mail. In other cases one must apply in person at a ranger station or park entrance. It can be a simple process, taking just a moment, or it may involve some red tape. If a daily quota of hikers has been met for a particular trail or region, you may be turned away. To be caught hiking without the proper permit means heavy penalties in some places.

Since many of us head for the wilderness in part to experience a feeling of freedom, and to get away from the hassles of daily life, some of us aren't enamored of permits (along with an ever-increasing number of other regulations). At the same time, permits often originate in response to serious problems, in areas which have been overused and sometimes abused by careless or thoughtless hikers.

Permits are not currently required in the majority of this country's hiking areas. We can limit our hiking to those places if we choose. Most important, by being careful to minimize our impact on the wilderness, we can greatly reduce the likelihood that permits will become more universal.

HIKING SEASONS

There are places in this country where you may hike twelve months of the year, but in most regions there's a hiking season, which can be short or long. In the highest mountains, where the trails may be buried under snow for much of the year, the season might last only two to three months. (You can hike on snow or ice using snowshoes and/or crampons, but this is a different matter. See the discussion of winter hiking that follows.)

Before traveling to an unfamiliar area to hike, it's a good idea to be aware of local climate and the seasonal variations which can be expected. Summer is often the best or the only feasible time to hike in many of the high mountain areas, whereas winter is sometimes preferable for low-lying areas with a hot climate. Spring and fall are great times to go hiking in some locations but not others.

Guidebooks will often offer seasonal advice. When they do not, contact a park agency or information center to learn whether hiking in a certain area is sensible at a particular time of year. If you fail to pay attention to such matters, you could unexpectedly find yourself trying to hike in 100° F temperatures, deep snow, or other inhospitable conditions.

WINTER HIKING

While winter may be a superb season for hiking in areas which have mild temperatures throughout the year, it's a different matter altogether in much of the rest of the country, especially in most mountain areas.

Along with spells of extreme cold, snow and ice present some particular problems and challenges if you wish to venture out into the wilderness. Extra-warm clothing and great care are required to avoid discomfort or danger. An injury on the trail or a major mistake with regard to clothing might mean one's life. Needless to say, winter hiking isn't for beginners.

A couple of inches of snow on the trail won't be much of a hindrance when hiking, although it will slow you down. Several inches or more change the picture completely. Snowshoes are usually required for walking in substantial amounts of snow. If it's extremely icy, crampons (accessories with spikes which attach to boots) may be necessary. Sometimes it's possible to walk on packed or crusted snow with ordinary boots, but this cannot be counted on.

While it's beyond the scope of this book, snowshoeing provides an enjoyable way to continue hiking during winter in those parts of the country that receive heavy snowfall. And at times when there's little or no snow in these areas, you can hike as you do at any other time of year—taking special care to bring sufficient clothing to keep warm and dry, and staying prepared for all possible weather.

HIGH MOUNTAIN HIKING

When heading for the high mountains, such as the Rockies or Sierras—including elevations over seven thousand feet and up to fourteen thousand feet—some special considerations enter in. First is the need to allow time to adjust to the altitudes, which can take a few days or more. Any hike will be much more difficult if you are not used to the elevations, and pushing too hard means risking altitude sickness. Taking it easy at first is advisable.

Second, the higher you go, the greater the likelihood of snow and ice. Some high trails are snow-free for as little as a few weeks each summer, such as mid-July through mid-September, and may include some snowbanks which rarely if ever melt. Calling ahead to check on conditions is a good idea when visiting such areas. On the trip itself one must always be prepared to turn around if hazardous trail conditions are encountered.

Finally, severe storms are not at all uncommon in the high mountains. It's vital to avoid being in an exposed place above timberline (the level above which trees don't grow) especially in the event of a thunderstorm, which may be accompanied by high winds. In some areas it's routinely recommended that one start hiking very early in the day so as to be back down below treeline by afternoon, when storms are most common. In any case, the first sign of a storm (such as a darkening sky with increasing winds) means it's time to return quickly to lower elevations.

DESERT HIKING

Summer temperatures in some desert areas are routinely 90° to 100° F or higher. It's not really sensible to hike under such conditions, where you can easily overheat and get into trouble. One alternative is to hike only early and late in the day. Better yet, avoid most desert areas altogether in the summer, visiting instead in the spring or fall (or winter, for some regions).

It's especially important to bring considerable quantities of water. This would seem to be quite obvious, yet less-experienced hikers are sometimes careless regarding water, not realizing the risks. Forgetting water can be inconvenient and lead to some discomfort elsewhere, but in the desert it could be fatal. The usual recommendation is for a minimum of one gallon of water per person, per day, in the desert.

The other vital consideration in the often shadeless desert is protection from the sun. Wearing a sun hat and sunscreen or lotion (and probably sunglasses) should be given especially high priority.

If it rains, flash floods can cause some danger in desert canyons. It's best to avoid creeks, drainages, and narrow canyons when there's a threat of rain, due to the risk of being trapped by suddenly rising water.

WEATHER

The weather is an ever-popular topic, and it's naturally a relevant one when you're spending time outdoors. Those who are new to hiking and other wilderness activities often have a special interest in the subject.

Weather forecasting is an inaccurate science, as most of us know. Sometimes the forecast is on target, and at other times it's dead wrong, especially in areas where the weather is very changeable. It's most difficult to get a good forecast for mountain and wilderness areas. The forecast you hear will usually be for a city or other low-lying area, often some distance from your hiking destination. Mountains frequently have their own unique weather patterns, with conditions sometimes markedly different from other areas.

Many of us have learned not to place much stock in forecasts or base our plans on them, except when there's strong evidence of dangerous storms or other unusually severe weather arising. If you stay home every time inclement weather is forecast or there's a risk of rain, you'll miss out on some fine days in the wilderness.

You do need to know what the range of possibilities could be, and you should always pack clothing and rainwear appropriate for any conceivable condition which could be encountered. It's best to go hiking with few assumptions or expectations regarding the weather. If you're ready for anything you won't get caught unprepared by surprise changes.

Fear about getting caught in the rain seems to be prevalent among the uninitiated. For many it's a deeply ingrained attitude, in part because of early childhood conditioning, and not easy to overcome. Some people imagine that walking in the rain must mean misery and getting sick. Our media often contribute to the problem by depicting wet weather in the worst possible light, and frequently exaggerating the likelihood of rain (we always hear about a "chance of rain" but never a "chance of sunshine"). Usually only the most perfect sunny days receive positive comments, and people are often encouraged to stay indoors at other times. Thus it's not surprising that some are hesitant to hike when there's a questionable forecast.

Also, except for those who live in dry climates with a special need of water, we're rarely thankful when it rains. Yet water is a vital element on earth, and rain is absolutely essential to the life cycle. Many of us love to swim (sometimes even in cold water), take baths or showers, and otherwise get near or into water as often as we can. The significant difference with rain is that it can't be controlled in any way, and sometimes comes at a time one wouldn't choose.

It's true that walking for a long distance in heavy rain can be a bit dispiriting, especially in lower temperatures, and it's important that you avoid getting simultaneously wet and cold. A strong likelihood of torrential rains, flooding, or gale-force winds does provide a good reason to consider staying home. But the vast majority of so-called rainy days often only amount to a little light rain, or a brief shower or two, or some mist or drizzle.

The wilderness can be extraordinarily lovely in the rain, the scents of the earth especially rich—and the flowers are rarely more beautiful or the vegetation more lush. As long as you're properly equipped with raingear and sufficient clothing, there's no reason rain has to interfere with your enjoyment of nature.

In any case, one certain fact is that the weather will frequently be different from what was predicted. It's surely a waste of energy to fret about less-than-perfect weather, and most sensible and satisfying to make the best of each day. While it may take some time to learn to enjoy wet-weather hiking, it's good to learn to accept whatever comes. Some of us discover that the unsunny days are beautiful in unimagined ways.

Walking Into the Wilderness

PARKING

You usually want to park where the trail begins, and often there's a clearly designated parking area right at the trailhead. In some locations you must park along the road. A good trail guidebook will often give instructions regarding parking. Roadside parking is prohibited in some places. When in doubt, it's a good idea to check with park authorities regarding regulations, to avoid the possibility of getting ticketed or towed.

Some guidebooks or authorities will advise against leaving your car in a remote location, because of the possibility of vandalism or theft. Such problems are virtually nonexistent in some regions, and more possible in others. If you're in doubt, it never hurts to ask. In any case, don't leave any valuables in the car (in the past too many hikers have done just that, rewarding those who break into cars).

ADMISSION FEES

Some state parks, most National Parks, and many private preserves charge an admission or parking fee. Always be prepared for a possible fee. The amount is often quite nominal, but in recent years such fees have increased consider-

ably in some areas (it's now up to ten dollars at some of our National Parks). Sometimes the fee is per person, sometimes per car. It may be good for a number of days or only for a single day. Often such fees are charged only in season.

FINDING THE TRAIL

Locating hiking trails from the road can be a simple process or a challenge. Well-known parks and hiking areas generally have prominent signs or other information which indicate trailheads quite clearly. In other places, trails may be

poorly marked along the road. Occasionally a considerable amount of searching is required. A good guidebook which includes precise directions for finding trails can help immeasurably here.

FOLLOWING TRAILS

Most of the hiking that's done in this country involves following marked trails. In certain areas, however, hiking trails are unmarked and easy to follow. Bushwhacking (off-trail travel) is another option which is practiced by some adventuresome hikers, especially in open areas such as in the desert where one isn't hindered by dense vegetation.

Trail markings vary widely. Commonly the trail is indicated by intermittent paint blazes on trees or rocks. Sometimes metal or plastic markers are used, nailed to the trees. In areas above timberline or where there are no trees, the trail is typically marked by "cairns," or small piles of rocks.

Each trail in a particular area may have markers of a different color. Sometimes, though, a single color or type of marker is used for all trails. The beginning or end of a trail is often indicated by three markers together. A turn is typically designated by two markers, with one above the other, the upper marker sometimes placed in the direction of the turn.

It's not uncommon for some easy-to-follow trails to be marked only by wooden signs at the trailhead and at intersections with other trails or roads. Unfortunately, in certain areas such signs have a way of disappearing, due to vandalism or theft by souvenir hunters.

On many trails, markers will be placed often enough so that one will be visible to a hiker almost all of the time (on some trails markers appear less frequently). If you walk more than a couple of minutes on such a trail without seeing a marker, it's a good idea to stop and backtrack to the last visible one. Continuing ahead for a distance on any trail without evidence of markers is one possible way to get lost—you could have missed a turn and might inadvertently be following a different trail.

It's important to develop the habit of watching for trail markers and other indications that you're on the intended path, especially when hiking alone. Such a habit becomes unconscious with experience, requiring little expenditure of energy, and doesn't need to distract from the enjoyment of hiking.

While some unmarked trails are easy to follow, others will present particular challenges, especially those which are overgrown or pass through rough terrain. It's best to forgo hiking on such trails unless or until you have lots of hiking experience.

BUSHWHACKING

A minority of hikers engage in bushwhacking, leaving the trails for cross-country travel. Bushwhacking can be fun and challenging, and it may have a special appeal if you're in search of solitude, since getting off the trails greatly reduces the likelihood of seeing another person. The activity has its risks, especially if you're alone, since there's very little chance of obtaining assistance should you sustain an injury or find yourself seriously lost.

Bushwhacking is easiest in relatively open areas which have limited undergrowth, such as one finds above timberline or in the desert, and when the terrain is not too rugged. In areas of dense forest and rough ground it can be difficult indeed. Bushwhacking is for those who are expert in the use of map and compass and have plenty of hiking experience under their belts.

AVOIDING GETTING LOST

Getting lost is one of those circumstances that's virtually always avoidable if you're reasonably conscientious and pay attention to what you're doing. Most of us have been "a bit lost" or turned around at some time or other, and this doesn't necessarily add up to a real problem. You may accidentally miss a turn and get off the trail for a short time, or find that you've somehow ended up on a trail which isn't on the map. In such a situation the solution is to retrace your steps to the starting point or the place where the trail was lost.

Getting *seriously* lost is another matter. If you lose the trail and continue to walk, and don't have a map and compass to reorient yourself, it could mean serious trouble. Without clothing and provisions for staying overnight, especially in cold weather, your life could literally be at stake. It's critical to avoid ever getting in such a spot. An essential way to accomplish this is to *always* carry a map and compass, and consult them as often as necessary. When going with others, one or more in the group must take this responsibility.

If you should somehow find yourself in the wilderness without these items, it's best to refrain from leaving the trail except for the shortest possible distances, and return to the highway exactly the way you came in. Any guesswork about which direction an unknown trail or trails may lead could be wrong.

You need not be obsessively concerned about the risk of getting lost, but it's good to have an awareness of your limitations in the wilderness, especially when it comes to orienting yourself without the aid of compass and map. Carelessness or excessive confidence regarding your ability to find the way could lead to a real predicament.

Whenever you leave the trail, such as to make a pit (bathroom) stop, it's wise to look around and note the appearances of nearby trees, rocks, or other natural objects—and look back toward the trail frequently as you move. If you get turned around, recognizable objects and scenery will help you to reorient yourself and find the way back.

If you should ever find yourself lost or disoriented, it's critical to avoid panicking, to stay as relaxed as possible and refrain from walking any further if you don't know the way. You can try to retrace your steps, looking closely for footprints or other signs of the way you came. If you don't have immediate success it's probably a good idea to rest for a few minutes before resuming.

Since you might be within earshot of others, it's also worth trying to call out, or using a whistle. Others may respond, and you can then follow the direction of their voices.

PACE

Hiking is most enjoyable when you go at a pace that's right for you. We each seem to have a natural best pace, which obviously differs from person to person. Some hikers are happiest walking briskly or fast, while others need to proceed much more slowly. What's comfortable can be affected by your level of fitness and also how you're feeling on a particular day.

Two friends with markedly different paces will probably not make the best hiking partners. On the other hand, most people can adjust their pace somewhat, which is sometimes necessary when hiking in a group.

You may have to experiment a bit to discover your best pace. Attempting to go too fast can lead to burnout long before the day is over, and undoubtedly less pleasure. Frequent stumbling or tripping is a sign that you may need to slow down. If you go a lot slower than your optimal pace, however, you may start to sense that you're losing the flow, and feel prematurely tired or lethargic. This can happen as well if you stop too frequently. We all need to slow down, of course, when the trail becomes rough and potentially hazardous, or steep and strenuous.

REST BREAKS

Periodic rest breaks are highly recommended. Often fatigue will tell you when it's time for a break. Generally speaking, a ten to fifteen minute stop every hour or so is probably a good idea, although those who are especially fit may need to rest less frequently. You're likely to feel noticeably reenergized when you proceed on your way again.

Some of us prefer to take an especially long break at lunchtime to spend some extra time relaxing, poking around a beautiful spot, stretching out and snoozing a bit, or going for a swim. Such an interval can be refreshing, providing a restful interlude to a day devoted in such good measure to exercise.

When the trail is extra challenging you may also want to take some brief stand-up breaks, pausing every now and then to catch your breath and allow the energy to return.

HIKING ON ROUGH TRAILS

Many of us have spent our lives walking almost exclusively on flat surfaces. Walking on irregular natural terrain, which may include rocks and tree roots, is obviously a somewhat different matter. Better balance is required, and most of us acquire this with experience. It's sensible to go slowly over rough areas. Some rocks and tree roots and old logs may be damp or wet and slippery, and whenever possible you may want to find footing around such obstacles. Otherwise, it's best to step very cautiously, putting your full weight down only when it's clear that an object or surface will hold you.

If you trip, slip, or stumble, you've probably been proceeding too fast for existing conditions, or haven't been paying enough attention to what's underfoot. When the trail is rough it's necessary to look or glance down nearly constantly.

Though one normally walks in a fully erect posture while hiking, when the footing is especially uncertain it's sensible to crouch a bit, lowering your center of gravity and reducing the likelihood of falling. On the most difficult trails you may occasionally even need to get down on all fours to proceed safely—for example, when crossing a jumble of angular rocks or boulders, which could be slippery or have few footholds, or when it's necessary to crawl through a narrow passage or tunnel.

HIKING ON STEEP TRAILS

Just as on a rough trail, on an especially steep trail it's advisable to stay very close to the ground, so if you should lose your balance, there would be a minimal distance to fall. Descending tends to be more hazardous than ascending, and requires special care. If necessary you might use small trees or rocks alongside the trail to hold onto, and occasionally back your way down a particularly difficult stretch. When in doubt, sitting and easing your way down on your rear end (facing downhill) is usually the safest of all ways to go.

A few trails will take you directly along the edge of a precipice or up a steep wall (with footing). By definition, no hiking trail should require ropes or special equipment to negotiate, or involve extreme danger. You may feel some fear, however, whether or not the trail presents any real risk. It's good to pay heed to your fear and not proceed before surveying the situation closely for a moment. There could indeed be a hazardous condition, or a level of difficulty that you're not yet prepared to deal with. You might decide to turn around and return the way you came, if that's feasible. On the other hand, scary spots are often simply places where there's a view of a steep drop, even though the trail itself may actually be quite wide and safe. Those among us who have a special fear of heights will probably want to avoid steeper trails at first (such fears are often overcome with time and experience).

When on steep terrain it's necessary to use special care to avoid dislodging stones or rocks which could fall on someone below. And since you can never know who might be below, it's obvious that stones should never be thrown over a cliff or downhill.

MILE-COUNTING, CLOCK-WATCHING, PEAK-BAGGING

Some hikers like to count miles, and may keep a frequent eye on their watches. Quite a few are extremely goal-oriented, including "peak-baggers" who attempt to climb as many different mountains as possible.

Everyone is of course free to approach hiking in any way he or she wishes, and there's certainly no single right way to go about it. Without question it's often interesting and sometimes important to know how far you've come, rewarding at times to climb mountains and set goals, and essential to know the time of day if you need to be out before sundown. Beyond that, however, if you focus constantly on measurements and goals there's a risk of losing a vital part of the experience, and you can end up programming much of the potential fun out of the day.

Some of us believe that it's worth trying to enjoy each moment in the wilderness as it comes—taking advantage of the potential for spontaneity and freedom, as well as the opportunity available to let go of our daily attachments and conceptions and measurements and schedules. A less programmed day can be wonderfully satisfying, and you may find yourself loosening up, relaxing, and letting yourself enjoy an experience in the natural world to the very fullest.

Avoiding Trouble
on the Trail

SAFETY

All outdoor activities involve risks. Life itself entails a succession of risks. Some activities require more risks than others. Hiking is a relatively safe endeavor, as long as you know how to take care of yourself in the outdoors and use caution when appropriate. Many of us believe that in most respects the wilderness is actually a much safer place than civilization (certainly more so than many of our urban areas or the nation's highways).

The point of this chapter is not to encourage you to focus on the negative, but rather to help you prevent any problem from arising which could get in the way of your enjoyment of hiking. Most potential problems can be avoided or nipped in the bud, as long as you know what to look out for and what steps to take when appropriate. Don't let any concerns you might have about these matters keep you from hiking!

Accidents and Injuries

Serious accidents while hiking are rare. Most accidents are entirely avoidable. If you're walking on a rough trail, carelessness or inattention could lead to stumbling or falling. Fortunately, most of us instinctively know when and where to be especially careful—such as when walking on rocks or boulders, or near a precipice, or if the footing is slippery.

The most common hiking injury is a twisted ankle. Most twisted ankles are not serious, and we're usually able to complete the hike unassisted. A major sprain, however, can be incapacitating. Good hiking boots and a reasonable degree of alertness will help prevent such an accident from happening to you.

An ankle is most likely to be twisted while hiking downhill, and also late in the day, when you're tired and often not as careful. It's wise to always *slow down* whenever descending on a trail. Hurrying downhill is asking for trouble. A loose stone or rock could move unexpectedly underfoot, causing you to lose your balance and perhaps fall. Or there might be a small tree root, partially hidden in the undergrowth, which could trip you. Staying aware of your footing and slowing down when appropriate are the best ways to guard against such an accident.

Hiking steeply downhill is also hard on the knees, especially if the trail is rocky. This is another good reason for descending slowly. It's easier on the knees if you step down gently, rather than pounding with the full force of your weight on each foot.

Most other injuries sustained while hiking tend to be minor affairs, such as scraping a knee or a finger on a rock. Fatal accidents are exceedingly rare, especially among responsible hikers. Most serious accidents that do occur may be attributed to extreme carelessness or recklessness, and the use of alcohol or drugs is sometimes implicated.

Animals

Fear of wild animals is fairly prevalent. Concern or anxiety seems to run the highest with respect to bears and snakes. The actual danger from such animals is minimal. The chances of being attacked or in any way injured by a wild animal are so slight that even those of us who spend much of our lives in the outdoors are unlikely to have such an experience.

Bears

Bears are among the most fearsome looking wild animals in this country, yet most bears will take every measure to avoid contact with human beings. The exception is those bears which have become used to people, as in some of the National Parks. In the unlikely event that you do meet up with a bear, the bear will probably depart quickly or at least keep his distance.

Especially feared is the grizzly, which has a reputation for unpredictable behavior and occasionally attacking human beings. In grizzly country (Alaska, Montana, Wyoming, and Idaho) it's sensible to be especially cautious. Read up on the subject if you'll be visiting these areas, and be aware that there is a certain risk involved. Nevertheless, millions of people hike and camp in grizzly territory each year without incident (the rare injuries or fatalities which occur are often heavily publicized).

If you do see a bear, you should stop, refrain from running or moving suddenly, and gently back off. The bear will probably do likewise.

Never try to approach a bear, as for instance to take photos. Your approach could be interpreted as a threat, especially if there are cubs nearby, and you'll be placing yourself in much more danger. Consult with rangers or other sources of information in advance of your hike for additional advice, which may differ depending on the kind of bear population present.

Snakes

The prevalence of poisonous snakes varies greatly depending on which part of the country you're hiking in. Such snakes are frequently seen in some areas, especially where the climate is hot, while in other places the poisonous varieties are extremely rare. In any case, few hikers are bitten by snakes. A reasonable degree of alertness and care, particularly when you're in an area known to harbor poisonous snakes, will usually suffice. Watching where you step is obviously wise, along with refraining from putting your hands where you can't see—such as in a crack or hole. If you're climbing, never reach above to grab a rock without looking. It's good to be extra cautious when walking on a trail overgrown with grass or bushes, if it's hard to see where you're stepping.

Snakebite kits are sold in most outdoor equipment stores, but there's disagreement about the value or necessity of such kits. Since the probability of sustaining a bite is so low, many of us don't carry them. There's also some question about how safe the kits are to use.

If you encounter a snake but can keep your distance, the snake will usually refrain from striking and retreat if permitted to do so. If you should be bitten, you would need to return to the nearest highway and obtain medical help as quickly as possible. If you're far from a road, assistance in getting out might be required. Snakebite is rarely fatal among healthy adults.

Other Animals

Sightings or encounters with most animals are not as common as some who are new to the wilderness expect. Keen senses allow many animals to avoid us, and with certain species a sighting is a rare and special pleasure. Yet sooner or later you're likely to cross paths with such animals as deer, elk, moose, porcupine, raccoon, skunk, fox, and woodchuck, among others.

Approaching any wild animal is always unwise. Most animals are capable of attacking when cornered, but will usually attempt to get away if permitted to do so. You should exercise special caution in the presence of any animal which is behaving strangely, as it could be rabid—but the likelihood of encountering such an animal is extremely small.

Insects

In some environments insects can be a nuisance, but they're rarely a serious problem in this country. An exception is for those who are allergic to bee stings or other bug bites. Anyone who believes he or she might be in this group should check with a doctor before heading for the wilderness during bug season.

When insects are present and biting, the obvious solution is to use bug repellent. In some cases, bugs may be so numerous and pesky that wearing a headnet is advisable or necessary. Insects are found only where temperatures are reasonably warm. In some of the higher mountain areas, where it's often cool and breezes or winds are common, bugs are scarce a good portion of the time.

One can never accurately predict the prevalence of insects, since recent local weather and rainfall will strongly influence the bug population. When in doubt, and except during the coldest seasons, it's best to bring along the bug repellent.

Some people consider bugs to be profoundly annoying, yet many of us find a degree of tolerance for insects developing as we spend time in the wilderness. It's to be expected that a few bugs may be buzzing around wherever you are in the summer, and assuming you're not being constantly bitten, there's no reason this should seriously interfere with your enjoyment of the outdoors.

While it's not easy for us to appreciate or accept them, we also need to remember that bugs are a part of the chain of life, have been around a lot longer than we have, and like all forms of life have a right to be here.

Ticks and Lyme Disease

Every few years there's a scare that succeeds in frightening some would-be hikers away from the wilderness. One of the most recent is Lyme Disease, which is carried by ticks. Everyone should know about Lyme Disease, but overreporting in the media has practically created a panic in some quarters of the country.

Most hikers do not get Lyme Disease, and most cases of Lyme Disease are not really serious as long as you receive proper treatment. A small number of people who contract it develop serious complications. For the vast majority of victims Lyme Disease is not much worse than the flu.

Lyme Disease has some flulike symptoms, and any case of summer flu should be suspect. When in doubt, see a doctor and get tested for the disease. There's also usually (but not always) a round red rash surrounding the area of the tick bite. Arthritic symptoms may develop weeks or months later if no treatment is received. Not everyone who comes down with the disease is aware of having been bitten, since the deer tick which carries it is very small, especially in the nymph stage.

Deer ticks are most often found in grassy or bushy areas at low elevations. You won't pick up a tick while hiking along an open trail. If the trail is overgrown the chances are greater. If you're hiking during the warmer months in an area known to harbor such ticks, check your body and hair for ticks during and after the hike. Not all ticks carry the disease, and it takes twelve to twenty-four hours for a tick to pass it on (if a tick is removed in time there will be no problem). Wearing light-colored pants makes it easier to spot a tick. Authorities generally recommend tucking pants into sock and spraying insect repellent on legs and feet.

In spite of all the recent warnings and alarm, however, on the vast majority of trails in this country the risk of picking up a tick or Lyme Disease is quite low.

Lightning

Most of us know that during an electrical storm it's dangerous to be in a high or exposed area, or under a lone tree. If you're on top of a mountain and can see or hear a thunderstorm coming, it's time to descend immediately to a lower and less exposed place—below timberline if at all possible, and away from open areas as well as prominent rocks or trees. If you're in a dense and relatively uniform forest the risk of being hit by lightning is exceedingly low.

In the higher mountains, storms occasionally strike with sudden fury. If you have only a short amount of time it may be necessary to leave the trail and get down into the bushes until it blows over. If lightning is striking nearby the recommended posture is to kneel, leaning forward all the way and placing your head on your knees (lightning sometimes travels horizontally upon striking, and this posture is safest by minimizing your contact with the ground).

Hypothermia

If you get badly chilled in cold, wet weather, there's a serious danger of hypothermia (popularly known as "exposure"). In this condition, your core body temperature begins to drop. Shivering becomes pronounced, your thought processes and speech may be confused, and you're at great risk. If you don't get immediate help, death could result.

Most cases of hypothermia are completely avoidable. As long as you know how to take care of yourself in the cold there's little need for concern. Whenever you're in the rain it's important to wear good quality (dependable) raingear, and when you feel cold, to put on additional clothing (some wool or synthetic fabrics like polypropylene are essential). Increasing the amount of exercise will sometimes help you to warm up. Eating something is also important, as the body needs fuel to stay warm. If you've had an adequate amount of sleep the night before you'll also be less susceptible to hypothermia.

Some people carelessly allow themselves to get wet and cold, having no idea that they could be risking their lives. Hypothermia can occur in temperatures as warm as 60° F. What's important to remember is to never let yourself become seriously chilled, whether you're wet or dry. It's also vital to tell others if you're feeling uncomfortably cold, to borrow additional clothing if necessary, and get whatever help you might need. If you're alone and unsuccessful in attempting to stay warm, it's time to head for the highway and the nearest source of heat as quickly as possible.

Heat Problems

Strenuous exercise in truly hot weather can be risky. If you're shaded or sheltered from the sun, as in forested areas, you're less likely to overheat. It's sensible to hike in cooler, shadier places when it's hot. In such weather you also need to carry and drink large quantities of water.

If you feel dizzy, weak or nauseated at any time while hiking in the heat, it's important to take a long rest and cool off. The hike should be shortened, if possible. It's foolish to try and push on when the body is telling you to stop.

Time is required for acclimating to higher temperatures. If you're not used to the heat it's sensible to refrain from setting ambitious hiking goals. In warm or hot areas where there's little or no protection from the sun the best time to hike is in the early morning and evening hours.

Altitude Problems

It takes time to adjust to high altitudes. If you'll be over five to six thousand feet but aren't accustomed to such elevations, it's best to limit yourself to a less-than-ambitious hike—which will usually feel much more tiring than one of similar distance and difficulty at a low elevation.

Even for the most fit among us, some initial shortness of breath is to be expected. This is especially true at heights over ten thousand feet. It's smart to go slowly and rest frequently. If you find yourself feeling weak, dizzy, or nauseated, it's time to conclude the hike as soon as possible—and get down to a lower elevation. Pushing on might mean a serious case of altitude sickness.

Hiking During Hunting Season

Hunting is permitted in many but not all parks and wilderness areas, most commonly for a period of several weeks in the late fall. The season can vary considerably from one state or region to another. Many hikers choose to avoid hiking in an area where hunting is going on, since there's always at least a slight risk of being accidentally mistaken for prey. The sounds of gunshots can also be very intrusive.

It's a good idea to inquire and be aware of hunting seasons and regulations. If you choose to visit an area during the actual season, always wear bright red or orange. A safer (and frequently quieter) alternative during hunting season is to restrict your hiking to those parks and preserves which are off-limits to hunters.

Poison Ivy, Poison Oak, Poison Sumac

Each of these plants is found in different parts of the country, and they're well worth avoiding. For many but not all people, contact will lead to a severe rash with uncomfortable itching. Symptoms may persist up to several weeks. Have someone point out these plants for you (or obtain an identification book) so you'll be able to spot them. Always take a look before sitting down in weeds or walking bare-legged through vegetation.

Blisters

Blisters aren't dangerous, to be sure, but they certainly will take the fun and pleasure out of walking and can help spoil a trip. The risk of blisters is often not taken seriously, but if you've ever had the experience of limping along in pain for some distance, you'll appreciate the need to take care in avoiding them.

Some people are more blister-prone than others, but be especially on the alert when wearing new boots, or older boots which haven't been worn in some time. Sweaty feet in hot weather are also more susceptible. Blisters can take you by surprise, and once you start to feel pain, the damage has probably been done. The key is prevention. When you feel the *slightest* rubbing or discomfort, it's time to stop, remove the boots and take a look at your feet. A piece of *moleskin* or *molefoam* (available from most pharmacies), which has adhesive on the back, should be cut to size and placed over any area where rubbing is taking place. The friction will be transferred to the moleskin, and a blister will usually be prevented.

If a blister has already been formed and broken, it's best to clean it and apply a bandage. For a minor blister, moleskin may sometimes be placed over the bandage. If it's a serious blister, molefoam (thicker foam with adhesive) can be placed around it. This will help take the pressure off and make walking easier. Molefoam is also useful for reducing any other uncomfortable or painful pressure inside a boot.

Walking Pains

A little lower-body muscle or joint soreness is normal after a long hike, especially if you haven't been hiking or exercising much. It's important to pay attention to any pain or discomfort which arises during the hike itself. Ignoring such messages from your body could increase the likelihood of an avoidable injury.

Poorly fitting boots or inadequate footwear are frequently responsible for foot or knee pain. In addition, some of us have structural imbalances in our feet, which can lead to knee or foot problems when we engage extensively in activities like walking, running, or hiking. Such difficulties may sometimes be corrected by wearing orthotics or insoles in boots or shoes.

Dealing With Discomfort

Wilderness activities like hiking certainly don't automatically entail discomfort, and the rewards and pleasures usually far outweigh any possible problems. Still, sooner or later we're likely to get soaked, pull a muscle, develop a blister, or perhaps find ourselves on a stretch of trail that's frustratingly difficult. Aside from physical demands, surprise changes in weather or unexpected obstacles can occasionally require a good measure of resilience and patience.

Anyone who has little or no tolerance for discomfort is probably not well suited for hiking.

Yet life in general is also going to present many problems for the person who insists that everything always be easy and comfortable.

Most of us don't deliberately choose difficult or uncomfortable situations, in or out of the wilderness—but once we're in one, there are some opportunities available. A sense of satisfaction and accomplishment can follow solving a tough problem or surmounting an obstacle. At some point we're likely to learn that we can deal with just about anything we're presented with. This knowledge will tend to diminish any fears we may have, and open the way to a more complete involvement and enjoyment of the activity.

Lamenting about and dwelling on whatever doesn't go right is a sure way to help spoil the day. On those relatively rare occasions when things seem to go awry and we may be feeling some discomfort, we'll find we can nevertheless survive, learn from the experience, feel competent and good about ourselves—and, to our possible amazement, perhaps even discover that we can still have a good time in the midst of it all.

SEVEN

The Pleasures of Hiking

. . . I step out of the car with more than a touch of heightened anticipation. I've been looking forward to this day all week, and it's great to be here. Just a short while ago I was on a busy, noisy highway, and now I'm in a world which couldn't be more different or more appealing. Since arriving in the park a few minutes ago I've already started to feel more relaxed, comfortable, at home.

The parking area sits amid an expanse of evergreen forest, with a grove of majestic tall pines nearby. The north-woods scent is pungent and delectable. Overhead the sky is bright blue with large billowing clouds which move steadily along. Where I'm standing it's pleasantly breezy and cool, with some sunshine providing added warmth. It's a spring day. I'm wearing a heavy wool shirt and a light parka, but if the sun stays out and the day warms up as expected, I'll probably be down to a T-shirt before long. My eyes turn to watch some small chirping birds darting about nearby. The air is fresher than any I've breathed or tasted in days.

In a couple of minutes I'm on my way, day pack on my back, parking lot gravel crunching beneath my boots. Just ahead is a wooden trail-head sign which lists the distances to several possible destinations, and I pull the trail map out of my shirt pocket for a look. My intention is to hike to the top of a small mountain several miles away, and I'll tentatively return by a different route, passing a sizable lake along the way.

There's a guidebook in my pack, but I don't need it right now. I already know that from here to the mountaintop the elevation gain is a thousand feet or so. Not very much by mountain standards, but it'll provide a nice little workout. Most of the climb should be pretty gradual, but I'm aware that it may be rough and rocky near the top. I haven't studied the guidebook too closely, since I'd rather get to know the area in my own way, without too many expectations, and perhaps enjoy a few surprises.

I step from gravel onto a nearly silent cushion of soft earth. The spruce-lined trail opens up before me. Here the path is a few feet wide, marked with an occasional white paint blaze on a tree. There's a trail register and I stop briefly to sign in, and then proceed on my way. At first it's almost flat, with just an occasional small rock or tree root in the path. Before long I find myself walking at a steady, comfortable pace. Moving along feels almost effortless.

As I walk, my eyes pass over an endless array of trees and bushes, plus patches of grass, scattered wildflowers, mushrooms and other fungi, and scores of other plants—some familiar, some unknown to me. Here and there a chipmunk darts, a squirrel scrambles up a tree, a toad hops, or there's a more distant rustle in the bushes as some larger mammal apparently retreats from the sound of my footsteps.

By now the early morning preparations and travels have just about faded from my mind. Once again I note with pleasure how wonderful it feels to be here. One foot goes before the other, almost automatically, and there's virtually nothing else to be done—except to look up every now and then for a trail marker and make sure I'm still on the right path.

In a while I reach a trail intersection, well-marked with a wooden sign. Not all trails or intersections are so clearly marked, and partly out of habit I stop to consult the map and pull out my compass to verify that I'm headed in the right direction. Since I've warmed up considerably, off comes my light parka and I stuff it into the day pack, where there's just enough room for it. I pause for a few moments before resuming my walk—taking a deep breath of mountain air, looking slowly around at the lush and shady green forest, glancing up through the leaves and branches at the still bright sky overhead—and then proceed on my way.

A few minutes later, walking along thoroughly engrossed in my thoughts, I'm suddenly startled as a large grouse noisily flutters up just a few feet ahead of me and then disappears. I instantly stop in my tracks, and then feel a touch of relief and amusement. This has happened before, and I know the grouse was probably trying to distract me away from a nearby nest.

I continue on. Soon the trail begins to climb and at the same time grows rockier. The footing has become a bit more difficult, so I'm glancing down at the ground much more frequently, watching carefully where I step. My pace slows only slightly, but remains steady, since I'm accustomed to walking on rough trails.

More time passes, but I have no need to keep track of it. The exact time of day seems truly unimportant here. The only consideration is that I'd like to be out of the woods before sunset, and prefer not to cut it too close at day's end. I'm delighted about having this whole day to myself, with no schedule to follow and complete freedom to roam at will.

I become conscious of a distant murmur. Is it the wind? As I move along it gradually grows louder, and I recognize clearly the sound of moving water. Before long a large stream comes into sight. Sunlight glitters on the rushing water. A short distance upstream on my right there's a fair-size waterfall, perhaps ten feet high and several feet wide, along with some smaller cascades. It's very full, probably swollen from recent rains, and since I'll need to cross the creek I'm glad to see a small, primitive wooden bridge to my left.

I'm already overdue for a break, and there's no question that this will be the place. I amble uphill to a spot just below the falls. On either side are large rock shelves and boulders, some of them covered with bright green moss. The area is shaded by massive high hemlocks. I climb onto a big round rock alongside the water, just beyond reach of the spray from the falls, remove my day pack and boots, take a few sips from my water bottle, and dangle my warm feet in the cold water. There's just a brief sting as my feet enter the churning water. In a moment, as expected, it feels utterly refreshing.

Some time passes, which I spend watching water-striders (bugs) skimming across the surface of a placid pool, thinking about assorted matters, and doing a bit of poking around. I could easily envision staying here all day, mesmerized by the sound of falling water, but after a while the trail and the mountain ahead begin to beckon once more. With my boots and day pack back on I rise, return downstream to the trail, cross the little log bridge, and continue on my way.

The path now grows slightly steeper, and there are some clusters of large boulders to negotiate. In a few places I need to hold on to maintain balance. I notice that my heart is beating faster and my breathing is deeper than before, mainly due to the exertion of hiking uphill. Yet everything feels just right. I'm sweating, but it's not an unpleasant sensation at all. I imagine I can feel the tension of recent days being slowly purged from my body. When I think about it, there's probably no place on earth I'd rather be than here right now.

The trail smooths out somewhat again, and after passing through a stretch of dense forest it starts to open up overhead. Trees are smaller, vegetation is more sparse, and some rays of sunshine now reach my face. It looks like I'm near the top of the mountain. After passing through some fragrant blooming bushes of mountain laurel I'm suddenly out in the open. I can instantly see that it's indeed a place to spend some time. The view is magnificent.

Although it's not a high mountain, the top is rocky and impressive, consisting of a jumble of massive rock slabs, barren except for some green lichen growing on the sides. Just below are expanses of open grassy meadow. I meander about the top for a few minutes and then sit on a rocky perch, soaking in the spectacular view, gazing off into distant valleys and following nearby ridgelines with my eyes, watching hawks circle in the distance. I feel a little tired but elated.

A few flies buzz around but otherwise it's supremely quiet and peaceful. After a while I move back down to the open grass, make myself comfortable, take off my wool shirt and socks, and retrieve my lunch from the day pack. I eat lunch in a leisurely fashion, and then stretch out lazily, watch the clouds move by for a while, and close my eyes.

Some time later I awaken. I hadn't planned a nap, but that doesn't matter. I feel rested and rather serene. It seems like time to move on, especially since I intend to stop at that lake on the way back. Off one side of the mountain in the distance I can see it, looking inviting from here, shimmering slightly in the sun.

Before rising I trim a couple pieces of moleskin to size, and place them over two sore spots on my feet which I'd noticed before dozing off. These boots are almost new, and it looks like some minor blisters might be on the way. The moleskin will hopefully nip them in the bud.

After one last long look across the panorama of mountains and valleys I resume my journey. The descent begins on a different trail, which angles off toward the lake. It's a little steep at first. My legs feel slightly stiff after the lengthy break so I start slowly, but soon my muscles have loosened up and all feels comfortable again.

In a short while I'm back in the cool shady forest. The trail levels off somewhat and becomes less rocky. Before I know it I glance up and discover the lake looming directly ahead through the trees. I realize I've probably traveled two or three miles and not even noticed the passage of time, which isn't an uncommon experience for me when hiking.

The lake is lovely, with several small rocky cliffs and blueberry bushes (too early for fruit) along the shore. I follow a short side trail down between two little cliffs to the lakeshore, and find a nice resting spot on a large smooth rock. The water ripples lightly in the breeze.

I hear a few geese squawking in the distance. My eyes are peeled along the opposite shoreline for signs of wildlife. Quite a few times I've seen deer or moose at lakes like this. I'd love to take a swim, but it's still early in the season, and the water's very cold. I don't mind. Sitting here is refreshing enough.

It's clear from the increasing angle of the sun (and a sneak at my pocketed watch) that the afternoon is on the wane, so it's time to resume walking. I check the map before setting off again, reminding myself to keep an eye out for an upcoming trail intersection. There I'll find the trail I came in on, and retrace my initial route. The intersection appears before long, clearly marked with a wooden sign. I turn once more, and now proceed down the last stretch of trail. A couple more miles and I'll be back at my car.

Since leaving the lake I hadn't been thinking about wildlife, and at a moment when I'm totally immersed in my thoughts a white-tailed deer bounds across the trail, perhaps thirty feet or so ahead of me—as usual, when I was least expecting it. We both stop almost simultaneously. I watch the deer and he looks me over for ten or fifteen seconds. Presumably he's trying to figure out if I present any danger, or perhaps he's just curious. Then off he goes again quickly through the brush. With a couple of flashes of white tail he's gone.

Continuing on my way, I can see the last of the sun's rays filtering through the trees just before disappearing behind a nearby mountain. Soon all will be in shadow and the day virtually over. I'm now feeling a bit weary, but it would be hard to come up with a real complaint. Frankly, I feel as fully alive and content right now as I'd ever want to be. Inside there's a warm glow that I know will last the evening and probably continue on into the week.

The road and my "other life" await just ahead. It will be good to get home . . . but at the same time, it's always a little hard to leave such a beautiful place. I know with virtual certainty that I'll be back again soon, the earliest that I can manage it—not to the exact same location, but to another place where I can roam the foot-trails and explore the wilderness freely to my heart's content. . . .

Minimizing our Impact on the Wilderness

PROTECTING THE WILDERNESS

The wilderness needs our help. We all know about some of the environmental problems which our planet faces, including air and water pollution and acid rain. Natural areas are very vulnerable to such threats. The health of some wild areas is currently in jeopardy. There have also been pressures to permit limited exploitation of the land within certain parks and preserves. The future of the wilderness depends on the efforts of all of us to see that it remains fully protected and unharmed.

Any measures we take to reduce the amount of waste and pollution which we directly or indirectly create in our lives will have a positive effect on the total environment, including the wilderness. We can also help by joining and supporting those groups and organizations which are working full-time to protect the environment in general and the wilderness in particular. Addresses and phone numbers of a few of these organizations will be found at the end of Part I.

The increased popularity of hiking and backpacking in the 1970s and '80s led to some special problems in the backcountry. The volume of litter increased, a number of streams and other water sources have been contaminated due to poor sanitation practices, and fragile vegetation has been damaged by careless hikers and others. It's vital that we all refrain from actions which could mar the wilderness in any way, and prevent any further deterioration from occurring. This means practicing minimal-impact hiking.

Litter

Few things are more disturbing to some of us than the sight of garbage or broken glass in a beautiful natural setting. It feels like an inexcusable desecration. Sadly, some people have little respect for their surroundings and minimal awareness of what they're doing in leaving a trail of refuse behind. These may be the actions of a relatively small number of people, but their impact is glaring.

While most hikers don't intentionally throw litter around, some do carelessly leave behind such things as tissues or candy wrappers or cigarette butts. It's essential that we all be as diligent as possible with regard to every bit of trash. *Everything we bring in must be carried out after using* (with the general exception of toilet paper, which can be buried in most but not all areas). Picking up litter left by others will also help. If a fire has been built, paper alone may be burned, but not those paper items which are plastic-coated or lined with foil.

Leftover food and orange or banana peels should usually be carried out as well. Bring an extra plastic bag for litter or leftovers. In some areas where the soil is rich and organic matter breaks down quickly, it's considered acceptable to leave leftover food or peels in the woods, but only well away from water sources and trails. No one wants to sit down at a lovely spot next to the decaying food scraps left by someone else.

For the sake of the wilderness as well as those who will follow us, we need to leave no sign of our passing.

Sanitation

When an outhouse or bathroom is available it's probably best to use it, assuming the conditions within are reasonably sanitary. Most of the time, however, you must use the "natural facilities," taking care of your needs in the woods. In some fragile areas special regulations apply (occasionally including the requirement to carry out human waste). In most wilderness areas there are just a couple of important guidelines. First, it's necessary to get well away from any and all water sources, preferably 150 feet or more. Second, solid waste must be buried. Dig a hole four to six inches deep, if possible, and cover it over afterward. In areas of moist earth a stick will usually suffice as a digging tool, or a small trowel may be carried for this purpose. If the soil is rocky or hard, dig as much of a hole as possible and rake some extra leaves or other organic matter over it. This should not be done at higher elevations where the vegetation is very fragile and the soil thin.

Poor sanitation practices are believed to be the single most important reason why water sources in the wilderness have been going bad. Unburied waste can wash downhill a considerable distance in heavy rain and end up in a stream or lake. Failing to follow the proper methods may mean harm to the wilderness and wildlife—and indirectly to ourselves as well.

Water

Water is vital to all forms of life. Pure clean water in the wilderness is a delicious and precious gift, and unpolluted water is sadly becoming more scarce. Years ago one could dip into practically any wild stream or lake for a refreshing drink, with little need to be concerned about contamination, but this is no longer true. Some water sources are undoubtedly still good, but in recent years record numbers of people have been getting sick from Giardia and other parasites. While not life-threatening, contracting a parasite or harmful bacteria can be quite an unpleasant experience, one well worth avoiding. Most of us are now very cautious about the water we drink.

On a day hike the easiest thing to do is to bring an ample supply of water for the day from home. It's also possible but less convenient to purify water on the trip itself, which is essential to do on an overnight trip. Boiling water for several minutes will destroy bacteria or parasites, but requires a stove or campfire. Iodine or other purification tablets added to water may do the trick, yet these are known to fail at times—and some of us don't carry them because of that fact. They also create an unpleasant taste, and may not be very healthy to ingest. Reasonably lightweight filter pumps have come on the market in recent years, and these have won considerable favor for purifying water. They work rather quickly and don't affect the taste.

The only source of water which may be considered reasonably safe without treating is that which flows out of the ground from a high mountain spring. If you get the water directly as it emerges from the earth high in a mountain wilderness, and are certain that there's no development or other potential source of pollution within many miles or at a higher elevation, the chances of contamination are almost nil.

When you're hiking near a lake or pond in warm weather you may want to stop for a swim and cool off. If you're washing up, it's important to avoid using soap or any other substance which doesn't belong in the water. Not everyone realizes that biodegradable soaps will still contaminate the water. Any cleaning with soap should be done on land some distance away (you can carry some water from the lake or stream for this purpose).

Contrary to practices of the past, no dishes or food containers should ever be washed in a stream or lake, with or without soap. Food scraps which end up in the water will rot and increase the bacterial count. It's essential that we do nothing which could contribute toward fouling a water source.

Noise

A range of sometimes conflicting needs are represented by those venturing into the wilderness. Many of us who hike and camp in the wilds wish to enjoy the peaceful quiet, and avoid human noise and distractions as much as possible during our stay. At the same time, children and others who are having fun outdoors often vocalize their excitement and pleasure loudly. In addition, some groups of teenagers and adults go into the woods with cases of beer to party and loudly let off steam.

You can't ask or expect others to be silent, but everyone should be aware that sound tends to travel a good distance in the wilderness. Shouting may sometimes be heard from as much as several miles away. To others within earshot, especially those who may be listening to natural sounds or resting, it may be experienced as disruptive. Noise also greatly reduces your chances of seeing wildlife.

Many wilderness areas are large enough, however, to handle numbers of people with different needs. Those who wish to make noise or are likely to be loud can show consideration by making an effort to seek a secluded area well off the trail, a good distance away from others who might be disturbed.

Reducing Our Visual Impact

While it may not be a matter of the foremost importance, wearing and using bright-colored clothing and gear does have an effect in the wilderness, making other hikers as well as wildlife much more aware of your presence—sometimes distractingly so. You can reduce your visual impact by wearing more muted colors (refraining especially from using day-glo-like colors. If you're camping, your tent will blend in with the surroundings much better if the color is natural). The exception is during hunting season, when it's best to wear the brightest possible garments if you're going to hike.

Staying on the Trail

When you're hiking in areas of heavy trail use and/or fragile terrain, try to stay on the trail as much as possible (unless bushwhacking off on your own). Sometimes mud or water will force you to the side, but walking unnecessarily alongside a trail will help to widen it and increase erosion. Likewise, cutting across switchbacks (the zigzags in a trail as it climbs the side of the mountain) is considered bad form. Taking a shortcut between switchbacks creates a steeper trail which will probably funnel rainfall and quickly erode. By watching where you're walking you'll avoid creating more work for trail maintainers or otherwise impacting negatively on the trail environment.

HIKING MISCELLANY

Longest Hiking Trails in the U.S.

Pacific Crest Trail—2,638 miles (CA/OR/WA)
Appalachian Trail—2,100 miles (13 eastern states)

Other Long Trails Currently Under Construction

North Country Trail—will be 3,200 miles
Continental Divide Trail—over 3,000 miles
American Discovery Trail—coast to coast
Florida Trail—1,300 miles
Ice Age Trail—1,000 miles

Major Trails with Alpine Scenery

Pacific Crest Trail
Continental Divide Trail
Colorado Trail

Most Spectacular and Challenging (and Varied) National Trail

Pacific Crest Trail

Most Spectacular Eastern Trail

Appalachian Trail (also the oldest long hiking trail in the country)

Easiest Long Trail

Florida Trail

Outstanding Lake Trails

Tahoe Rim Trail (CA)
Superior Hiking Trail (MN)
Lakeshore Trail (MI)—in Pictured Rocks National Lakeshore

Oceanside Trails

Oregon Coast Trail (OR)
Parks along the coast of California and Maine

Outstanding River Trail

North Umpqua Trail (OR)

Highest Elevation in the U.S.

Mt. McKinley—20,320 ft.—in Denali National Park (AK)

Highest Elevation in the "Lower 48"

Mt. Whitney—14,495 ft.—in Sequoia National Park (CA)
(Terminus of the 210-mile John Muir Trail)

Highest Elevation in the Eastern U.S.

Mt. Mitchell—6,684 ft.—in Mt. Mitchell State Park (NC)

Lowest Elevation in the U.S.

Badwater Basin— −282 ft.—in Death Valley National Monument (CA)

Most Magnificent National Parks in the U.S. For Hiking

Yosemite National Park (CA)
Yellowstone National Park (WY)
Grand Teton National Park (WY)
Rocky Mountain National Park (CO)
Glacier National Park (MT)
Olympic National Park (WA)
Sequoia & Kings Canyon National Parks (CA)
Great Smoky Mountains National Park (NC/TN)

Areas With the Most Miles of Hiking Trails in the U.S.

Bridger-Teton National Forest (WY)—2,800 miles
Nez Perce National Forest (ID)—2,600 miles
Wenatchee National Forest (WA)—2,500 miles

Largest National Forests in the U.S.

Tongass National Forest (AK)—16,800,000 acres
Chugach National Forest (AK)—5,800,000 acres
Toiyabe National Forest (NV/CA)— −3,855,960 acres

Largest National Park in the U.S.

Wrangell—St. Elias National Park and Preserve (AK)—13,000,000 acres

Largest Park in the U.S. Outside of Alaska

Adirondack (State) Park (NY)—6,000,000 acres

Largest Wilderness Area in the Lower 48

Frank Church—River of No Return Wilderness (ID)/Located in 6 contiguous National Forests—
2,361,767 acres

Largest Areas Above Timberline in the Eastern U.S.

In White Mountain National Forest (NH)

World Record for Highest Windspeed (231 miles per hour)

On Mt. Washington, in White Mountain National Forest (NH)

Most Extensive Prairie Wilderness in the U.S.

Badlands National Park (SD)

Most Spectacular Canyons

Grand Canyon (AZ)—Grand Canyon National Park
Hells Canyon (ID/OR)—Hells Canyon National Recreation Area, in Nez Perce National Forest and
    Wallowa–Whitman National Forest

Subtropical Hiking

In Everglades National Park (FL)

Rainforest Hiking

In Hawaii Volcanoes National Park (HI)
Haleakala National Park (HI)
Olympic National Park (WA)
Olympic National Forest (WA)

Island Hiking

Isle Royale National Park (MI)
Parks in Hawaii

SOME HIKING RESOURCES

MAGAZINES WITH HIKING INFORMATION

American Hiker, 1015 31st Street N.W. Washington, DC 20007.

Appalachian Trailway News, P.O. Box 807, Harpers Ferry, WV 25425.

Backpacker, 33 East Minor Street, Emmaus, PA 18098.

Outside, 1165 North Clark Street, Chicago, IL 60610.

MAIL-ORDER SOURCES OF HIKING GUIDE-BOOKS

The Nature Library, 150 Nassau Street, Room 1020, New York, NY 10038; (212)608-3327.

Backcountry Bookstore, P.O. Box 191, Snohomish, WA 98290; (206)568-8722.

Chessler Books, P.O. Box 4267, Evergreen, CO 80439; (800)654-8502.

The Wilderness Bookshelf, 5128 Colorado Avenue, Sheffield Village, OH 44054; (216)934-4143.

MAIL-ORDER SOURCES OF HIKING GEAR

REI (Recreational Equipment, Inc.), P.O. Box 88125, Seattle, WA 98138; (800)426-4840.

L.L. Bean, Inc., Freeport, ME 04033; (800)543-9072. Request their "Sportings Specialties" catalog.

Campmor, P.O. Box 998, Paramus, NJ 07653; (201)445-5000.

Don Gleason's Campers Supply, Inc., 411 Pearl Street, Northampton, MA 01061; (413)584-4895.

A NATIONAL ORGANIZATION FOR HIKERS AND TRAILS

American Hiking Society, 1015 31st Street. N.W., Washington, DC 20007; (703)385-3252. This group needs your support to help protect existing trails and develop new trails. Please join!

WILDERNESS-ORIENTED ENVIRONMENTAL GROUPS WORTH SUPPORTING

The Adirondack Council, P.O. Box D-2, Elizabethtown, NY 12932; (518)873-2240

Alliance for the Wild Rockies, 415 North Higgins Avenue, Missoula, MT 59802: (406)721-5420.

Oregon Natural Resources Council, 522 S.W. Fifth Avenue, Suite 1050, Portland, OR 97204; (503)223-9001.

Sierra Club, 730 Polk Street, San Francisco, CA 94109; (415)776-2211.

Southern Utah Wilderness Alliance, Box 518, Cedar City, UT 84721; (801)586-8242.

The Wilderness Society, 900 17th Street N.W., Washington, DC 20006; (202)833-2300.

PART II

WHERE TO HIKE: THE BEST AREAS AND TRAILS

Along with Hiking Resources For Each State

MAJOR TRAILS AND BEST HIKING AREAS

There are thousands of parks, forests, preserves, reservations, sanctuaries, and other natural areas located throughout the United States. Many are publicly owned, others are private. Within these tracts (and outside of them as well) are found an enormous number of hiking trails, adding up to many tens of thousands of miles. In some parts of the country the range of choices is truly fantastic.

The intent of the following fifty-state guide is to list and briefly describe the important "Major Trails," along with the "Best Hiking Areas," meaning especially attractive areas which offer the most extensive hiking. In addition, for many states "Other Recommended Locations" are given. These are often smaller areas which nevertheless offer some fine scenery and good hiking.

Locations selected for this book generally have at least twenty miles or more of marked hiking trails. Major trails singled out for special attention (which often are found outside of park boundaries) usually run forty miles or longer. The cut-off points inevitably have a certain arbitrariness, but most of the country's best hiking areas and most important trails should be found here.

Priority is given to those places and trails which involve wilderness or other unspoiled natural surroundings. Some trails which pass through minimally developed rural countryside are included, especially for states which have limited hiking available. Urban or suburban parks and trails are generally omitted from the book, as are some trails which mostly follow roads. These may provide pleasant walking, but don't offer the kind of experience in nature that some of us consider a vital part of hiking.

Parks and other wild areas which have few or no marked hiking trails have not been included, regardless of how attractive the scenery or extensive the wilderness. Many parks which have short trails or very small trail systems are certainly still worth a visit. See each state's "Hiking Resources" section regarding information about state parks, forests, and other areas where there may be shorter or lesser-known trails. Also consult any available guidebooks for additional alternatives.

With regard to major trails and hiking areas, every attempt was made to make the listings as complete as possible. A handful of omissions have occurred because adequate information could not be obtained (a small number of parks did not respond to repeated inquiries, or information may not have reached the author in time to be included). A few others could have inadvertently been missed. If you're aware of a trail or hiking area which seems to belong in this book, please see the next-to-the-last page for an address to write to. Your submissions and suggestions will be gratefully received, and can help to make the next edition of the book even more complete.

To the extent possible, selections are listed in the order of importance for hiking, with the most spectacular areas and those with the most trails presented first. The task of prioritizing is difficult for those states which have a large number of outstanding areas. When in doubt, order has been based on the size of trail networks, with some priority given to unusually magnificent areas such as National Parks.

The reader is advised to keep in mind a couple of drawbacks in focusing on the largest, best, or most spectacular areas. First of all, good hiking doesn't require that one go solely to such places. There are plenty of attractive little parks and preserves throughout the country, for instance, which can provide a thoroughly satisfying day of hiking. And being out in nature can be rewarding in itself, regardless of the particulars of scenery.

In addition, more than a few of the best-known areas already draw plenty of hikers. Some of us feel that a wilderness experience is diminished when too many people are present, and we're personally happiest when we encounter relatively few others during a day on the trail. The wilderness environment as well would benefit if we limit the frequency of our visits to the most popular places, and favor more of the lesser-known areas, where the trails are sometimes almost deserted.

There's no denying, though, that it's a special treat to periodically visit the great parks, which often have truly awe-inspiring scenery. Some wilderness areas are so vast that almost unlimited solitude is available. Such places provide a rich and memorable experience which may be difficult to achieve elsewhere.

USING THIS PART OF THE BOOK

You'll find a chapter for every state. Each begins with a brief overview of the state including the hiking opportunities available, along with a state map. Please note that these maps offer approximations of trail routes and park locations, drawn from the best available information, but do not have the precision of trail maps. Next is a listing of "Major Trails" (if any)—long distance trails of outstanding scenic interest—followed by "Best Hiking Areas" (the most spectacular places with the most trails) and "Other Recommended Locations" (additional areas offering good hiking). At the end of the chapter are some "Hiking Resources" for the state.

Be sure to obtain more detailed trail information as well as local maps before heading for a particular area or trail. Use the addresses provided, and also try to obtain a hiking guidebook for the region or trail, if one exists. Many of the available guidebooks are listed under "Hiking Resources" for each state. If a particular book is for an area in your state, local bookstores or sporting goods stores may carry it. Otherwise, you'll probably need to order it by mail. See *Some Hiking Resources* at the end of Part I, for a listing of some mail-order companies which sell guidebooks.

If you're not thoroughly experienced in hiking or in using maps, be sure to read Part I. Gain some experience in going with others before you consider a trip on your own or trying it with an inexperienced friend. You'll find a listing of local hiking clubs and other organizations which offer hikes at the end of the "Hiking Resources" sections.

If you'd like to get off the beaten path and visit some lesser-known areas, or explore as thoroughly as possible all the options in your locality (including places which are not listed in this book), check your state's "Hiking Resources" section for the appropriate agency to contact regarding state parks and forests. Also contact any existing trail associations for leads about lesser-known trails.

THE DIFFERENT CATEGORIES OF PUBLIC LANDS

Most hiking takes place on public lands. However, many people do not fully understand the differences between National Parks and National Forests, state parks and state forests, as well as other varieties of public lands. Since these differences have a bearing on the kind of hiking experience you may have, they are addressed here.

National Parks

Most of us know about our National Parks, which receive a great deal of publicity. There are some fifty-four National Parks in the United States, and they're administered by the U.S. Department of the the Interior. The majority are in the western states, with just a few located in the East. National Parks preserve some of the most spectacular natural areas in the country, and virtually all are worth a visit. Many of them are wonderful places.

National parklands are generally kept in a wilderness state. The only intrusion commonly permitted involves visitor facilities. In a few parks such facilities are extensive and clearly excessive, sometimes including small villages and vast parking lots, and thus have come under criticism. At the same time, these tend to take up only a small portion of the total park area.

For some of us, there's one major problem involved in visiting a National Park: the crowds of people attracted. Solitude is generally hard to come by, although some parks are much more popular than others. Most visitors don't venture far from their cars and there are far fewer hikers than tourists, but many trails still receive heavy use. The best time to visit is off-season or mid-week, if possible. Most parks will typically have some lesser-used and more remote trails, which may require overnight backpacking to reach. Permits are commonly required for camping, and quotas are frequently set.

Most National Parks tend to issue excellent literature, and any park with a substantial trail system tends to have a trail guidebook or pamphlet available, along with maps. A request for information will usually be met by an attractive packet of useful materials, often with a map.

National Monuments, Recreation Areas, and Historical Parks

These are other kinds of parks run by the National Park Service. National Monuments tend to be smaller than National Parks (but not always), and are frequently areas of extraordinary scenic interest. Some are very similar to National Parks but for various reasons haven't been accorded full National Park status.

National Recreation Areas are usually places which have a particular recreational focus, and which may not be completely in a wilderness condition. Many of these areas tend to center around rivers or large lakes. National Historical Parks are areas of special historic interest, yet some of these have expanses of wild lands similar to other kinds of parks.

There are additional categories of parks which have appeared in recent years: National Seashores, National Lakeshores, and National Wild and Scenic Rivers. Most send out attractive and high-quality literature, often with useful information about trails.

National Forests

National Forests contain many more of the most splendid and desirable areas in the country for hiking. There are 156 National Forests in the United States, with the majority in the western states, and they are administered by the U.S. Department of Agriculture. Unlike National Parks, which protect most of the land as wilderness, National Forests are multi-use lands, where logging and a wide variety of recreational uses are permitted.

Within most National Forests there are designated "Wilderness Areas" which have been set aside. Here vehicles are banned and entry is only on foot or by horseback. Many of these wilderness areas are comparable in beauty (and occasionally in size) to many of our National Parks, and thus make especially desirable destinations for hikers.

Some of the most spectacular National Forests are as popular and crowded as National Parks, but most are not. Wilderness areas tend to draw the majority of hikers. This is understandable since in other parts of the forest one may encounter logging, motorcycles or other motorized vehicles, and other sources of noise which some of us find intrusive. This will not always be the case, and some trails outside of wilderness areas offer exceptional hiking. Wilderness areas in some popular National Forests require permits for overnight use, and occasionally even for day hiking. Some National Forests and accompanying wilderness areas do not receive many visitors.

The literature mailed out by National Forests tends to include much spottier and less complete information than that obtainable from National Parks—presumably in part due to current budgetary limitations. A few National Forests issue attractive glossy brochures, free maps, and extensive useful information about trails, but most do not. Maps are generally available for a fee.

Some National Forests are covered by hiking guidebooks, but many are not. The most complete information may usually be obtained in person at a ranger station or information center, where a large "Recreational Opportunity Guide" is normally maintained, containing information about many or most of the trails. Sometimes photocopies of information regarding a specific trail or trails will be sent by mail upon request.

National Wildlife Refuges

Wildlife refuges are of course devoted to protecting wildlife. Most National as well as state wildlife refuges do not have marked hiking trails, although there are exceptions. Some are closed to the public. Of the many that are open, some permit free walking or hiking, although you must frequently find your own path.

BLM Lands

Bureau of Land Management (BLM) lands are other federal lands, located mostly in the west-

ern states. Some of these lands include outstanding wilderness areas and other beautiful natural scenery. There are very few marked trails, however, so they're mainly for the knowledgeable and adventuresome hiker. Relatively few guidebooks list BLM lands, information isn't easy to obtain, and access is sometimes difficult. The Sierra Club series of "Guides to Natural Areas" in the western states, by John and Jane Perry, list a selection of these lands. Due to the near-absence of marked trails, only a handful of such areas appear in this book.

State Parks

In general, state parks (like National Parks) tend to be developed at least minimally for tourism and recreation, but otherwise exist to protect a natural area. This country has an enormous variety of state parks, which have great differences in size, scenery, and hiking options. Some states have very small parks with only short paths, while others have enormous state parks with a truly vast array of trails. In general, far more hiking is done in state parks in the eastern United States than in the West (with the exception of California, which has loads of opportunities on state lands). Presumably this is partly because federal lands are so much more limited in the East, whereas the western states have many more National Parks and Forests.

Information about trails in larger state parks will sometimes be included in hiking guidebooks, when available. In some cases one must write the individual park for information and a map, which may or may not be available. Most states have some sort of "Division of State Parks," and by contacting this agency, information regarding the entire state's parks or individual parks may sometimes be obtained. Addresses for these agencies are generally given in the "Hiking Resources" section following each state listing in this book. The address is omitted for some states which have little hiking available in state parks.

State Forests

State forests tend to be less developed for tourism. Some are virtually unidentified and difficult to locate without good instructions. As with National Forests, logging and other uses are commonly permitted. With notable exceptions, in most states the number of hiking trails in state forests is not significant, and information can be hard to obtain. Those that offer hiking and a considerable amount of other recreational use may issue brochures, maps, and other information.

County and Local Parks

County and local parks are often well-developed for popular recreational use. Many such parks are rather small and don't offer extensive trail systems, and sometimes aren't suitable for hiking at all. The most comprehensive guidebooks often cover such parks, and a few will be found in this book's listings.

PRIVATE LANDS

Preserves, Reservations, and Sanctuaries

While the words "preserve," "reserve," "reservation," or "sanctuary" are sometimes applied to public lands, most often these refer to private lands owned by organizations devoted to preservation. There are thousands of such preserves across the country, and many are open to the public. The majority are relatively small and have only short nature trails, but quite a few offer a significant amount of hiking, with good-size trail systems. Some of the larger areas are included in this book.

Other Private Lands

In some states a number of hiking trails are found on privately owned lands which fall outside of preserves or other such entities. Sometimes relevant information will be found in local guidebooks. There's an ongoing problem, however, in that land can change hands and the trails be closed at any time. Sometimes special permission must be obtained to enter the area. For these and other reasons most such trails and areas have been omitted from this book.

NATIONAL TRAILS

There are several kinds of nationally designated trails. Of special interest to hikers are National Scenic Trails, which are often long multistate wilderness trails offering spectacular natural scenery. A total of eight such trails are currently in existence, and among these are the country's longest and greatest trails.

Granddaddy of them all is the 2,100-mile Appalachian Trail, completed in 1937 and designated our first National Scenic Trail in 1968. This famous trail runs the length of the Appalachian Mountains from Georgia to Maine. Another especially important National Scenic Trail is the 2,600-mile Pacific Crest Trail, which extends from the Mexican border through California, Oregon, and Washington to Canada—following the high

crest of the Sierras, the Cascades, and other mountain ranges.

Still another high mountain route is provided by the as-yet-uncompleted 3,100-mile Continental Divide Trail, which follows the Divide from New Mexico (Mexican border) through Montana to Canada. Much of the time this trail stays at extremely high elevations, and runs through some very remote country.

The network of major National Scenic Trails continues to grow with the ongoing construction of the 3,200-mile North Country Trail, which will run from New York to North Dakota. There are other new trails in the offing as well, and not all of these have National Scenic Trail status. Included are the Great Western Trail, which will

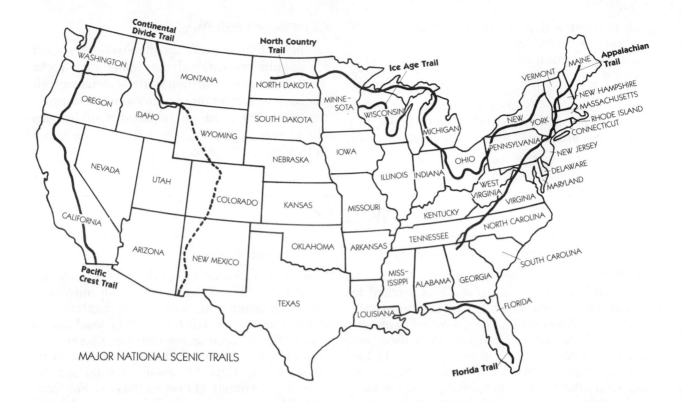

MAJOR NATIONAL SCENIC TRAILS

run from Arizona to Canada, and the American Discovery Trail (currently being scouted) which will run from coast to coast. You'll find more information about many of these trails under the listings for each state. Only those trails which have portions open and marked have been included in this book.

National Recreation Trails are much shorter than National Scenic Trails, running from less than a mile to ten or twenty miles, and occasionally longer. Not all are hiking trails. National Recreation Trails often lie within a single park or forest, and tend to traverse an especially scenic area.

National Historic Trails are usually multi-use trails. These generally follow a path of special historic significance, commemorating a famous trip or an early American cross-country route. At times the trails will provide a wilderness hiking experience, but some of them also pass through developed areas and may follow well-traveled roads, or sometimes rivers.

ALABAMA

Hiking has a limited history in Alabama, and there still aren't lots of trails, but the number of appealing options is growing. Quite a few state parks have rather good trail systems, and four National Forests in the state provide hiking opportunities amid some wild and lovely scenery. Especially notable is the eighty-mile-long-and-growing Pinhoti Trail in Talladega National Forest.

MAJOR TRAILS

PINHOTI TRAIL—80 miles. When completed, this National Recreation Trail will be over 100 miles long. The trail is within 377,000-acre Talladega National Forest in northeastern Alabama, with attractive forested terrain which includes small ridges, rocky bluffs, and valleys with streams and a few lakes. Difficulty is easy to moderate. Trail information: National Forests in Alabama, 1765 Highland Avenue, Montgomery, AL 36107; (205)832-7630.

BEST HIKING AREAS

BANKHEAD NATIONAL FOREST—P.O. Box 278, South Main Street, Double Springs, AL 35553. 179,654 acres. Located in northwest Alabama, Bankhead National Forest is an area of low ridges, sandstone cliffs, gorges and waterfalls, and the scenic Sipsey River. There are hardwood forests, wildlife including deer, and the beautiful and somewhat remote 12,726-acre Sipsey Wilderness, which has over 23 miles of hiking trails.

CONECUH NATIONAL FOREST—U.S. Forest Service, P.O. Box 310, 1100 South 3-Notch Street, Andalusia, AL 36420; (205)222-2555. 82,883 acres. Situated along the southern border of Alabama, this National Forest has stands of longleaf pine, cypress, hardwoods, and several streams. Among the wildlife are deer and alligator. Located here is the Conecuh Trail, an easy 20-mile hiking trail which includes two large loops and passes several attractive ponds.

OAK MOUNTAIN STATE PARK—P.O. Box 278, Pelham, AL 35124; (205)663-6771. 10,000 acres. Located in the north-central part of the state, scenic Oak Mountain is Alabama's largest state park and has over 30 miles of hiking trails. Terrain is hilly to mountainous with pine and hardwood trees and four lakes.

DESOTO STATE PARK—Route 1, Box 210, Fort Payne, AL 35967; (205)845-0051. 5,067 acres. This attractive park in northeast Alabama has mountain ridges, a river canyon, waterfalls, and 20 miles of hiking trails.

De Soto ▲
State Park

Bankhead
National Forest

BIRMINGHAM
●

▲
Oak Mountain
State Park

Pinhoti Trail

Talladega
National Forest

MONTGOMERY
●

ALABAMA

Conecuh
National Forest

MOBILE
●

ALABAMA HIKING RESOURCES

INFORMATION ABOUT STATE PARKS

Division of State Parks, Alabama Department of
Conservation and Natural Resources, 64 North
Union Street, Montgomery, AL 36130.

INFORMATION ABOUT NATIONAL FORESTS

National Forests in Alabama, 1765 Highland
Avenue, Montgomery, AL 36107; (205)832-
7630.

STATE HIGHWAY MAP AND TRAVEL INFORMATION

Alabama Bureau of Tourism and Travel, 532
South Perry Street, Montgomery, AL 36104;
1(800)ALABAMA.

CLUBS AND OTHER ORGANIZATIONS WHICH OFFER HIKES

Appalachian Trail Club of Alabama, P.O. Box
360213, Birmingham, AL 35236.

Sierra Club, P.O. Box 55591, Birmingham, AL
35255.

ALASKA

The magnitude and magnificence of Alaska's wilderness is almost beyond comprehension for those of us who live in the lower forty-eight. This state has the highest and most spectacular mountains on the continent—including 20,320-foot Mount McKinley—along with gigantic glaciers, vast areas of alpine tundra, active volcanoes, glacier-carved gorges and canyons, and perpetual icefields. There are 8 National Parks and other National Monuments and Preserves totaling 51 million acres, two National Forests comprising 23 million acres, 77 million acres of National Wildlife Refuges—and 26 National Wild and Scenic Rivers.

Only the National Forests and some state parks have significant numbers of marked hiking trails. Most National Parks are relatively new, quite remote, practically trailless, and require considerable resourcefulness and expertise to safely enter and explore. For those with an adventuresome spirit, however, Alaska offers an experience of some of the greatest wilderness remaining in the world.

BEST HIKING AREAS

TONGASS NATIONAL FOREST—16,800,000 acres. This National Forest is so vast that there are three separate headquarters: Chatham Area, 204 Siginaka Way, Sitka, AK 99835; (907)747-6671. Ketchikan Area, Federal Building, Ketchi-

kan, AK 99901; (907)225-3101. Stikine Area, 201 12th Street, P.O. Box 309, Petersburg, AK 99833; (907)772-3841.

Located on Alaska's southeast panhandle, Tongass is by far the largest National Forest in the United States. It includes an incredibly beautiful landscape of spectacular snow-covered peaks, glaciers, icefields and snowfields, gorges and canyons, high ridges and volcanoes, islands and fjords. There are precipitous granite walls and rocky outcroppings, numerous alpine lakes, major rivers, streams with waterfalls, and sandy ocean beaches.

The region has 14 designated wilderness areas totaling over 5 million acres. Within the forest boundaries is the splendid 2,285,000-acre Misty Fiords National Monument, almost all of which is designated wilderness. There are lush old-growth rain forests of Sitka spruce and Western hemlock, with some 1,000-year-old trees—along with cedar, lodgepole pine, cottonwood, and alder—and lots of boggy areas ("muskegs") with small ponds.

Timberline here is only 2,500 to 3,000 feet in elevation, above which is alpine tundra. Wildflowers are rampant in season. Wildlife includes brown and black bear, moose, deer, mountain goat, wolf, lynx, fox, and wolverine. Among the local marine mammals are whale, porpoise, seal, and sea lion.

Tongass has more than 400 miles of hiking trails. Many are short and not often interconnected, and some areas are accessible only by boat or plane. Difficulty varies from easy to strenuous. Some trails offer gorgeous vistas.

CHUGACH NATIONAL FOREST—201 East 9th Avenue, Suite 206, Anchorage, AK 99501; (907)271-2500. 5,800,000 acres. Located in southeast Alaska, east and south of Anchorage, Chugach is the second largest National Forest in the United States—a truly enormous area of absolutely splendid wild land, with spectacular mountains, massive glaciers, lofty lakes and streams. It includes part of the Copper River Delta, nesting area for millions of birds, and Prince William Sound, with 3,500 miles of shoreline (partially damaged by the 1989 oil spill). There's also a 2.1 million-acre wilderness study area.

Most hiking trails are on the Kenai Peninsula, where one finds the Kenai Mountains, some impressive glaciers, and open alpine tundra above timberline. The area also has thick spruce and hemlock forests. Among the wildlife are moose, black and brown bear, Dall sheep, mountain goat—and whale offshore.

There are more than 200 miles of hiking trails in this National Forest, including the scenic and easy 39-mile Resurrection Pass National Recreation Trail. Difficulty generally ranges from easy to moderate. The hiking season for the majority of trails is May to October, with a few trails feasible only from July to September.

OTHER RECOMMENDED LOCATIONS

CHUGACH STATE PARK—Alaska Division of Parks and Outdoor Recreation, P.O. Box 107001, Anchorage, AK 99510; (907)345-5014. 495,000 acres. This is a huge state park in south-central Alaska, next to Chugach National Forest. It's an area of mountains up to 8,000 feet, broad valleys, glaciers and lakes, forests and alpine tundra. Grizzly and black bear, wolf, and mountain goat are among the wildlife. There are many miles of maintained and unmaintained trails here, including the 26-mile Iditarod/Crow Pass Trail. Difficulty varies from easy to strenuous.

CHENA RIVER STATE RECREATION AREA—Alaska Division of Parks and Outdoor Recreation, 3700 Airport Way, Fairbanks, AK 99709; (907)451-2695. 254,080 acres. Located east of Fairbanks, this very large State Recreation Area in the Chena River Valley has hilly terrain with low ridges, rock formations and outcroppings, spruce forests, and alpine tundra. Wildlife includes moose, grizzly and black bear, wolf, and lynx. Among a number of hiking trails here are three well-marked trail-loops adding up to nearly 50 miles. Longest is the 29-mile Chena Dome Trail.

STEESE/WHITE MOUNTAINS DISTRICT—Bureau of Land Management, 1150 University Avenue, Fairbanks, AK 99708; (907)474-2350. This BLM-administered district in central Alaska has two trails of note: the 27-mile Pinnell Mountain Trail, located in the Steese National Conservation Area, and the 19-mile White Mountains Trail, in the White Mountains National Recreation Area. Both trails cross alpine ridges and tundra and offer great views. Among the wildlife in the region are grizzly bear, wolf, and wolverine.

DENALI STATE PARK—Alaska Division of Parks and Outdoor Recreation, HC 32, Box 6706, Wasilla, AK 99687; (907)745-3975. 324,240 acres. Denali State Park stands next to Denali National Park and Preserve in south-central Alaska. Within the park boundaries are mountain ridges with alpine meadows and tundra, valleys with glacial streams, and magnificent views. There are also spruce and birch forests, and wildlife which includes grizzly and black bears, moose, coyote, and wolf. Over 40 miles of trails extend through the park. Difficulty ranges from easy to strenuous.

KACHEMAK BAY STATE PARK—Alaska Division of Parks and Outdoor Recreation, P.O. Box 1247, Soldotna, AK 99669; (907)262-5581. 250,000 acres. This large state park is located on the Kenai Peninsula in south-central Alaska. Access is by boat or airplane. Terrain is ruggedly mountainous with glaciers, spruce forests, alpine tundra, and ocean shoreline. Moose, bear, and wolf are among the local wildlife, along with

ALASKA

Steese/White
Mountains District

FAIRBANKS ●

Chena River
State Recreation
Area

▲ Denali State Park

Chugach
ANCHORAGE ● State Park

Chugach
National Forest

Kachemak Bay
State Park

● JUNEAU

Tongass
National Forest

marine animals including seal, sea otter, and whale. There are over 20 miles of hiking trails, some of which offer great views. Difficulty varies from easy to strenuous.

ALASKA HIKING RESOURCES

HIKING GUIDEBOOKS
55 Ways to the Wilderness in South Central Alaska—Nienhueser, Helen, & Simmerman, Nancy. Seattle: The Mountaineers, 1985.

INFORMATION ABOUT STATE PARKS
Alaska Division of Parks and Outdoor Recreation, P.O. Box 107001, Anchorage, AK 99510.

INFORMATION ABOUT NATIONAL PARKS
Alaska Regional Office, National Park Service, 2525 Gambell Street, Room 107, Anchorage, AK 99503; (907)271-2643.

INFORMATION ABOUT PUBLIC LANDS
Alaska Public Lands Information Center, 605 West 4th Avenue, Suite 105, Anchorage, AK 99501; (907)271-2737.

STATE HIGHWAY MAP AND TRAVEL INFORMATION
Alaska Division of Tourism, Box E, Juneau, AK 99811; (907)465-2010.

ALASKA HIKING CLUBS
Sierra Club, P.O. Box 103–441, Anchorage, AK 99501.

ARIZONA

Major areas of Arizona are arid desert, but the state is also home to high rugged mountains and plateaus, steep red-rock cliffs and spectacular canyons—most dramatic of which is the famous and awesome Grand Canyon. Public landholdings in Arizona are truly vast, with six enormous National Forests containing some of the richest and most enticing scenery. Trails are widespread here, especially in the wilderness areas, and just about every conceivable kind of hiking experience is available in this beautiful state.

MAJOR TRAILS

ARIZONA TRAIL—This is a new trail, currently under construction. When completed it will run the length of Arizona from Utah to Mexico, passing through some of the state's finest scenery. Ninety-five percent of the trail will be on public lands, in many cases utilizing previously existing trails. Total distance will be more than 700 miles. So far over 100 miles have been completed and dedicated. Trail information: Arizona Trail Coordinator, Kaibab National Forest, 800 South 6th Street, Williams, AZ 86046.

BEST HIKING AREAS

GRAND CANYON NATIONAL PARK—P.O. Box 129, Grand Canyon, AZ 86023; (602)638-7888. 1,215,735 acres. Situated on the Colorado Plateau in northern Arizona, the magnificent mile-deep and 200-mile-long Grand Canyon of the Colorado River is a world-famous tourist attraction, offering a natural spectacle which many find truly awe-inspiring. There are endlessly varied views from the rims as well as throughout the enormous desert canyon, with its exposed and multicolored layers of rock.

Elevations range from 7,000 to 9,000 feet on the South and North Rims to 2,400 feet or less along the Colorado River—with major differences in temperature, climate, and vegetation from top to bottom. There are spruce fir and ponderosa pine forests on the rim, some piñon pine and juniper below, and sagebrush plus other desert plants further down into the canyon. Wildlife here includes mule deer, bobcat, coyote, and fox.

The Grand Canyon has many hiking trails. Some are very steep and challenging. The South Rim draws extremely large crowds, and some trails receive heavy use. Summer hiking is not recommended due to the extreme temperatures at lower elevations. Water is very scarce, and so is shade on some trails. Except for those who are exceptionally fit, day hiking far into the canyon is risky, due to the long and difficult ascent required in returning to the rim.

CORONADO NATIONAL FOREST—300 West Congress, Tucson, AZ 85701; (602)670-6483. 1,780,196 acres. Located in southeastern Arizona and comprised of several separate units, Coronado National Forest encloses some extremely varied terrain and diverse vegetation. There are no less than twelve mountain ranges, with many elevations exceeding 9,000 feet. Mount Graham is the highest point at 10,717 feet. Some of the area is extremely rugged, with rocky summits and massive cliffs, pinnacles and rock outcroppings, steep-sided canyons and gorges—and wonderful panoramic views.

Several wilderness areas are included. Spruce, pine and fir forests are found in the mountains, with grasslands and desert vegetation including saguaro cactus at lower elevations. There are lakes and streams in some locations. Among the wildlife are black bear, bighorn sheep, deer, pronghorn, mountain lion, and bobcat.

Coronado National Forest has more than 900 miles of hiking trails, including a section of the new Arizona Trail. Difficulty ranges from easy to strenuous. Some trails are not well marked and difficult to follow.

APACHE–SITGREAVES NATIONAL FORESTS—P.O. Box 640, Springerville, AZ 85938; (602)333-4301. 2,004,819 acres. Situated in east-central Arizona, these two extremely large National Forests include major expanses of desert, high mountains, plateaus, and rugged canyons. Elevations range from 3,500 feet to over 10,000 feet, with wonderful vistas from high lookouts. Among the mountains here is Escudilla Peak (10,912 feet), Arizona's third highest.

Vegetation varies from subalpine plants, mountain meadows, and conifers—including an enormous ponderosa pine forest—to desert scrub, yucca, and prickly pear. Among the area's mammals are elk, antelope, deer, and mountain lion.

There are several wilderness areas, including the 174,000-acre Blue Range Primitive Area. A number of lakes and a great many streams are also here. An estimated 875 miles of hiking trails extend throughout the region. The 29-mile Eagle National Recreation trail is among them. Difficulty ranges from easy to strenuous. Most trails are open to horseback riding, and not all are maintained.

TONTO NATIONAL FOREST—P.O. Box 5348, 2324 East McDowell Road, Phoenix, AZ 85010; (602)225-5200. 2,874,580 acres. Enormous Tonto National Forest is located in central Arizona,

enclosing parts of several sizable desert mountain ranges. There are 8 wilderness areas here, which include the 252,000-acre Mazatzal Wilderness and the 160,000-acre Superstition Wilderness. The scenery is diverse and striking, with jagged summits and rugged ridges, painted cliffs and bluffs, precipitous canyons, rock outcrops and pinnacles, buttes and mesas.

Vegetation includes Sonoran Desert scrub, saguaro cactus, chaparral and manazanita, piñon-juniper, and forests of fir and pine at some higher elevations. There are scenic creeks, an area of Indian cliff dwellings, and many superb views. Among the wildlife are deer, bear, and mountain lion.

Over 800 miles of trail are found here. Included is the 51-mile Highline National Recreation Trail, the 29-mile Mazatzal Divide Trail, and the 28-mile Verde River Trail. Difficulty ranges from easy to strenuous. Summer hiking is not recommended due to high desert temperatures. Some trails are unmaintained and not easy to follow.

COCONINO NATIONAL FOREST—2323 East Greenlaw Lane, Flagstaff, AZ 86004; (602)527-7400. 1,835,913 acres. This important National Forest is located in north-central Arizona. It includes an unusually rich range of scenery and terrain, and several wilderness areas. Along with the high desert of the Colorado Plateau are the volcanic snow-capped San Francisco Peaks, and Arizona's highest mountain—12,633-foot Humphrey's Peak—with alpine tundra and bristlecone pine at treeline.

There are also countless rocky cliffs and gorgeous colored canyons, great red sandstone buttes and spires. Especially splendid are 21-mile-long Sycamore Canyon and 16-mile Oak Creek Canyon, which is 2,500 feet deep. The area has numerous lakes and creeks, meadows and coniferous forest, piñon-juniper woodlands, and desert grasslands with cholla and cactus. Local wildlife includes elk, mule deer, black bear, mountain lion, coyote, and bobcat.

There are over 300 miles of trails. Among them is a 53-mile section of the rugged 133-mile General Crook State Historic Trail. Some trails receive heavy use. Difficulty ranges from easy to strenuous. Spring and fall are the best seasons to hike (summer not recommended due to the heat).

PRESCOTT NATIONAL FOREST—344 South Cortez Street, Prescott, AZ 86303; (602)445-1762. 1,250,613 acres. Prescott National Forest consists of two large tracts in central Arizona, with several fine wilderness areas and elevations from 3,000 feet to over 7,000 feet. There are some rugged mountain ranges, pine and fir-forested ridges, and giant mesas with outstanding vistas—plus limestone and sandstone-walled canyons, and gigantic granite boulders. Vegetation includes piñon-juniper woodlands, chaparral and manzanita, and desert mesquite and cactus. Among the local wildlife are black bear, deer, mountain lion, and coyote.

Over 300 miles of hiking trails are available here. Some trails are heavily used, others are unmaintained. Difficulty varies from easy to strenuous. Due to summer heat, spring and fall are best for hiking.

OTHER RECOMMENDED LOCATIONS

KAIBAB NATIONAL FOREST—800 South 6th Street, Williams, AZ 86046; (602)635-2681. 1,556,465 acres. Divided into three substantial tracts of land in northern Arizona, located north as well as south of the Grand Canyon, Kaibab National Forest is situated primarily on a forested plateau. A few prominent peaks include 10,418-foot Kendrick Mountain.

There are also some cliffs and steep canyons, a small part of the Grand Canyon's rim, and some great views. Vegetation ranges from subalpine meadows and conifer forest to desert varieties. Elk and mule deer are among the mammals here.

Approximately 77 miles of hiking trails are found in this National Forest, including 37 miles of the new Arizona Trail, with difficulty ranging from easy to strenuous. Summer hiking is inadvisable because of the heat.

SAGUARO NATIONAL MONUMENT—3693 South Old Spanish Trail, Tucson, AZ 85730; (602)296-8576. 83,651 acres. Consisting of two separate tracts near Tucson in southeast Arizona, this National Monument features stands of giant saguaro cactus. Elevations range from 2,700 feet to 8,666 feet (Mica Mountain). Over 71,000 acres are designated as wilderness.

Along with saguaro there are cholla and prickly pear in the desert, with some grasslands and oak-pine woodlands at higher elevations, and pine and fir forests in the mountains. Wildlife includes mule deer and coyote. A number of hiking trails are found in this National Monument. Summer hiking is not recommended due to the often extreme heat.

MCDOWELL MOUNTAIN REGIONAL PARK—3475 West Durango Street, Phoenix, AZ 85009; (602)272-8871. 21,099 acres. Located in the desert northeast of Phoenix, this regional park includes small mountains with elevations from 1,600 feet to 3,000 feet, offering some great views. There are over 50 miles of hiking trails, some of which are open to horses.

ESTRELLA MOUNTAIN REGIONAL PARK—3475 West Durango Street, Phoenix, AZ 85009; (602)272-8871. 19,200 acres. Situated in the Sierra Estrella Mountains and desert, Estrella Mountain Regional Park has elevations from 900 feet to 3,650 feet. Vegetation includes saguaro cactus, creosote, and cholla—with mule deer and bighorn sheep among the wildlife. There are over 33 miles of trails here, most of which are open to horseback riding.

ARIZONA HIKING RESOURCES

HIKING GUIDEBOOKS

Arizona Trails—Mazel, David. Berkeley, CA: Wilderness Press, 1989.

Grand Canyon Treks—Volumes I, II, & III—Butchart, J. Harvey. Glendale, CA: La Siesta Press, 1983.

The Hiker's Guide to Arizona—Aitchison, Stewart, & Grubbs, Bruce. Helena, MT: Falcon Press.

Hiking the Grand Canyon—Annerino, John. San Francisco: Sierra Club Books, 1986.

Hiking Guide to the Santa Rita Mountains of

Arizona—Martin, Bob & Dotty. Boulder, CO: Pruett.

Hiking the Southwest—Ganci, Dave. San Francisco: Sierra Club Books, 1983.

Hiking the Southwest's Canyon Country—Hinchman, Sandra. Seattle, WA: The Mountaineers.

On Foot in the Grand Canyon—Spangler, Sharon. Boulder, CO: Pruett.

Tucson Hiking Guide—Leavengood, Betty. Boulder, CO: Pruett, 1990.

INFORMATION ABOUT STATE PARKS

Arizona State Parks, 800 West Washington, Phoenix, AZ 85007; (602)255-4174.

STATE HIGHWAY MAP AND TRAVEL INFORMATION

Arizona Office of Tourism, 1100 West Washington, Phoenix, AZ 85007; (602)542-TOUR.

CLUBS AND OTHER ORGANIZATIONS WHICH OFFER HIKES

Central Arizona Backpackers Association, 5 South Pueblo Street, Gilbert, AZ 85234.

Green Valley Hiking Club, 909 Quail Drive, Green Valley, AZ 85614.

Huachuca Hiking Club, 3705 Shawnee Drive, Sierra Vista, AZ 85635.

Sierra Club, c/o Dawson Henderson, Route 4, Box 886, Flagstaff, AZ 86001.

Southern Arizona Hiking Club, Box 12122, Tucson, AZ 85732.

ARIZONA

ARKANSAS

Until fairly recently there were few hiking trails in Arkansas, but now that situation has changed, and new trails continue to be built. Along with shorter paths in some state parks, there's especially fine hiking and superb scenery to be found within two notable National Forests in the Ozark and Ouachita Mountain regions—and traversing these forests are two outstanding National Recreation Trails.

MAJOR TRAILS

OUACHITA NATIONAL RECREATION TRAIL—225 miles. The Ouachita Trail is the longest trail in Arkansas. One hundred eighty-six miles lie within Ouachita National Forest in west-central Arkansas, with the western end in Oklahoma. As it crosses the Ouachita Mountains (elevations from 600 feet to 2,600 feet) this beautiful trail offers varied and sometimes rugged scenery. Difficulty varies from easy to strenuous. Trail information: Ouachita National Forest, P.O. Box 1270 Hot Springs, AR 71902; (501)321-5202.

OZARK HIGHLANDS TRAIL—168 miles. This fine National Recreation Trail runs the length of Ozark National Forest in northwest Arkansas, traversing wild mountainous terrain and offering a wide range of lovely scenery. At times the trail follows streams and also offers some great views. Difficulty varies from easy to strenuous. Trail information: Ozark National Forest, P.O. Box 1008, 605 West Main, Russellville, AR 72801; (501)968-2354.

BEST HIKING AREAS

OUACHITA NATIONAL FOREST—P.O. Box 1270, Hot Springs, AR 71902; (501)321-5202. 1,600,000 acres. Situated in west-central Arkansas with a small portion in southeast Oklahoma, Ouachita is the largest National Forest in this part of the country. It's an area of medium-size mountain ridges and rugged terrain, lovely lakes and streams—and dense oak and pine forest, with some old-growth stands. There are seven wilderness areas, and more than 235 miles of hiking trails—including the 30-mile Womble Trail, and 175 miles of the 225-mile Ouachita Trail.

OZARK NATIONAL FOREST—P.O. Box 1008, 605 West Main, Russellville, AR 72801; (501)968-2354. 1,300,000 acres. Consisting of several separate tracts in northwestern Arkansas, this large National Forest encompasses quite a variety of beautiful Ozark mountain scenery. Mount Magazine (2,823 feet) the highest point in Arkansas, is found here. Several wilderness areas are also included.

There are hardwood forests of oak-hickory, a number of creeks and small lakes, and some

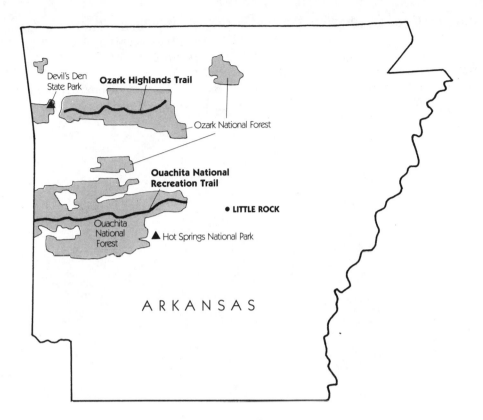

underground caverns. The steadily expanding trail system now has over 220 miles of hiking trails, with varying degrees of difficulty. Foremost among them is a 160-mile segment of the Ozark Highlands Trail.

OTHER RECOMMENDED LOCATIONS

HOT SPRINGS NATIONAL PARK—P.O. Box 1860, Hot Springs, AR 71902; (501)623-1433. 4,787 acres. This small National Park, which includes a number of natural hot springs, is located alongside the city of Hot Springs in the Ouachita Mountains. There are pine and oak forests, wildflowers, elevations up to 1,405 feet, and over 35 miles of trails. This is not remote country, and some trails offer views of the city, yet there remains some appealing scenery.

DEVIL'S DEN STATE PARK—Route 1, Box 118,

West Fork, AR 72774; (501)761-3325. Devil's Den is a wild and secluded state park in the Ozark Mountains of northwest Arkansas. The park has numerous rock formations, caves, a mountain stream, some great views—and 25 miles of hiking trails, including the 15-mile Butterfield Trail.

ARKANSAS HIKING RESOURCES

INFORMATION ABOUT STATE PARKS
Arkansas Department of Parks and Tourism, One Capitol Mall, Little Rock, AR 72001; (501)682-1301.

TRAIL INFORMATION
Arkansas Trails Council, One Capitol Mall, Little Rock, AR 72001; (501)682-1301.

STATE HIGHWAY MAP AND TRAVEL INFORMATION
Arkansas Department of Parks and Tourism, One

Capitol Mall, Little Rock, AR 72001; (501)682-1301.

CLUBS AND OTHER ORGANIZATIONS WHICH OFFER HIKES

Ouachita Mountain Hikers, P.O. Box 371, Hot Springs, AR 71902.

Ozark Highlands Trail Association, P.O. Box 1074, Fayetteville, AR 72702.

Ozark Society, P.O. Box 2914, Little Rock, AR 72203.

Sierra Club, c/o George Oleson, 1669 Carolyn Drive, Fayetteville, AR 72701.

CALIFORNIA

California offers an amazing array of choices to the hiker, more than any other state, with a natural landscape which is often spectacularly wild and at times irresistibly beautiful. A number of high mountain ranges are here, including the famous Sierra Nevada, the Cascades, and the Coast Range—along with valleys and foothills, dramatic canyons, enormous expanses of desert, and magnificent wild coastline. Public landholdings are vast, with 18 National Forests, several National Parks, and 16 million acres of BLM lands. There are over 10,000 miles of trails on National Forest lands alone, and many of the 255 state parks also have substantial trail systems. A hiker is faced with almost limitless possibilities in this extraordinarily interesting and varied state.

MAJOR TRAILS

PACIFIC CREST TRAIL—1680 miles in California (2,638 total). This is one of our greatest and most spectacular National Scenic Trails, running from Mexico to Canada. The California section offers an enormous range of wild and often remote high mountain scenery, with countless lakes and magnificent panoramas. It runs the length of the Sierras, traverses some other mountain ranges, and includes a stretch in the Mojave Desert. Most of the time the trail is on National Forest and National Park lands. Elevations range from about 1,000 feet to 13,180 feet near Mount Whitney. Permits are required for hiking the trail in some National Forests and National Parks. In the Sierras the trail is snow-free only from July through September, but in southern California it's usable even in winter. Horses are permitted. Difficulty ranges from easy to extremely strenuous. Trail information: Pacific Crest Trail Conference, 365 West 29th Avenue, Eugene, OR 97405.

JOHN MUIR TRAIL—210 miles. The John Muir Trail is among the most spectacular in the country, and it's the longest which is uncrossed by any road, providing an entry into some incredibly remote wilderness. The trail runs from Yosemite Valley in Yosemite National Park to 14,495-foot Mount Whitney in Sequoia National Park. It generally remains at high elevations, with scores of lakes and many magnificent views along the way. Some parts are extremely strenuous. Wilderness permits are required. Much of the trail is now also the route of the Pacific Crest Trail. Trail information: *Guide to the John Muir Trail*—Winnett, Thomas. Berkeley: Wilderness Press, 1984.

THE TAHOE–YOSEMITE TRAIL—185 miles. While this trail does not yet have official status, it's become well-established, and most of the route is marked. The trail runs from the Desolation Wilderness at Lake Tahoe along the Sierra Nevada to Yosemite National Park, where it connects with the John Muir Trail. It's less remote than the latter, offering numerous day hiking options. Terrain is very diverse, with a good range of elevations. There's some magnificent wilderness scenery, including a great many lakes and splendid views. A wilderness permit is required for some sections. Difficulty varies from easy to strenuous. Trail information: *The Tahoe–Yosemite Trail*—Winnett, Thomas. Berkeley: Wilderness Press, 1987.

TAHOE RIM TRAIL—This new trail will run about 150 miles when finished. It completely encircles magnificent Lake Tahoe, America's largest alpine lake, on the Nevada border. Much of the time it remains on National Forest lands in California and Nevada. The terrain is mountainous and sometimes rugged, with great views of Lake Tahoe. Trail information: The Tahoe Rim Trail, P.O. Box 10156, South Lake Tahoe, CA 95731.

BEST HIKING AREAS

YOSEMITE NATIONAL PARK—P.O. Box 577, Yosemite National Park, CA 95389; (209)372-0264. 748,542 acres. Located in the high mountains of east-central California's Sierra Nevada, and surrounded by National Forest lands, Yosemite is justly famous and unquestionably one of our most magnificent National Parks. John Muir's name is associated with the park, as his efforts helped lead to its establishment in 1890 (Muir also founded the Sierra Club).

Most visitors head for Yosemite Valley, which is one of the most spectacular mountain valleys in the country. This part of the park is unfortunately overcrowded and overdeveloped, with many stores and extensive facilities in Yosemite Village—but 95 percent of Yosemite remains wilderness, and solitude is still available here if you hike some distance from the highways. The beauty and often awe-inspiring grandeur of this region cannot be overstated.

Elevations range from 2,000 feet to over 13,000 feet—with Mount Lyell (13,114 feet) the highest point. Some of the scenery comes on an enormous scale here. There are steep peaks and rock formations, high vertical walls and massive granite domes, giant glacial U-shaped canyons and valleys.

Along with many lakes and streams are a number of high waterfalls, several of which are in the 1,000- to 2,000-feet range—including 1,430-foot Upper Yosemite Falls. Wildlife includes black bear, mule deer, bighorn sheep, mountain lion, and coyote. There are alpine flora, open meadows and abundant wildflowers, forests of fir and pine, and giant sequoias.

The park has about 800 miles of hiking trails, many of which are open to horses. Included is a section of the 210-mile John Muir Trail, which is utilized by the 2,600-mile Pacific Crest Trail. Difficulty ranges from easy to very strenuous. High elevation trails may be under snow until July. Some trails tend to be crowded, especially in the summer.

SEQUOIA AND KINGS CANYON NATIONAL PARKS—Three Rivers, CA 93271; (209)565-3307. 864,118 acres. Situated in east-central California and surrounded by National Forest lands, these two jointly administered National Parks include some of the most spectacular high country scenery of the Sierras. On the east side the parks border along the Sierra crest, with elevations up to 14,495 feet on Mount Whitney, which is the highest mountain in the United States outside of Alaska. Most of the region is wilderness, with a considerable amount of remote backcountry.

There are great snow-covered high peaks and precipitous granite-walled canyons, including the 8,000-foot canyon of the Kings River (South Fork), said to be the deepest in the country. Here too are many stands of the once widespread giant sequoia—among them the 2,500-year-old General Sherman Tree, thought to be the largest and one of the oldest trees on the earth.

There are also virgin forests of mixed conifers, chaparral and oak woodlands, and lovely mountain meadows. Black bear, bighorn sheep, mule deer, mountain lion, coyote, and bobcat are among the mammals here. The region has many rivers and glacial lakes, streams and waterfalls—and wonderful panoramic vistas.

Six Rivers
National Forest

Pacific Crest Trail

Lava Beds
National Monument

Modoc National Forest

Redwood
National Park

a

Shasta-Trinity
National Forest

a—Klamath National Forest
b—Inyo National Forest
c—Sequoia National Forest
d—San Bernadino National Forest
e—Cleveland National Forest

Humboldt Redwoods
State Park

King Range
National
Conservation Area

Lassen National Forest

Lassen Volcanic National Park

Mendocino
National Forest

Plumas National Forest

Tahoe National Forest

Sugarloaf Ridge
State Park

Tahoe Rim Trail

Eldorado
National Forest

Lake Tahoe Basin Management Unit

Annadel State Park

SACRAMENTO

Point Reyes
National Seashore

**Tahoe-
Yosemite
Trail**

Stanislaus National Forest

Mt. Tamalpais State Park

Yosemite
National
Park

Mt. Diablo
State Park

SAN FRANCISCO

b

Butano State Park

Henry Coe
State Park

Sierra
National Forest

b

Big Basin Redwoods
State Park

John Muir Trail

Castle Rock State Park

c

Pinnacles
National
Monument

Death Valley
National
Monument

Sequoia & Kings
Canyon National
Parks

c

CALIFORNIA

Los Padres National Forest

c

Angeles National Forest

Mt. San Jacinto
State Park &
Wilderness

Point Mugu State Park

Joshua Tree
National Monument

d

LOS ANGELES

d

e

Anza-Borrego
Desert State
Park

e

Cuyamaca Rancho
State Park

e

SAN DIEGO

Pacific Crest Trail

CALIFORNIA

Sequoia and Kings Canyon National Parks have a combined total of over 800 miles of hiking trails—including parts of the 210-mile John Muir and 2,600-mile Pacific Crest Trails (which coincide) and the 49-mile High Sierra Trail. Difficulty varies from easy to strenuous. High trails tend to be snow-free from July to October.

SHASTA–TRINITY NATIONAL FOREST—2400 Washington Avenue, Redding, CA 96001; (916)246-5443. 2,159,001 acres. This vast National Forest in northern California is a splendid area of lofty granite peaks and cliffs, canyons and picturesque lakes, glaciers and lava flows, talus slopes and rock pinnacles—and includes snow-and-glacier-covered Mount Shasta (14,162 feet), second highest volcano in the Cascades.

Several beautiful wilderness areas are found here, including a portion of the 500,000-acre Trinity Alps Wilderness, which extends into two other National Forests—plus the 38,000-acre Mount Shasta Wilderness centering around Mount Shasta. The area has many fine rivers and creeks with waterfalls, mixed forests of fir, pine, and cedar (with virgin stands), chaparral, and high mountain meadows with wildflowers. Wildlife includes such mammals as mule deer, black bear, coyote, mountain lion, bobcat, and fox.

Shasta–Trinity has a network of trails which extends some 1,400 miles, and includes a 154-mile section of the 2,600-mile Pacific Crest Trail. Difficulty ranges from easy to quite strenuous. High trails may be under snow until July.

LOS PADRES NATIONAL FOREST—6144 Calle Real, Goleta, CA 93117; (805)683-6711. 1,724,000 acres. Los Padres National Forest is located along the south-central coast of California, and consists of two separate tracts—with land northwest of Los Angeles, as well as in the Big Sur area farther to the north. Much of the terrain is ruggedly mountainous, with some steep ridges and peaks, cliffs and canyons, and sculpted rock formations. There are several mountain ranges, and five designated wilderness areas, including the 149,000-acre San Rafael Wilderness and the 164,000-acre Ventana Wilderness. The scenery is often quite beautiful, and superb views plentiful.

The highest point is barren-summited Mount Pinos (8,831 feet). There's also some desert, and lands along the ocean include part of the famous and spectacular Big Sur coastline. A section of the San Andreas Fault crosses the forest, and there are also lovely rivers and streams with waterfalls, and natural hot springs. Vegetation includes extensive chapparal, oak woodlands, wildflowers, and some forested areas with pine, fir, and cedar—and some stands of redwoods. Among the local mammals are deer, bear, bobcat, mountain lion, coyote, and fox. The endangered California condor, which has a 9-foot wingspan, is also here.

There are approximately 1,200 miles of trails, which are also open to horses. Difficulty ranges from easy to strenuous. Some trails are closed from July through November due to the fire hazard in the region. Winter and spring are the best hiking seasons for some lower-elevation areas where summer can be hot. A permit is required to enter wilderness areas for day hiking. Some trails are heavily used.

SEQUOIA NATIONAL FOREST—900 West Grand Avenue, Porterville, CA 93257; (209)784-1500. 1,115,375 acres. Situated in the southern Sierras of south-central California, Sequoia National Forest consists of several units, the largest of which is next to Sequoia National Park. Elevations range from 1,000 feet to over 12,000 feet. Mount Florence (12,432 feet) is the highest peak. There are many magnificent views—with several wilderness areas, including the 95,000-acre Dome Lane Wilderness and 111,000 acres of the 303,000-acre Golden Trout Wilderness (which continues into Inyo National Forest).

Terrain in this extremely scenic area ranges from foothills and areas of desert to the high mountains along the ridge of the Sierra Nevada, with some steep canyons, granite domes, and unusual rock formations. There are lovely lakes, rivers, creeks, and waterfalls.

Vegetation varies from grasslands and brush fields with chapparal to oak woodlands and forests of mixed conifers. Of special interest in this National Forest are the many giant sequoias, some of which run over 270 feet high and with diameters of over 30 feet. Mule deer, black bear, mountain lion, bobcat, coyote, and fox are among the local wildlife.

More than 900 miles of hiking trails are found here, including a segment of the Pacific Crest Trail and the 40-mile Silver Knapsack Trail, both of which extend into Sequoia National Park. Difficulty varies from easy to strenuous. Motorized vehicles are permitted on some trails. Certain routes receive heavy use.

INYO NATIONAL FOREST—873 North Main Street, Bishop, CA 93514; (619)873-5841. 1,798,638 acres in California. This elongated National Forest stretches along the east slope of the Sierras north and east of Sequoia, Kings Canyon, and Yosemite National Parks. Some outstanding high mountain scenery and remarkable views are found here.

Elevations range from 5,000 feet to 14,495-foot Mount Whitney—highest mountain in the United States outside of Alaska—which is on the border with Sequoia National Park. The terrain includes many lofty jagged peaks, rock domes and giant boulders, sheer cliffs and deep granite canyons, glaciers and rolling hills.

There are six wilderness areas, including parts of the 584,000-acre John Muir Wilderness, the 305,000-acre Golden Trout Wilderness, and the 228,000-acre Ansel Adams Wilderness. The region has hundreds of beautiful lakes, lush meadows with wildflowers, streams with falls—along with stands of fir and pine, hemlock and aspen, plus sagebrush desert. Of particular interest is an ancient forest of bristlecone pine, considered to be the oldest living things on the earth. Local animals include deer, black bear, bighorn sheep, coyote, fox, and bobcat.

Over 1,100 miles of hiking trails extend through the area. Among them are sections of the John Muir Trail and the Pacific Crest Trail. Difficulty varies from easy to very strenuous. Some trails receive quite heavy use. High trails may only be snow-free from July to October.

SIERRA NATIONAL FOREST—1600 Tollhouse Road, Clovis, CA 93612; (209)487-5155. 1,303,120 acres. This beautiful National Forest is situated in the western Sierras of central California, between Kings Canyon and Yosemite National Parks. There are five wilderness areas here, including 138,000 acres of the 228,000-acre Ansel Adams Wilderness, and about half of the 584,000-acre John Muir Wilderness (which extends into Inyo National Forest).

The terrain includes rugged and striking snow-covered peaks with some small glaciers, granite outcroppings and steep canyons. The highest point is Mount Humphreys (13,986 feet). The area has many wild lakes, rivers, and streams, and wildlife including black bear, mule deer, coyote, bobcat, and gray fox. There are high meadows and grassy foothills, virgin forest with fir, pine, and cedar, plus giant sequoias and some hot springs.

Sierra National Forest has about 1,100 miles of trails. Among them are sections of the John Muir and Pacific Crest Trails (which coincide). Some trails are quite heavily used. Difficulty ranges from easy to strenuous. Horses are permitted on most trails. High elevations are often under snow until July.

KLAMATH NATIONAL FOREST—1312 Fairlane Road, Yreka, CA 96097; (916)842-6131. 1,671,053 acres. Consisting of two tracts near and alongside California's northern border, Klamath National Forest encompasses segments of several mountain ranges, and includes some outstanding scenery. Elevations range from under 1,000 feet to over 8,000 feet—with some magnificent views available. Especially notable is the 215,000-acre Marble Mountain Wilderness, with 8,299-foot Boulder Peak, along with two additional small wilderness areas.

The area has steep mountain peaks of marble and granite, glacial bowls and rocky canyons, mountain meadows and extensive grasslands. There are mixed conifer forests with ponderosa pine and virgin fir, plus hardwoods—along with many alpine lakes, numerous creeks, and several major rivers. Among the region's wildlife are antelope, wild horse, elk, black bear, mule and black-tailed deer, wolverine, and gray fox.

Over 1,100 miles of trails are found in this National Forest, including a section of the Pacific Crest Trail. Many trails are open to horseback riding. Difficulty varies from easy to strenuous. Some high country trails may be under snow until July.

STANISLAUS NATIONAL FOREST—19777 Greenley Road, Sonora, CA 95370; (209)532-3671. 899,894 acres. Located north and west of Yosemite National Park on the western slopes of the Sierras, Stanislaus National Forest is a region of ruggedly scenic granite ridges and volcanic peaks, rock formations and deep gorges, high meadows and glacial lakes. There are several major rivers, numerous streams, and superb panoramic views.

Vegetation ranges from alpine varieties with wildflowers to low woodlands and forests of fir, pine, cedar, including some old-growth stands. Among the wildlife are black bear, mule deer, coyote, bobcat, and gray fox. There are three wilderness areas: the 113,000-acre Emigrant Wilderness, plus part of the 105,000-acre Mokelumne Wilderness and the 160,000-acre Carson-Iceberg Wilderness. Elevations range from under 2,000 feet to 11,520-foot Leavitt Peak.

Stanislaus has about 700 miles of trails, including a section of the Pacific Crest Trail along the boundary with Toiyabe National Forest, plus the Tahoe-Yosemite Trail. Higher elevations may only be snow-free from July through September. Some trails receive heavy use. Difficulty ranges from easy to strenuous.

SAN BERNARDINO NATIONAL FOREST—1824 South Commercenter Circle, San Bernardino, CA 92408; (714)383-5588. 658,664 acres. Consisting of two tracts in southern California, this popular National Forest offers a range of scenery from high peaks and ridges to hilly lowlands and desert. There are many creeks and some rivers, granite gorges and canyons, and great vistas. Three wilderness areas total 111,000 acres. Elevations run from 1,000 feet to over 11,000 feet. The highest point in southern California is here, 11,502-foot San Gorgonio Mountain.

Part of the region is forested with ponderosa and lodgepole pine, white and Douglas fir, juniper and piñon. Other areas are covered with chaparral, and at high elevations, subalpine meadows and vegetation. Among the local mammals are mule deer, bighorn sheep, black bear, mountain lion, coyote, and bobcat.

There are more than 500 miles of hiking trails here, including a section of the Pacific Crest Trail. Difficulty ranges from easy to strenuous. Most trails are open to horseback riding, and some to bikes or motorcycles. During fire season certain trails and areas may be closed. Some trails receive heavy use, and a permit is required for day hikes into wilderness areas.

ANGELES NATIONAL FOREST—701 North Santa Anita Avenue, Arcadia, CA 91006; (818)574-5200. 652,704 acres. Angeles National Forest is situated north and northeast of Los Angeles, in southern California. It's an area of often rugged mountains, with elevations from 1,200 feet to over 10,000 feet. The highest point is Mount Baldy (10,064 feet), and there are many outstanding vistas. Three wilderness areas add up to over 81,000 acres, and include the 44,000-acre Sheep Mountain Wilderness and the 36,000-acre San Gabriel Wilderness.

Along with the high peaks of the San Gabriel Mountains are beautiful canyons and cliffs, rock outcrops and formations, and part of the San Andreas Fault. There are several rivers and many small streams and waterfalls—and vegetation ranging from chaparral, manzanita, and yucca to pine, cedar, and fir forests. Of interest are some 2,000-year-old Limber pines. Mule deer, bighorn sheep, black bear, and coyote are among the wildlife.

This National Forest has about 525 miles of hiking trails, including the 53-mile Silver Moccasin Trail and 131 miles of the Pacific Crest Trail. Some trails are heavily used. Difficulty varies from easy to strenuous. A wilderness permit is required to use certain wilderness trails.

TAHOE NATIONAL FOREST—Highway 49 & Coyote Street, Nevada City, CA 95959; (916)265-

4531. 811,740 acres. Located northwest of Lake Tahoe in the Sierra Nevada of north-central California, Tahoe National Forest has elevations from 1,500 feet to 9,400 feet along the crest of the Sierras. The region includes high peaks and basins, knobs and saddles, rocky knolls, outcrops, and giant boulders, and deep glaciated river canyons with massive sheer-walled cliffs. There are spectacular panoramic views, and one designated wilderness area, the Granite Chief Wilderness.

The forest has many small alpine lakes, streams, and some thundering waterfalls. Among several rivers is the North Fork American National Wild and Scenic River. There are meadows with wildflowers, forests of fir, pine, hemlock, and hardwoods—with some old-growth stands. The wildlife includes mule deer, bear, mountain lion, coyote, and bobcat.

About 500 miles of hiking trails are found here. Among them is a section of the Pacific Crest Trail. Most are open to horses, and some trails are heavily used. Difficulty ranges from easy to strenuous. Some high trails are snow-covered until July.

ELDORADO NATIONAL FOREST—3070 Camino Heights Drive, Camino CA 95709; (916)644-6048. 668,947 acres. Eldorado is an extremely scenic National Forest southwest of Lake Tahoe, in north-central California. It encloses some mountains of the High Sierra, including 9,983-foot Pyramid Peak, with outstanding views. There are also canyons and creeks, and a number of lakes and meadows with wildflowers. The area nearest Lake Tahoe is also part of the Lake Tahoe Basin Management Unit.

There are two wilderness areas, the 63,000-acre Desolation Wilderness plus part of the 105,000-acre Mokelumne Wilderness. The region has forests of lodgepole pine, whitebark fir, and hemlock, including some virgin stands. Mule deer, black bear, mountain lion, coyote, bobcat, and gray fox are among the wildlife.

This National Forest has about 350 miles of trails. Included are segments of the Pacific Crest Trail and the partially-completed Tahoe Rim Trail. Mountain bikes are permitted on some trails. Difficulty ranges from easy to strenuous. Some trails are very heavily used.

REDWOOD NATIONAL PARK—1111 Second Street, Crescent City, CA 95531; (707)464-6101. 106,000 acres. Located along the coast of northern California, 50-mile long and narrow Redwood National Park was established to protect the state's magnificent virgin stands of redwoods—tallest trees in the world, with the highest at 368 feet. Some live to be 2,000 years old.

Directly associated with this park are three adjacent state parks: Jedediah Smith Redwoods State Park, Del Norte Coast Redwoods State Park, and Prairie Creek Redwoods State Park. A trail network connects all four parks. The area includes rugged coastline scenery with some beaches, beautiful creeks, prairies, and conifer forests. Among the wildlife are elk, black-tailed deer, and mountain lion—plus marine mammals such as whale, seal, and sea lion.

Redwood National Park has over 50 miles of hiking trails, and the three state parks have a total of nearly 100 additional miles of trails (trail information regarding all four parks may be obtained from the National Park). Difficulty ranges from easy to strenuous.

LASSEN VOLCANIC NATIONAL PARK—P.O. Box 100, Mineral, CA 96063; (916)595-4444. 106,372 acres. Surrounded by the lands of Lassen National Forest in the southern Cascades of northern California, this National Park is the home of volcanic 10,457-foot Lassen Peak, which erupted earlier this century. There are many other mountains as well, and most of this volcanic-landscaped park is wilderness.

Scenery includes craters and cinder cones, lava flows and pinnacles, and steep canyons. There are thermal areas with steaming sulphur vents and also hot springs—plus beautiful lakes and streams, meadows and forests of pine and fir. Wildfire includes bear, deer, mountain lion, and coyote.

Lassen Volcanic National Park has 150 miles of trails, which includes a 17-mile portion of the Pacific Crest Trail. Difficulty ranges from easy to strenuous. Higher elevations may only be snow-free from July through September.

PLUMAS NATIONAL FOREST—159 Lawrence Street, Quincy, CA 95971; (916)283-2050. 1,409,986 acres. Plumas National Forest is located in northeast California, at the northern end of the Sierras, with elevations from 1,000 feet to over 8,000 feet. There's one 21,000-acre wilderness area (Bucks Lake Wilderness), with 7,017-foot Spanish Peak, and some wonderful views. The region includes rocky ridges and slopes, cliffs and canyons.

There are many lakes, creeks, some rivers, and waterfalls—highest of which is 640-foot Feather Falls. Vegetation includes sagebrush and manzanita, brush fields, conifer forests, and meadows. Mule deer, black bear, mountain lion, coyote, and bobcat are among the wildlife.

This National Forest has more than 300 miles of trails, with about 75 miles of the Pacific Crest Trail. Most trails are open to horses, and motorbikes are permitted on some. Difficulty varies from easy to strenuous.

MENDOCINO NATIONAL FOREST—420 East Laurel Street, Willows, CA 95988; (916)934-3316. 876,236 acres. This National Forest is located in northwest California, and includes numerous mountains with elevations up to 8,000 feet, great views, deep canyons, and some lowlands. The area is forested with fir and pine (including some old-growth stands), juniper and hemlock, with grasslands and brushlands, plus meadows and many streams. Among the local mammals are black-tailed deer, black bear, mountain lion, coyote and bobcat.

Within Mendocino National Forest are two wilderness areas, the 37,000-acre Snow Mountain Wilderness and 74,000 acres of the 111,000-acre Yolla Bolly–Middle Eel Wilderness (the rest of which is in Shasta–Trinity National Forest). All told there are over 600 miles of trails here, varying in difficulty from easy to strenuous.

CLEVELAND NATIONAL FOREST—880 Front Street, San Diego, CA 92188; (619)557-5050. 419,841 acres. Situated near the southern border of California, Cleveland National Forest covers some low mountain ranges with elevations up to 6,000 feet, deep canyons with streams (most of which dry up during the year) and has four wilderness areas, including the 39,000-acre San Mateo Wilderness. Much of it is arid country with chaparral, plus pine-oak woodlands and conifer forests at higher elevations. Wildlife consists of mule deer, mountain lion, bobcat, coyote, and many other species.

There are about 200 miles of trails here, including a section of the Pacific Crest Trail. Difficulty ranges from easy to strenuous. A free permit is required for day hiking into some wilderness areas. Certain areas are subject to closure due to fire hazard.

SIX RIVERS NATIONAL FOREST—507 F Street, Eureka, CA 95501; (707)442-1721. 980,285 acres. Located in the mountains of northwest California, this extremely long and narrow National Forest includes several rivers and an estimated 200 miles of trails. The National Forest did not respond to repeated requests for information.

DEATH VALLEY NATIONAL MONUMENT—Death Valley, CA 92328; (619)786-2331. 2,048,851 acres. This enormous National Monument is located along the Nevada border, in south-central California. It includes below-sea-level desert with often extremely high temperatures in Death Valley itself—but there are also rugged snow-capped peaks, steep canyons, and craters as well as sand dunes. At 11,049 feet Telescope Peak is the highest point, 11,300 feet higher than the valley floor.

At higher elevations there are pine and juniper forests, with some bristlecone pine, and among the wildlife are mule deer, bighorn sheep, mountain lion, and coyote. The area has over 50 miles of trails, but most are primitive and not maintained. Difficulty ranges from easy to strenuous. Hiking in Death Valley is inadvisable between May and October because of the heat.

LASSEN NATIONAL FOREST—55 South Sacramento Street, Susanville, CA 96130; (916)257-2151. 1,060,588 acres. Located in northern California and surrounding Lassen National

Park, this National Forest includes some high mountains of the northern Sierras and southern Cascades as well as foothills and plateaus, rugged canyons and sagebrush flats. Some of the landscape is volcanic, with crater peaks and lava formations. There are also caves, open meadows, lakes and ponds, and forests of pine and fir.

Elevations range from 1,500 feet to over 8,600 feet. The highest point is 8,677-foot Crater Peak. There are three wilderness areas totaling 78,000 acres, including the 41,000-acre Ishi Wilderness. Among the local wildlife are mule and black-tailed deer, antelope, black bear, mountain lion, and coyote.

Lassen National Forest has about 135 miles of hiking trails, with parts of the 2,600-mile Pacific Crest Trail and the 30-mile Bizz Johnson Trail. Difficulty varies from easy to strenuous. Outstanding views are available from some trails.

JOSHUA TREE NATIONAL MONUMENT—74485 National Monument Drive, Twentynine Palms, CA 92277; (619)367-7511. 547,790 acres. Joshua Tree National Monument is situated east of San Bernardino National Forest in southern California. This is a region of Mojave and Colorado desert environments, with widespread stands of Joshua Trees, along with other desert vegetation including cactus and seasonal wildflowers and oases with palms.

There are also some rugged mountains, canyons, massive boulders and rock formations, and scenic views. Elevations range from 1,000 feet to nearly 6,000 feet. Among the wildlife are bighorn sheep, coyote, and bobcat.

The area has well over 50 miles of trails, including 35 miles of the California Riding and Hiking Trail. Only a few trails are marked. Summer hiking at low elevations is not recommended due to the high temperatures.

MODOC NATIONAL FOREST—441 North Main Street, Alturas, CA 96101; (916)233-5811. 1,651,232 acres. Modoc National Forest is located in the northeast corner of California, and includes the Warner Mountains, with elevations from 4,300 feet to nearly 9,900 feet. The mountainous terrain consists of peaks and volcanoes, great cliffs and canyons, glacial lakes and streams. Among the wildlife are mule deer, pronghorn antelope, and wild horse.

There's one wilderness area, the 70,000-acre South Warner Wilderness, and some exceptional views. Vegetation ranges from high desert to alpine plants, with meadows and grasslands, pine and fir forests, juniper and sagebrush. The area has more than 100 miles of hiking trails, easy to strenuous in difficulty.

CUYAMACA RANCHO STATE PARK—12551 Highway 79, Descanso, CA 92016; (619)765-0755. 30,000 acres. Cuyamaca Rancho State Park is located east of San Diego, in southern California. It's a region of mountains and mesas, with elevations from 3,500 feet to over 6,500 feet. The highest point is 6,512-foot Cuyamaca Peak. Some of the area is forested with pine, fir, cedar, and oak. There are also meadows, grasslands, and some desert.

Wildlife here includes mule deer, coyote, mountain lion, bobcat, and fox. There are 110 miles of hiking trails, most of which are open to horseback riding, and some fine vistas available. A section of the California Riding and Hiking Trail crosses the park.

LAKE TAHOE BASIN MANAGEMENT UNIT—870 Emerald Bay Road, Suite 1, South Lake Tahoe, CA 96150; (916)573-2600. 148,000 acres. This unit of the Forest Service in north-central California was created to help protect the lands around beautiful 21-mile-long Lake Tahoe—an area which has experienced substantial development over the years. Much of the unit consists of lands near the south and west shores of the lake. It includes a portion of the Desolation Wilderness, the rest of which is in Eldorado National Forest.

Elevations range from under 6,300 feet to over 10,000 feet. There are well over 100 miles of hiking trails in the area. Difficulty varies from easy to strenuous.

HUMBOLDT REDWOODS STATE PARK—P.O. Box 100, Weott, CA 95571; (707)946-2311. 51,000 acres. This large state park is located near the coast of northern California, and includes the largest forest of old-growth redwoods to be found anywhere. Many are over 300 feet high. In addition to these awesome trees are some Douglas fir and oak, and wildlife including mule deer. In the area are some low ridges, prairies, and a stretch of the Eel River. All told the park has over 100 miles of hiking trails.

POINT REYES NATIONAL SEASHORE—Point Reyes, CA 94956; (415)663-1092. 65,303 acres. Located on the coast of California about 40 miles north of San Francisco, Point Reyes National Seashore has miles of beautiful beaches, bays, and lagoons, high seaside cliffs, and includes Inverness Ridge with 1,407-foot Mount Wittenberg. There are Douglas fir and pine forests, some grasslands, and a section of the San Andreas Fault crosses the area. Among the wildlife are deer, mountain lion, and bobcat, with whale and seal off the coast. There are over 75 miles of maintained hiking trails. Difficulty varies from easy to strenuous.

BIG BASIN REDWOODS STATE PARK—21600 Big Basin Way, Boulder Creek, CA 95006; (408)338-6132. 16,000 acres. Big Basin Redwoods State Park is situated near the ocean in the Santa Cruz Mountains south of San Francisco. There are 1,500-year-old virgin redwoods here, some over 300 feet high, along with mixed conifer forest, chaparral, and manzanita—and a number of streams. Among the wildlife are black-tailed deer, coyote, and mountain lion. The park has about 100 miles of hiking trails, including a section of the Skyline to the Sea Trail.

ANZA–BORREGO DESERT STATE PARK—P.O. Box 299, Borrego Springs, CA 92004; (619)767-5311. 600,000 acres. Anza–Borrego is California's largest state park, located in the southern part of the state east of San Diego. It's a desert park with varied scenery including many mountain peaks over 5,000 feet, canyons, badlands, cliffs, sandstone formations, and streams—with spring wildflowers and scores of palm oases. Wildlife includes bighorn sheep, mule deer, and mountain lion.

This park has nearly 20 miles of short trails, along with longer segments of the Pacific Crest Trail and the California Riding and Hiking Trail. Summer hiking is not recommended due to the high temperatures.

KING RANGE NATIONAL CONSERVATION AREA—Bureau of Land Management, 555 Leslie Street, Ukiah, CA 95482; (707)462-3873. 52,000 acres. One of the few BLM-administered areas with a substantial trail system, the King Range National Conservation Area is a wild and rugged region along the coast of northern California. Elevations run from sea level to 4,087-foot King's Peak. The coastline includes high cliffs and sandy wilderness beaches with some boulders.

The area has Douglas fir forests, grassy areas, and coastal chapparal. Among the wildlife are black-trailed deer, black bear, and coyote—plus sea lion, seal, and whale offshore. There are over 60 miles of hiking trails, including the 24-mile Lost Coast Trail, which follows the shoreline, and the 23-mile King Mountain National Recreation Trail.

MOUNT TAMALPAIS STATE PARK—801 Panoramic Highway, Mill Valley, CA 94941; (415) 388-2070. 6,400 acres. Located just north of San Francisco, this state park is dominated by 2,571-foot "Mount Tam," which offers wonderful views. The park surrounds Muir Woods National Monument, and there are redwoods, forests of Douglas fir, oak woodlands, grassy areas, chaparral, and wildflowers.

Wildlife includes black-tailed deer, mountain lion, and bobcat. Over 50 miles of hiking trails extend through the area, and these connect with additional trails on nearby public lands. Difficulty ranges from easy to strenuous.

MOUNT DIABLO STATE PARK—P.O. Box 250, Diablo, CA 94528; (415)837-2525. 14,500 acres. Situated east of San Francisco, this state park is dominated by 3,849-foot Mount Diablo, which has some great views. There are other peaks as well, along with canyons, rock formations and caves, and some beautiful streams.

Vegetation consists of oak woodlands along

with pine, plus grasslands and chaparral. Black-tailed deer, mountain lion, bobcat, and gray fox are among the wildlife. The park has well over 50 miles of trails, most of which are open to horses. Difficulty varies from easy to strenuous.

POINT MUGU STATE PARK—c/o Santa Monica Mountains District, 2860A Camino Dos Rios, Newbury Park, CA 91320; (818)706-1310/(805) 987-3303. 15,000 acres. Located along the coast of southern California in the edge of the Santa Monica Mountains, this state park includes some rugged terrain—with two canyons, plus over three miles of shoreline with rocky bluffs and a beach.

Mule deer, coyote, and bobcat are among the wildlife, and the varied vegetation includes slopes with chaparral and grassy areas with scattered trees. There are also streams, waterfalls, ponds, and a wilderness area. Point Mugu has more than 50 miles of hiking trails, some of which offer fine views.

HENRY COE STATE PARK—P.O. Box 846, Morgan Hill, CA 95038; (408)779-2728. 67,000 acres. Henry Coe is California's second largest state park, located southeast of San Jose in west-central California. There's a 22,000-acre wilderness area, and the terrain is often rough, with steep ridges and canyons. Included are oak woodlands, grasslands, some pine forest, and several creeks. The park has over 45 miles of trails.

MOUNT SAN JACINTO STATE PARK & WILDERNESS—P.O. Box 308, Idyllwild, CA 92349; (714)659-2607. 13,000 acres. This state park is located east of Los Angeles in southern California, surrounded by the lands of San Bernardino National Forest, in the San Jacinto Mountains. Elevations start at 5,400 feet, and there are several peaks over 10,000 feet. Highest is 10,804-foot San Jacinto Peak. The area has forests of pine, fir, and oak, and over 10,000 acres are designated wilderness.

Within the park are about 35 miles of trails, including a section of the Pacific Crest Trail, with access available to other trails in San Ber-

nardino National Forest. A permit is required for day hiking here.

ANNADEL STATE PARK—6201 Channel Drive, Santa Rosa, CA 95409; (707)539-3911. 5,000 acres. This wild state park, located 60 miles north of San Francisco, has hilly terrain with areas of chaparral, meadows, and forests of Douglas fir. Elevations range from 360 feet to 1,880 feet. There are 35 miles of trails, most of which are moderate in difficulty. Some trails are open to horses and mountain bikes.

CASTLE ROCK STATE PARK—15000 Skyline Boulevard, Los Gatos, CA 95030; (408)867-2952. 3,600 acres. Situated in the Santa Cruz mountains south of San Francisco and San Jose, Castle Rock is a wild state park with rugged terrain and great views. There are steep slopes, rock outcrops, and sandstone caves—with meadows and forests of Douglas fir, pine, and redwood. Thirty-two miles of trails are found here, including a section of the Skyline to the Sea Trail. Some trails are open to horses.

PINNACLES NATIONAL MONUMENT—Paicines, CA 95043; (408)389-4485. 16,251 acres. Located east of Monterey in west-central California, Pinnacles National Monument is an area of craggy volcanic rock spires and formations, with precipitous rock cliffs and caves. Vegetation is dominated by chaparral, with limited grasslands and woodlands. Wildlife includes black-tailed deer, mountain lion, and fox. There are about 30 miles of trails, easy to strenuous in difficulty. Due to summer heat, spring and fall are the best times to hike here.

LAVA BEDS NATIONAL MONUMENT—P.O. Box 867, Tulelake, CA 96134; (916)667-2282. 46,239 acres. Located in northern California near the Oregon border, Lava Beds National Monument protects a volcanic landscape with cinder cones and almost 200 caves. There are grasslands with juniper and a ponderosa pine forest, with wildlife including mule deer, mountain lion, and coyote. The Monument has over 25 miles of hiking trails.

SUGARLOAF RIDGE STATE PARK—2605 Adobe Canyon Road, Kenwood, CA 95452; (707)833-5712. 2,500 acres. Located east of Santa Rosa and Annadel State Park, Sugarloaf Ridge State Park has 25 miles of trails, which connect with trails in nearby Mount Hood Regional Park. Some are open to mountain bikes and horses. Elevations range from 600 feet to 2,729-foot Mount Baldy. Within the park are meadows, ridges with chaparral, fir and oak forest, and some redwoods.

BUTANO STATE PARK—P.O. Box 9, Pescadero, CA 94060; (415)879-0173. 2,200 acres. This small state park is situated in the Santa Cruz Mountains near the coast of north-central California. There are lots of redwoods here, including 400 acres of virgin forest. Mule deer, coyote, and fox are among the wildlife. The park has about 20 miles of hiking trails.

CALIFORNIA HIKING RESOURCES

HIKING GUIDEBOOKS

Best Short Hikes in California's Northern Sierra—Whitehill, Karen & Terry. Seattle: The Mountaineers.

Carson-Iceberg Wilderness—Schaffer, Jeffrey P. Berkeley, CA: Wilderness Press, 1987.

Emigrant Wilderness—Schifrin, Ben. Berkeley: Wilderness Press, 1990.

Guide to the John Muir Trail—Winnett, Thomas. Berkeley: Wilderness Press, 1984.

Hiker's Hip Pocket Guide to the Humboldt Coast—Lorentzen, Ben. Berkeley: Wilderness Press, 1988.

Hiker's Hip Pocket Guide to the Mendocino Coast—Lorentzen, Ben. Berkeley: Wilderness Press, 1989.

Hiker's Hip Pocket Guide to Sonoma County—Lorentzen, Ben. Berkeley: Wilderness Press, 1990.

Hiker's Guide to California—Adkinson, Ron. Helena, MT: Falcon Press.

Hiking the Big Sur Country—Schaffer, Jeffrey P. Berkeley: Wilderness Press, 1988.

Marble Mountain Wilderness—Green, David.

Berkeley: Wilderness Press, 1980.

The Mount Shasta Book—Selters, Andy, & Zanger, Michael. Berkeley: Wilderness Press, 1989.

The Pacific Crest Trail—Volume 1: California—Schaffer, Jeffrey P. Berkeley: Wilderness Press, 1989.

Peninsula Trails—Rusmore, Joan, & Spangle, Frances. Berkeley: Wilderness Press, 1989.

San Bernardino Mountain Trails—Robinson, John W. Berkeley: Wilderness Press, 1986.

Sierra North—Winnett, Thomas, & Winnett, Jason. Berkeley: Wilderness Press, 1985.

Sierra South—Winnett, Thomas, & Winnett, Jason. Berkeley: Wilderness Press, 1990.

South Bay Trails—Spangle, Frances, & Rusmore, Joan. Berkeley: Wilderness Press, 1984.

Starr's Guide to the John Muir Trail and the High Sierra Region—Starr, Walter A. San Francisco: Sierra Club Books.

The Tahoe Sierra—Schaffer, Jeffrey P. Berkeley: Wilderness Press, 1987.

The Tahoe–Yosemite Trail—Winnett, Thomas. Berkeley: Wilderness Press, 1987.

Trails of the Angeles—Robinson, John W. Berkeley: Wilderness Press, 1990.

The Trinity Alps—Linkhart, Luther. Berkeley: Wilderness Press, 1986.

Yosemite National Park—Schaffer, Jeffrey P. Berkeley: Wilderness Press, 1983.

INFORMATION ABOUT STATE PARKS

California Department of Parks and Recreation, P.O. Box 942896, Sacramento, CA 94296; (916)322-7000.

STATE HIGHWAY MAP AND TRAVEL INFORMATION

California Office of Tourism, P.O. Box 9278, Department T-99, Van Nuys, CA 91409; (800)862-2543, ext. 99.

CLUBS AND OTHER ORGANIZATIONS WHICH OFFER HIKES

Berkeley Hiking Club, Box 147, Berkeley, CA 94701.

Contra Costa Hills Club, c/o YMCA, 1515 Webster, #434, Oakland, CA 94612.

Diablo Hiking Club, c/o A. B. Barton, 3424 Sentinel, Martinez, CA 94553.

Hayward Hiking Club, 18573 Reamer Road, Castro Valley, CA 94546.

Sierra Club, 1013 Hogan Way, Bakersfield, CA 93309.

Sierra Club, P.O. Box 5667, Carmel, CA 93921.

Sierra Club, P.O. Box 5396, Fresno, CA 93755.

Sierra Club, 3550 West 6th Street, Suite 321, Los Angeles, CA 90020.

Sierra Club, c/o David Sheehan, 1411 Ramona Drive, Newbury Park, CA 91320.

Sierra Club, 6014 College Avenue, Oakland, CA 94618.

Sierra Club, 2448 Watson, Palo Alto, CA 94303.

Sierra Club, P.O. Box 8096, Reno, NV 89507.

Sierra Club, P.O. Box 1335, Sacramento, CA 95812.

Sierra Club, 568 North Mountain View Avenue, Suite 130, San Bernardino, CA 92401.

Sierra Club, 3820 Ray Street, San Diego, CA 92104.

Sierra Club, P.O. Box 15755, San Luis Obispo, CA 93406.

Sierra Club, P.O. Box 466, Santa Rosa, CA 95402.

Trails Club of Rossmoor, 4139 Terra Grenada Drive, #18, Walnut Creek, CA 94595.

COLORADO

Few states can compete with Colorado when it comes to truly spectacular high mountain scenery. Some of the loftiest peaks in the country are located here in the Rockies, with fifty-three mountains over fourteen thousand feet, amid magnificent expanses of wilderness. Much of the land in central and western Colorado falls within several enormous National Forests—offering a vast array of often splendid trails and some of the most thrilling high-country hiking in the United States.

MAJOR TRAILS

THE COLORADO TRAIL—469 miles. This new trail, dedicated in 1988, stretches from southwest of Denver to Durango, Colorado. It passes through several National Forests and wilderness areas, in a region which has some of the state's finest mountain scenery. The trail remains at high elevations a great deal of the time, offering spectacular views. Difficulty ranges from easy to very strenuous, with many major gains and losses of elevation. Much of the trail is open to mountain biking and horseback riding as well as hiking. Trail information: The Colorado Trail Foundation, 548 Pine Song Trail, Golden, CO 80401.

BEST HIKING AREAS

ROCKY MOUNTAIN NATIONAL PARK—Estes Park, CO 80517; (303)586-2371. 265,200 acres. Located in north-central Colorado and nearly surrounded by National Forest lands, Rocky Mountain National Park stands among this country's finest National Parks. Some of the highest elevations of the Rockies are found here, with an indescribably splendid array of rugged snow-covered peaks—59 of them over 12,000 feet—and some truly wonderful wilderness scenery. Magnificent views seem to be everywhere.

Long's Peak (14,255 feet) is the highest point. Valleys are at about 8,000-foot elevation. The Continental Divide crosses in a southeast to northwest direction. Over a third of the park is above timberline, with major areas of alpine tundra. Below are forested mountainsides, with juniper and ponderosa pine, spruce, and fir. There are high-walled canyons and cliffs, several small glaciers, and scores of lakes. Some of the many creeks and wild rivers have beautiful waterfalls and cascades. Among the wildlife are elk, moose, mule deer, black bear, bighorn sheep, and mountain lion.

The park has 355 miles of hiking trails. Difficulty ranges from easy to extremely strenuous. Among the trails is a challenging route to the top of Long's Peak. The park draws large crowds in the summer, and some trails receive heavy use. Higher trails may only be snow-free from mid-summer through early fall. Time should be allotted to adjust to the unusually high altitudes.

WHITE RIVER NATIONAL FOREST—P.O. Box 948, Glenwood Springs, CO 81602; (303)945-2521. 1,960,760 acres. Situated near Glenwood Springs in west-central Colorado, White River National Forest consists of two separate and enormous tracts of splendid Rocky Mountain landscape. Over one-third is wilderness, with many high peaks and vast areas above treeline. Some elevations exceed 14,000 feet, and views are fantastic.

In addition to rugged mountainous terrain, there's a 400-square-mile, 10,000-foot high plateau (the White River Plateau) with some steep canyons—and also rock formations, rolling grasslands, slopes forested with conifers, and a large number of beautiful mountain lakes and streams, some with waterfalls. There are seven different wilderness areas. Especially spectacular and popular is the 174,000-acre Maroon Bells–Snowmass Wilderness, which extends into Gunnison National Forest. Wildlife includes elk, black bear, mule deer, bobcat, mountain lion, and coyote.

The area has over 1,400 miles of hiking trails, some of which are open to horseback riding. Difficulty ranges from easy to very strenuous. Some trails are crowded, and the National Forest as a whole receives heavy use. Most trails are free of snow only from July through September.

RIO GRANDE NATIONAL FOREST—1803 West Highway 160, Monte Vista, CO 81144; (303)852-5941. 1,851,792 acres. Situated in the south-central and southwestern parts of the state, with

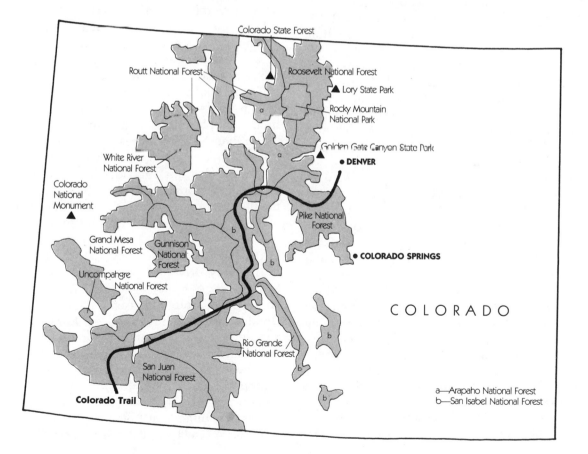

a portion along the New Mexico border, Rio Grande National Forest is a huge area of high-country Colorado—a spectacular region of rugged mountains with barren rocky peaks, precipitous canyons and high volcanic cliffs, gorgeous lakes, rivers, and streams, many with waterfalls.

Included are segments of the San Juan, La Garita, and Sangre de Cristo Mountain Ranges, with a few elevations exceeding 14,000 feet. Some major portions of the Continental Divide are here, with unbelievably beautiful panoramic views. This National Forest is also the source of the Rio Grande River.

There are several wilderness areas—including the 463,000-acre Weminuche Wilderness Area, Colorado's largest, which extends into San Juan National Forest. The terrain includes high talus slopes, interesting rock outcrops, and natural arches. There are forests of spruce and fir, pine and aspen, plus alpine meadows and tundra with an array of wildflowers. Among the wildlife are black bear, mule deer, elk, mountain lion, bobcat, and coyote.

Over 1,300 miles of trails are found here, with a 235-mile stretch of the 3,100-mile Continental Divide Trail. Many trails are open to horseback riding. Some are not well-marked. Difficulty varies from easy to very strenuous. High elevations are generally snow-free only from mid-July through mid-September.

GRAND MESA, UNCOMPAHGRE, AND GUNNISON NATIONAL FORESTS—2250 Highway 50, Delta, CO 81416; (303)874-7691. 2,953,191 acres. These three National Forests, now administered as a single entity, are clustered in west and southwest Colorado, adding up to almost three million acres of magnificent wild land. Along with rough and steep rocky peaks, there's an area of high plateaus and sprawling mesas, including gigantic Grand Mesa (largest in the country), which has 300 lakes and is located at about 10,000-foot elevation. Gunnison National Forest borders on the Continental Divide, with some peaks over 14,000 feet.

There are several wilderness areas. Terrain includes high alpine country, unusual rock formations, deep canyons, and other superb scenery. The area has a multitude of mountain lakes and streams, spruce forests, meadows, and grasslands with countless wildflowers. Outstanding vistas are common. The three National Forests have a large number of hiking trails, totaling many hundreds of miles. Some trails are open to horseback riding.

SAN JUAN NATIONAL FOREST—701 Camino del Rio, Room 301, Durango, CO 81301; (303)247-4874. 1,860,931 acres. Located west of the Continental Divide in southwest Colorado, this massive National Forest has a magnificent array of Rocky Mountain scenery. There are several wilderness areas, including a major portion of the 463,000-acre Weminuche Wilderness (part of which is in Rio Grande National Forest)—Colorado's largest, with some remote areas. There are towering and spectacular snowy peaks, several over 14,000 feet.

You find large areas above treeline, high mountain lakes and alpine meadows, forests of spruce and ponderosa pine, rugged rock formations, mesas and deep canyons. There are several major rivers, countless creeks and waterfalls. Elk, mule deer, bear, bighorn sheep, mountain lion, and bobcat are among the local wildlife.

San Juan National Forest has more than 1,100 miles of hiking trails. Some receive heavy use. Trails are also open to horseback riding. Difficulty ranges from easy to very strenuous. Frost is possible at any time, and snow generally remains at high elevations till mid-July.

PIKE AND SAN ISABEL NATIONAL FORESTS—1920 Valley Drive, Pueblo, CO 81008; (719)545-8737. 2,217,446 acres. Located in central and west-central Colorado, east of the Continental Divide, these two huge National Forests encompass several high mountain ranges, including the Sawatch, Rampart, and Sangre de Cristo ranges, along with the prominent twin Spanish Peaks.

Mount Elbert (14,433 feet) is here, Colorado's highest peak and the second highest elevation in the country outside of Alaska—plus Mount Massive (14,421 feet) and Mount Harvard (14,420 feet), second and third highest in the state. A total of 22 peaks are over 14,000 feet. Among these spectacular mountains is famous and popular Pike's Peak (14,110 feet). The views here, of course, are absolutely magnificent.

There are several wilderness areas. The alpine scenery includes many high lakes and mountain meadows, countless creeks, rock pinnacles and outcrops, talus slopes with boulders, and deep canyons—with forests of spruce, lodgepole and ponderosa pine, and aspen. The wildlife includes antelope, deer, elk, bear, mountain goat, bighorn sheep, and mountain lion.

Over 1,200 miles of trails extend through these National Forests, including about half of the 400-mile Colorado Trail. Trail difficulty varies from easy to extremely strenuous.

ARAPAHO AND ROOSEVELT NATIONAL FORESTS—240 West Prospect Road, Fort Collins, CO 80526; (303)498-1100. 1,813,493 acres. Arapaho and Roosevelt National Forests are situated in north-central and northern Colorado, surrounding Rocky Mountain National Park and on both sides of the Continental Divide. It's a magnificent area of stunning, snow-covered peaks, with some elevations over 14,000 feet. There are several wilderness areas, including the splendid and popular Indian Peaks Wilderness Area.

This is a land of high alpine lakes and tundra, glaciers, meadowed basins and boulder fields, rocky ridges, deep canyons, and striking rock formations. There are steep slopes with spruce fir and lodgepole pine forests, aspen groves, and many creeks with waterfalls and plenty of spectacular panoramas. Wildlife includes deer, elk, bear, bighorn sheep, and coyote.

These National Forests have over 900 miles of hiking trails, which vary in difficulty from easy to strenuous. Some trails receive heavy use, especially in the Indian Peaks Wilderness. There are snowbanks on some of the high trails well into July.

ROUTT NATIONAL FOREST—29587 West U.S. 40, Steamboat Springs, CO 80487; (303)879-1722. 1,127,164 acres. Consisting of three separate tracts of land in northwest Colorado, and bisected by the Continental Divide, this sizable National Forest includes plenty of impressive Rocky Mountain scenery, with many peaks over 10,000 feet. Highest of all here is Mount Zirkel (12,180 feet), located in the 140,000-acre Mount Zirkel Wilderness.

In addition to lofty peaks with gorgeous vistas, there are deep canyons with precipitous cliffs, legions of lakes, boulder-strewn streams, and some waterfalls—along with alpine meadows and tundra, spruce fir forests, stands of lodgepole pine and aspen, and sagebrush hills. Elk, mule deer, black bear, coyote, bobcat and fox are among the wildlife here.

The area has over 600 miles of trails, including a section of the Continental Divide Trail. Difficulty ranges from easy to strenuous. Snow generally covers the high trails until July.

OTHER RECOMMENDED LOCATIONS

COLORADO NATIONAL MONUMENT—Fruita, CO 81521; (303)858-3617. 19,919 acres. Located on the Colorado Plateau near the state's western border, this impressive National Monument has steep-walled and multicolored canyons, beautiful towering rock formations and spires, arches and domes. There are wonderful views, with semidesert vegetation, and wildlife including mule deer, elk, bighorn, and coyote. Approximately 45 miles of trails are found here. Not all trails are marked or maintained.

GOLDEN GATE CANYON STATE PARK—Route 6, Box 280, Golden, CO 80403; (303)592-1502. 10,200 acres. Located 30 miles west of Denver, this beautiful and popular park on the edge of the Front Range of the Rockies has elevations up to 10,400 feet. There are open mountain meadows, forests of pine and aspen, great views, and about 60 miles of easy to strenuous hiking trails. The area receives heavy use.

LORY STATE PARK—708 Lodgepole Drive, Bellvue, CO 80512; (303)493-1623. 2,479 acres. Situated in the foothills of the Rockies in northern

Colorado near Fort Collins, Lory State Park has grassy plains, a forest of ponderosa pine, and some fine views. Among the wildlife are mule deer, black bear, and mountain lion. There are about 30 miles of marked hiking trails, some of which are open to horseback riding. Difficulty ranges from easy to strenuous.

COLORADO STATE FOREST—Star Route, Box 91, Walden, CO 80480; (303)723-8366. 70,708 acres. This state-owned park northwest of Rocky Mountain National Park has high mountains, alpine lakes and streams, and over 20 miles of hiking trails. Difficulty ranges from moderate to strenuous.

COLORADO HIKING RESOURCES

HIKING GUIDEBOOKS

The Hiker's Guide to Colorado—Boddie, Caryn & Peter. Helena, MT: Falcon Press.

Hiking Trails of the Boulder Mountain Parks and Plains—De Haan, Vici. Boulder, CO: Pruett.

Hiking the Trails of Central Colorado—Hagon, Mary. Boulder, CO: Pruett.

Hiking Trails of Southwestern Colorado—Pixler, Paul. Boulder, CO: Pruett.

Telluride Hiking Guide—Kees, Susan. Boulder, CO: Pruett, 1990.

Trails of the Front Range—Kenofer, Louis. Boulder, CO: Pruett, 1980.

INFORMATION ABOUT STATE PARKS

Colorado Division of Parks and Recreation, 1313 Sherman Street, Room 618, Denver, CO 80203; (303)866-3437.

STATE HIGHWAY MAP AND TRAVEL INFORMATION

Colorado Tourism Board, 1625 Broadway, Suite 1700, Denver, CO 80202; (303)592-5410.

HIKING CLUBS

Colorado Mountain Club, Box 1105, Boulder, CO 80306.

Colorado Mountain Club, 2530 West Alameda Avenue, Denver, CO 80219.

Sierra Club, 777 Grant Street, Suite 606, Denver, CO 80203.

CONNECTICUT

Connecticut has no large parks or extensive wild areas, yet in spite of its relatively small size and substantial population it offers a surprising amount of hiking. A major system of blue-blazed trails, totaling several hundred miles, extends throughout much of the state. Significant portions of the trails are on private land. Although you are never far from development while hiking in Connecticut, the woodland and forest scenery is quite attractive here.

MAJOR TRAILS

APPALACHIAN TRAIL 61 miles in Connecticut (2,100 total). The Appalachian Trail winds over hills and small mountains through the northwestern part of the state. Before entering Massachusetts the trail climbs into the wilder and more rugged terrain of the Taconic Mountains, ascending Bear Mountain (2,316 feet), Connecticut's highest mountain. Difficulty varies from easy to strenuous. Trail Information: Appalachian Trail Conference, P.O. Box 807, Harpers Ferry, WV 25425.

METACOMET TRAIL—45 miles in Connecticut (117 miles total). This scenic trail, part of the Metacomet–Monadnock Trail, runs from Meriden in south-central Connecticut up through Massachusetts into New Hampshire. It passes through some beautiful forest, and crosses diverse and sometimes rocky terrain, with nice views from cliffs and small mountains. Trail information: Connecticut Forest and Park Association, 16 Meriden Road, Middletown, CT 06457; (203)346-2372.

MATTABESETT TRAIL—52 miles. Located in south-central Connecticut, the Mattabesett Trail follows along ridges and over high ledges, offering fine views of the Connecticut River—and descends through ravines and crosses many streams. Trail information: Connecticut Forest and Park Association (see address above).

TUNXIS TRAIL—59 miles. This trail leads through the woodlands of north-central Connecticut, with some nice views from open ledges and the tops of small mountains. The trail (which is currently broken in places) passes through diverse woodland and forest. Trail information: Connecticut Forest and Park Association (see address above).

In addition to the trails listed above, Connecticut has a number of other blue-blazed trails which run 20 to 40 miles in length. For information consult the *Connecticut Walk Book* or contact the Connecticut Forest and Park Association, 16 Meriden Road, Middletown, CT 06457; (203)346-2372.

BEST HIKING AREAS

PACHAUG STATE FOREST—Connecticut Office of State Parks and Recreation, 165 Capitol Ave-

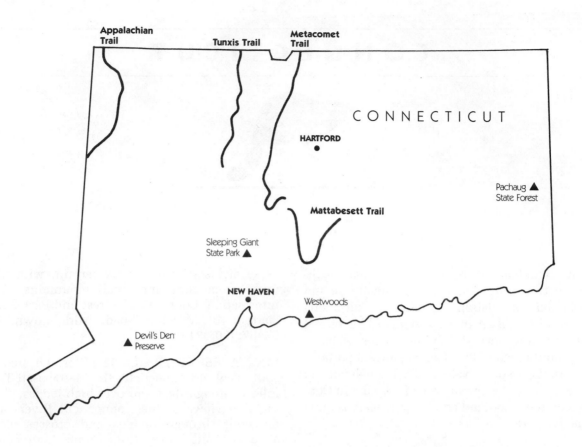

CONNECTICUT

HARTFORD

Pachaug ▲
State Forest

Mattabesett Trail

Sleeping Giant
State Park ▲

NEW HAVEN

Westwoods ▲

Devil's Den ▲
Preserve

nue, Hartford, CT 06106; (203)566-2304. 22,937 acres. Situated in eastern Connecticut, Pachaug State Forest is the largest area of public land in the state. The forest includes rocky terrain with many streams, meadows, cedar swamps, and stands of rhododendron. There are over 35 miles of hiking trails.

SLEEPING GIANT STATE PARK—Connecticut Office of State Parks and Recreation, 165 Capitol Avenue, Hartford, CT 06106; (203)566-2304. 1,331 acres. This state park is in north-central Connecticut, north of New Haven. It's an area of small rocky hills and mountains (elevations from 100 feet to over 700 feet) which form the profile of a sleeping giant, with some fine views from open areas. The region is forested with hardwoods, and there are about 28 miles of hiking trails. Difficulty ranges from easy to strenuous.

WESTWOODS—Guilford Land Conservation Trust, P.O. Box 200, Guilford, CT 06437. 2,000 acres. Westwoods is a beautiful and unexpectedly wild area which lies near the Long Island Sound in south-central Connecticut. Some of the terrain is quite rocky, with granite outcroppings and caves. The area includes forests of hemlock and oak-hickory, swamps and a large lake—and over 40 miles of hilly trails, easy to moderate in difficulty.

DEVIL'S DEN PRESERVE—Box 1162, Weston, CT 06883; (203)226-4991. 1,558 acres. Located in southwestern Connecticut and owned by the Nature Conservancy, this beautiful and wild forested preserve has 20 miles of winding, hilly trails. Difficulty ranges from easy to moderate. Terrain includes low rocky ridges with nice views, and there are a number of streams.

CONNECTICUT HIKING RESOURCES

HIKING GUIDEBOOKS

Connecticut Walk Book—Middletown, CT: Connecticut Forest and Park Association, 1984.

Fifty Hikes in Connecticut—Hardy, Gerry and Sue. Woodstock, VT: The Countryman Press, 1984.

Guide to the Appalachian Trail in Massachusetts–Connecticut—Harpers Ferry, WV: The Appalachian Trail Conference, 1990.

TRAIL INFORMATION

Connecticut Forest and Park Association, 16 Meriden Road, Middletown, CT 06457; (203)346-2372.

New England Trail Conference, 33 Knollwood Drive, East Longmeadow, MA 01028; (203)342-1425 or (413)732-3719.

INFORMATION ABOUT STATE PARKS AND FORESTS

Connecticut Office of Parks and Recreation, 165 Capitol Avenue, Hartford, CT 06106; (203)566-2304.

STATE HIGHWAY MAP

Connecticut Department of Transportation, P.O. Drawer A, Wethersfield, CT 06109.

CLUBS AND OTHER ORGANIZATIONS WHICH OFFER HIKES

American Youth Hostels, 118 Oak Street, Hartford, CT 06110.

Appalachian Mountain Club, c/o Douglas Christie, 11 Colton Road, West Hartford, CT 06107.

Green Mountain Club, c/o Richard Krompegal, 142 Churchill Drive, Newington, CT 06111.

New Haven Hiking Club, c/o Jacqueline T. Collimore, 1838 Boulevard, New Haven, CT 06511.

Sierra Club, 118 Oak Street, Hartford, CT 06106.

DELAWARE

Hiking options are limited in Delaware, our second smallest state, although a number of little state parks, forests, and wildlife refuges offer some pleasant walking and beautiful coastal scenery—with barrier islands and beaches, marshes and woodlands. While most of these areas won't provide a long day hike, a couple of state parks have several miles or more of attractive trails.

DELAWARE HIKING RESOURCES

HIKING GUIDEBOOKS
Walks and Rambles on the Delmarva Peninsula— Woodstock, VT: The Countryman Press.

INFORMATION ABOUT STATE PARKS AND FORESTS
Delaware Division of Parks and Recreation, 89 Kings Highway, P.O. Box 1401, Dover, DE 19903; (302)736-4702.

STATE HIGHWAY MAP AND TRAVEL INFORMATION
Delaware Tourism Office, 99 Kings Highway, P.O. Box 1401, Dover, DE 19903; (302)736-4271 or (800)441-8846 (out of state)/(800)282-8667 (in state).

DELAWARE HIKING CLUBS
Brandywine Valley Outing Club, Box 134, Rockland, DE 19732.
Sierra Club, 1116 C West Street, Annapolis, MD 21403.
Wilmington Trail Club, P.O. Box 1184, Wilmington, DE 19899.

FLORIDA

Florida is emerging as an increasingly attractive destination for hikers. A surprising number of trails now wind through this beautiful state, which has several million acres of public lands. Except for parts of northern Florida, most of the terrain is flat, and frequently wet—with many exotic plants and birds, and areas of subtropical wilderness in the southern reaches. The most important trail by far is the partially-completed 1,300-mile Florida Trail, which will put this state permanently on the country's hiking map.

MAJOR TRAILS

FLORIDA TRAIL—When it's finished the Florida National Scenic Trail will run 1,300 miles—from the panhandle of northwest Florida to Big Cypress National Preserve in southern Florida. It passes through much of the state's wildest and loveliest scenery, including three National Forests. Major segments are now open, adding up to over 700 miles. There are also a number of side trails and loops. Sections which cross private lands may only be used by Florida Trail Association members. Most of the trail is easy, and parts of it are often wet. Trail information: Florida Trail Association, P.O. Box 13708, Gainesville, FL 32604.

BEST HIKING AREAS

EVERGLADES NATIONAL PARK—P.O. Box 279, Homestead, FL 33030; (305)247-6211. 1,400,855 acres. Everglades is the largest National Park in the eastern United States, located at the southern end of Florida, and extending out to include Florida Bay and scores of keys (small islands). Much of this magnificent wilderness park is wet or under water, but there are still many miles of hiking trails here. Most trails are nearly flat and generally follow old roads.

Scenery includes subtropical vegetation, pinelands and hardwood hammocks (clusters of trees), mangroves and marshlands, and coastal prairies. Among the wildlife are alligator, crocodile, manatee, and Florida panther. There's also an enormous and fascinating bird population. Due to the climate and insects, winter and early spring are the best times to hike here.

WITHLACOOCHEE STATE FOREST—15023 Broad Street, Brooksville, FL 33512. 113,431 acres. Withlacoochee State Forest in central Florida is an area of sandy hills, hardwood hammocks, pine plantations and flatlands, prairies, swamps and cypress ponds, along with the Withlacoochee River. Wildlife includes deer, black bear, bobcat, fox, alligator, and armadillo. Over 90 miles of trails are found here, including the 41-mile Citrus Trail and 31-mile Richloam Trail.

APALACHICOLA NATIONAL FOREST—P.O. Box 309, Crawfordville, FL 32327. 557,729 acres. Apalachicola National Forest is located in northwestern Florida. It's the largest National Forest in the state, and includes six major rivers and many more streams, small lakes, sand ridges,

swamps and savannahs. In the region are stands of longleaf and slash pine, with cypress and magnolia.

The wildlife here includes white-tailed deer, black bear, alligator, Florida panther, and many beautiful birds. The forest has two designated wilderness areas, one of which is the 24,000-acre Bradwell Bay Wilderness, an area of swamplands and ponds. The major trail here is the 60-mile Apalachicola Trail, part of the Florida Trail.

OCALA NATIONAL FOREST—Route 2, Box 701, Silver Springs, FL 32688. 367,254 acres. A major National Forest in north-central Florida, Ocala has some varied scenery including prairies and slash pine forests, hardwood hammocks, cypress swamps, little ponds, lakes and streams—with white-tailed deer among the wildlife. Crossing the forest is the 66-mile Ocala

Trail, which is also a segment of the Florida Trail.

ST. MARKS NATIONAL WILDLIFE REFUGE—P.O. Box 68, St. Marks, FL 32355. 96,500 acres. This large and scenic National Wildlife Refuge is situated along the Gulf of Mexico in northwest Florida. It has forests of longleaf pine, marshes, swamps with hardwoods, streams and ponds, and a substantial amount of wilderness. White-tailed deer, black bear, fox, and alligator are among the wildlife, along with a large bird population. There are over 60 miles of trails, most of which follow old roads or railroad beds.

OTHER RECOMMENDED LOCATIONS

BIG CYPRESS NATIONAL PRESERVE—Star Route Box 110, Ochopee, FL 33943; (813)695-

2000. 570,000 acres. This large National Preserve which lies northwest of Everglades National Park is almost entirely wilderness. It's an area of swamps and marshes, prairies and hardwood hammocks, and mangrove forests. Among the local wildlife are deer, black bear, alligator, and Florida panther. There are 42 miles of trails, including a section of the Florida Trail.

MYAKKA RIVER STATE PARK—13207 S.R.72, Sarasota, FL 34241; (813)924-1027. 28,876 acres. Florida's largest state park, located in the southwestern part of the state, Myakka River State Park offers varied scenery including pine flatwoods, prairie marshes, and oak-palm hammocks—with some ponds, a good-size lake, and 12 miles of the Myakka River. Deer, bobcat, and alligator are among the wildlife. There are over 40 miles of easy hiking trails.

OSCEOLA NATIONAL FOREST—Route 7, Box 95, Lake City, FL 32055. 157,230 acres. Osceola National Forest in northeastern Florida has cypress swamps, pine forests, and a stretch of the Suwannee River. Wildlife includes deer and black bear. A 39-mile segment of the Florida Trail passes through the forest.

TOSOHATCHEE STATE RESERVE—3365 Taylor Crook Road, Christmas, FL 32709, (407)568-5893. 28,000 acres. This wild state reserve is situated along a 19-mile stretch of the St. Johns River in central Florida. It's an area of pine flatwoods and hammocks, swamps, and marshes—with wildlife including white-tailed deer, black bear, bobcat, and fox. There are 27 miles of easy loop trails here.

BLACKWATER RIVER STATE FOREST—Route 1, Box 77, Milton, FL 32570; (904)957-4111. 183,155 acres. This sizable state forest in northwestern Florida has cypress swamps, forests of longleaf pine, oak, and other hardwoods, and wild azalea. Deer and fox are among the wildlife. There are several streams, the beautiful Blackwater River, and 26 miles of easy trails, including a section of the Florida Trail.

ST. VINCENT NATIONAL WILDLIFE REFUGE— P.O. Box 447, Apalachicola, FL 32320; (904)653-8808. 12,358 acres. St. Vincent is a beautiful barrier island off the gulf coast of northwestern Florida, with dunes, hardwood hammocks, marshes and ponds, and a rich birdlife. It's accessible by boat. Old roads and beach offer many miles of trails.

FLORIDA HIKING RESOURCES

HIKING GUIDEBOOKS

A Hiking Guide to the Trails of Florida—Carter, Elizabeth F. Birmingham: Menasha Ridge Press, 1987.
Walking the Florida Trail—Keller, Jim. Gainesville: Florida Trail Association, 1985.

MAPS

Florida Atlas and Gazetteer—Freeport: DeLorme Mapping Company, 1987.

INFORMATION ABOUT STATE PARKS

Florida Department of Natural Resources, Division of Recreation and Parks, 3900 Commonwealth Boulevard, Tallahassee, FL 32399; (904)487-4784.

INFORMATION ABOUT NATIONAL FORESTS

National Forests in Florida, 227 North Bronough Street, Suite 4001, Tallahassee, FL 32301; (904)681-7265.

STATE HIGHWAY MAP AND TRAVEL INFORMATION

Florida Division of Tourism, 107 West Gaines, Suite 543, Tallahassee, FL 32399; (904)488-8230.

TRAIL INFORMATION

Florida Trail Association, P.O. Box 13708, Gainesville, FL 32604.

CLUBS AND OTHER ORGANIZATIONS WHICH OFFER HIKES

Appalachian Trail Club of Florida, c/o Grace Tyner, 1310 Quail Drive, Sarasota, FL 34231.
Florida Trail Association, P.O. Box 13708, Gainesville, FL 32604. This organization has a number of chapters throughout Florida.
Sierra Club, c/o Beth Ann Brick, 462 Fernwood, Key Biscayne, FL 33149.

GEORGIA

Georgia has quite diverse scenery ranging from rugged mountains in the north to swamplands in the southeast. Hiking opportunities on state lands are somewhat limited, although a few state parks have attractive little trail networks. The most impressive hiking is found in northern Georgia's Chattahoochee National Forest—a large and important National Forest which offers a wonderful array of trails in an unusually wild and beautiful mountain setting.

MAJOR TRAILS

APPALACHIAN TRAIL—75 miles in Georgia (2,100 total). This is the southernmost section of the famous Appalachian Trail. It falls entirely within Chattahoochee National Forest. Beginning on top of 3,782-foot Springer Mountain (accessible by an approach trail from Amicalola Falls State Park), the trail heads north over a number of rugged mountains with elevations as high as 4,430 feet. There are fine views from a few open mountaintops as well as overlooks in this scenic wilderness. Most of the trail is moderate to strenuous in difficulty. Trail information: Appalachian Trail Conference, P.O. Box 807, Harpers Ferry, WV 25425.

BENTON MACKAYE TRAIL—75 miles in Georgia. This partially completed trail is named after the man who fathered the Appalachian Trail. It will eventually run about 250 miles, forming a large loop with the Appalachian Trail from Springer Mountain to the Great Smoky Mountains National Park in North Carolina and Tennessee. Most of the trail will be on public lands. The Georgia portion is basically completed, and leads through the wild mountains of Chattahoochee National Forest, including the Cohutta Wilderness. Difficulty ranges from easy to strenuous. Trail information: Benton MacKaye Trail Association, P.O. Box 53271, Atlanta, GA 30355.

BEST HIKING AREAS

CHATTAHOOCHEE NATIONAL FOREST—508 Oak Street N.W., Gainesville, GA 30501; (404)536-0541. 740,000 acres. Chattahoochee National Forest is a major tract of wild land which lies along the mountainous northern border of Georgia, at the southern end of the Blue Ridge Mountains. Georgia's highest mountain, 4,784-foot Brasstown Bald, is here. The landscape also contains steep slopes and gorges, high cliffs and tall pines, diverse deciduous forests of oak, hickory and maple, with rhododendron and mountain laurel.

Wildlife includes white-tailed deer, black bear, bobcat, and gray fox. There are countless creeks, many with waterfalls, and beautiful mountain lakes and rivers—including the Chattooga National Wild and Scenic River. Also here is the rugged 37,000-acre Cohutta Wilderness, which

extends into Tennessee's Cherokee National Forest.

There are nearly 400 miles of hiking trails. Among them are the 37-mile Bartram National Recreation Trail, the 35-mile Duncan Ridge National Recreation Trail, 75 miles of the Benton MacKaye Trail, and 75 miles of the Appalachian Trail.

OTHER RECOMMENDED LOCATIONS

CUMBERLAND ISLAND NATIONAL SEA-SHORE—P.O. Box 806, St. Marys, GA 31558; (912)882-4336. 37,000 acres. Located on the southeast coast of Georgia, this beautiful 16-mile long barrier island (accessible by ferry) has many miles of wilderness trails. Scenery includes attractive mixed forests of oak, magnolia and pine—with dunes, salt marsh, and great stretches of white sand beach. Deer and alligator are among the wildlife here.

GEORGIA HIKING RESOURCES

HIKING GUIDEBOOKS
Guide to the Appalachian Trail in North Carolina and Georgia—Harpers Ferry, WV: The Appalachian Trail Conference, 1989.

The Hiking Trails of North Georgia—Homan, Tim. Atlanta: Peachtree Publishers, Ltd., 1987.

INFORMATION ABOUT STATE PARKS

Georgia Department of Natural Resources, 205 Butler Street, S.E., Atlanta, GA 30334; 1(800)342-7275 (in Georgia) or 1(800)542-7275 (outside Georgia).

STATE HIGHWAY MAP AND TRAVEL INFORMATION

Georgia Tourist Division, P.O. Box 1776, Atlanta, GA 30301; (404)656-3590.

CLUBS AND OTHER ORGANIZATIONS WHICH OFFER HIKES

Georgia Appalachian Trail Club, P.O. Box 654, Atlanta, GA 30301.

The Georgia Conservancy, 781 Marietta Street, N.W., Atlanta, GA 30318.

Georgia Rails into Trails Society, c/o First Peoples Bank, 63 Barrett Parkway, Marietta, GA 30066.

Sierra Club, P.O. Box 467151, Atlanta, GA 30346.

HAWAII

Hawaii's volcanic islands offer a magnificent mountainous landscape which includes some active volcanoes with slow-moving lava. There are also deep canyons and valleys with rain forests and jungles, lovely waterfalls and pools—and a rugged coastline with high fluted cliffs and beautiful beaches. Two National Parks have the most extensive trail systems, while shorter trails lead through a number of forest reserves and state parks, permitting one to sample the striking natural scenery of this lovely island state.

BEST HIKING AREAS

HAWAII VOLCANOES NATIONAL PARK—Hawaii, HI 96718; (808)967-7311. 229,117 acres. Located on the island of Hawaii, this National Park includes two active volcanoes, which periodically erupt with slow lava flows: 4,077-foot Kilauea and 13,667-foot Mauna Loa. These are actually the tops of enormous volcanic masses which extend down 18,000 feet beneath the ocean surface.

The park is a landscape of barren craters, massive lava flows, and steaming vents—but also has some grassy meadows and lush rain forests. There are over 130 miles of hiking trails, easy to strenuous in difficulty. Especially challenging is the rough 18-mile Mauna Loa Trail,

which ascends 6,600 feet to the top of Mauna Loa.

HALEAKALA NATIONAL PARK—P.O. Box 369, Makawao, Maui, HI 96768; (808)572-9306. 28,665 acres. Situated on the island of Maui, this National Park is dominated by 10,023-foot Mount Haleakala, a dormant volcano with a crater that's seven miles across. Along with beautiful volcanic wilderness scenery which includes cinder cones, old lava flows, and magnificent views, the park also encompasses the lush Kipahula Valley—with luxuriant rain forest and steep coastal cliffs. There are four streams, with some waterfalls and lovely pools. Thirty-six miles of hiking trails extend throughout the park. Difficulty ranges from easy to strenuous.

OTHER RECOMMENDED LOCATIONS

KULA & KAHIKINUI FOREST RESERVES—Hawaii Division of Forestry and Wildlife, P.O. Box 1015, Wailuku, Maui, HI 96793; (808)244-4352. These two adjacent reserves on the island of Maui are located next to Haleakala National Park and Polipoli State Park. It's a mountainous region of 6,000 to 7,000 foot elevations with some great views, and dense mixed forests which include pine and cedar, redwood and ash—along with open grassy areas. There are over 30 miles of hiking trails in the two reserves.

HAWAII HIKING RESOURCES

HIKING GUIDEBOOKS
Hawaiian Hiking Trails—Chisholm, Craig. Lake Oswego, OR: The Fernglen Press, 1989.

INFORMATION ABOUT STATE PARKS
Hawaii Division of State Parks, P.O. Box 621, Honolulu, HI 96809.

INFORMATION ABOUT STATE FORESTS
Hawaii Division of Forestry and Wildlife, 1151 Punchbowl Street, Room 325, Honolulu, HI 96813; (808)548-2861.

HAWAII HIKING CLUBS
Sierra Club, P.O. Box 2577, Honolulu, HI 96803.

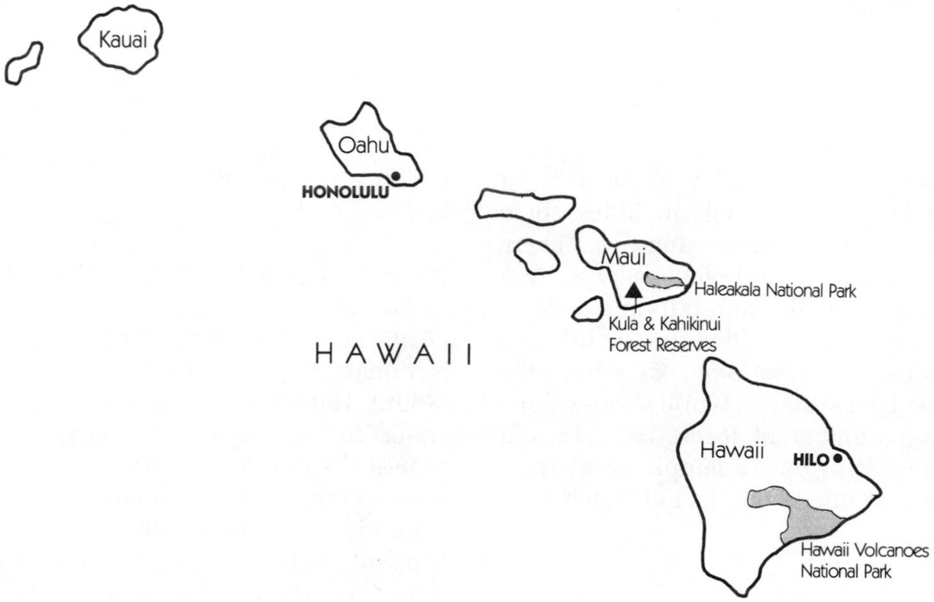

Kauai

Oahu
HONOLULU

Maui
Haleakala National Park
Kula & Kahikinui
Forest Reserves

HAWAII

Hawaii
HILO

Hawaii Volcanoes
National Park

IDAHO

Idaho is a ruggedly mountainous state with many steep jagged peaks, deep canyon gorges, and an incredible number of wild lakes, streams, and spectacular rivers. Almost three-fourths of Idaho is public land, and while there's no National Park here, ten sizable and splendidly scenic National Forests more than compensate. Altogether there are an estimated seventeen thousand miles of trails in the state, offering some of the richest and most rewarding hiking in the country.

MAJOR TRAILS

CONTINENTAL DIVIDE TRAIL—325 miles (3,100 total). This segment of the magnificent Continental Divide Trail straddles the Montana border, and parts of it are in that state. Although it's essentially completed, some trail work remains to be done. Scenery includes rugged and spectacular high peaks, along with forested hills and grasslands. At times the trail follows the crest of the Divide, and for other stretches it runs along jeep roads. Elevations are as high as 10,000 feet, with some absolutely splendid views. The trail is open to horseback riding as well as hiking. It's generally free of snow only from July through September. Difficulty varies from easy to strenuous. Trail information: Continental Divide Trail Society, P.O. Box 30002, Bethesda, MD 20814.

BEST HIKING AREAS

NEZ PERCE NATIONAL FOREST—Route 2, Box 475, Grangeville, ID 83530, (208)983-1950. 2,218,333 acres. Nez Perce is an enormous National Forest in north-central Idaho—an area of extremely rugged and scenic mountains (some over 9,000 feet), steep canyons, and extensive forests of ponderosa pine and Douglas fir. There are subalpine flora at high elevations, and many mountain lakes plus scores of streams. Wildlife includes elk, moose, white-tailed and mule deer, black bear, bighorn sheep, mountain goat, and mountain lion.

Especially notable is spectacular 7,000-foot-deep Hells Canyon on the Snake River, said to be the deepest gorge in the country. Here too are the splendid Salmon and Selway National Wild and Scenic Rivers. There are four wilderness areas, adding up to over 900,000 acres, including 560,000 acres of the vast 1,340,681-acre Selway-Bitterroot Wilderness—plus the 206,000-acre Gospel Wilderness.

This National Forest has approximately 2,600 miles of trails. Many are open to horseback riding, and some to other uses. Included are several National Recreation Trails. Difficulty ranges from easy to very strenuous. Some trails are unmaintained. High trails are often under snow until mid-July, and snow typically returns by late September.

IDAHO PANHANDLE NATIONAL FORESTS—
1201 Ironwood Drive, Coeur d'Alene, ID 83814;
(208)667-2561. 2,479,245 acres. This is a group
of three National Forests—Kaniksu, Coeur
d'Alene, and St. Joe—located in Idaho's northern
panhandle. Even though there are no official
wilderness areas, it's an attractive and often wild
region which encompasses several mountain
ranges, including the Bitterroot Mountains on
Montana's border.

The St. Joe National Wild and Scenic River is
here. There are rugged mountain ridges with
steep peaks over 7,000 feet, dense evergreen
forests, open meadows, and a great many lakes,
ponds, rivers, and streams with waterfalls. Trees
include 1000-year-old cedars and old-growth
hemlocks, along with pine and fir, larch and
spruce. Among the wildlife are grizzly and black
bear, caribou, elk, white-tailed and mule deer,
moose, mountain goat, coyote, and lynx.

The Idaho Panhandle National Forests have a
combined total of over 2,000 miles of trails.
About half receive regular maintenance, and
some are open to motorized use. There are a
number of National Recreation Trails, including
the 41-mile Big Creek Trail. Also here is the
northern part of the new Idaho Centennial Trail.
Difficulty varies from easy to strenuous.

SAWTOOTH NATIONAL FOREST—2647 Kim-
berly Road East, Twin Falls, ID 83301; (208)737-
3200. 1,347,422 acres. Consisting of several
tracts in south-central Idaho, Sawtooth National
Forest encompasses some of Idaho's most spectacular mountain ranges—notably the jagged-
peaked Sawtooth Mountains, along with the
White Cloud and Boulder Mountains. Seven
hundred and fifty-six thousand acres are set
aside as the Sawtooth National Recreation Area,
an especially magnificent region which includes
the 217,000-acre Sawtooth Wilderness.

Some 40 peaks are over 10,000 feet, with a few
over 11,000 feet. Hyndman Peak is the highest at
12,009 feet. Along with lofty granite peaks there
are limestone cliffs and impressive rock formations, mountain meadows, deep canyon gorges,
over 1,000 lakes, thousands of miles of streams,
and some outstanding rivers. Vegetation ranges

from alpine plants to forests of conifers and
sagebrush hills. Elk, deer, bighorn sheep, black
bear, antelope, mountain goat, and coyote are
among the mammals here.

An estimated 1,600 miles of trails are found in
this National Forest. Some offer superb panoramic views. Nearly half are in the Sawtooth
National Recreation Area. Not all trails are maintained, and many are open to horseback riding.
Difficulty ranges from easy to strenuous. High
mountain passes are sometimes under snow until mid-July.

CHALLIS NATIONAL FOREST—HC 63, Box
1671, Challis, ID 83226; (208)879-2285.
2,516,191 acres. Situated in south-central Idaho,
Challis is a massive National Forest which encloses several lofty mountain ranges. The highest point in Idaho is here, 12,655-foot Borah
Peak. There are also vast areas of roadless land,
with 782,000 acres of the 2,361,767-acre Frank
Church–River of No Return Wilderness—which
extends into five other National Forests, and is
the largest such wilderness in the country outside of Alaska.

The scenery includes barren, sheer-faced
peaks, cirque basins and canyons, high mountain lakes, hundreds of miles of creeks, and
magnificent views. Vegetation varies from valley
grasslands and conifer forests to elevated meadows and alpine tundra. Elk, deer, antelope, bighorn sheep, mountain goat, moose, and black
bear are among the mammals found in this
National Forest.

There are over 1,600 miles of trails, including
the 59-mile Highline Trail. Some are open to
horseback riding. Difficulty ranges from easy to
strenuous. Most trails are lightly used. Trails at
high elevations may be under snow until July.

PAYETTE NATIONAL FOREST—P.O. Box 1026,
McCall, ID 83638; (208)634-8151. 2,314,436
acres. Payette National Forest consists of two
huge parcels of land in central Idaho. It's a
beautifully wild and mountainous region, with
some elevations exceeding 9,000 feet. There are
two wilderness areas, including 780,000 acres of

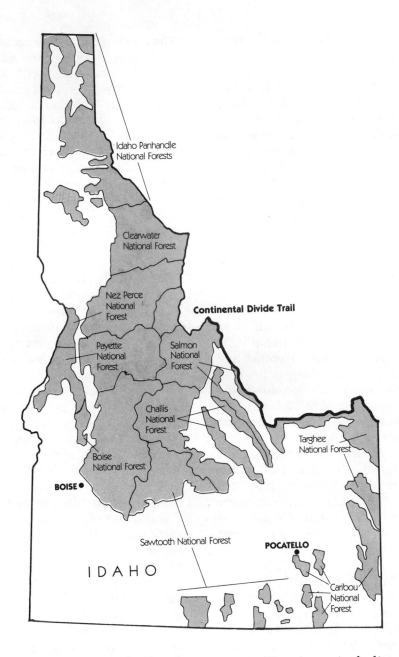

Idaho Panhandle
National Forests

Clearwater
National Forest

Nez Perce
National
Forest

Continental Divide Trail

Payette
National
Forest

Salmon
National
Forest

Challis
National
Forest

Targhee
National Forest

Boise
National Forest

BOISE ●

Sawtooth National Forest

POCATELLO

Caribou
National
Forest

IDAHO

the magnificent 2,361,767-acre Frank Church–River of No Return Wilderness, which stretches into five other National Forests.

This is an area of steep peaks, ridges, and slopes with great open views, cirques and horns, rock domes, terraces, and granite walls. There are rugged river canyons and gorges with rock outcrops, and glaciated valleys—plus a multitude of lakes, an endless number of streams, and some major rivers, including the Salmon River and parts of several other Wild and Scenic Rivers. Among the wildlife are elk, deer, mountain goat, moose, bighorn sheep, black bear, and gray wolf. Vegetation ranges from meadows and grasslands to forests of pine and spruce, fir and aspen.

Payette contains more than 1,400 miles of hiking trails. Many are open to horseback riding.

Some are unmaintained. Difficulty varies from easy to strenuous.

TARGHEE NATIONAL FOREST

TARGHEE NATIONAL FOREST—P.O. Box 208, St. Anthony, ID 83445; (208)624-3151. 1,557,792 acres in Idaho (296,448 in Wyoming). With attractive tracts in southeast Idaho which extend into western Wyoming, Targhee National Forest borders on Yellowstone National Park and Wyoming's Tetons, and includes a section of the Continental Divide. There are rugged mountain ranges here with high peaks and fantastic views (many elevations over 10,000 feet), steep ridges and saddles, deep canyons and cliffs, and massive glacial cirques. The area contains countless creeks with waterfalls, rivers, high lakes and ponds.

One of two wilderness areas is the 116,000-acre Jedediah Smith Wilderness, which is in Wyoming alongside Grand Teton National Park. Vegetation varies from semidesert sagebrush and forests of lodgepole pine and Douglas fir, with stands of aspen, to high grassy meadows and alpine tundra. Elk, grizzly and black bear, deer, bighorn sheep, moose, and mountain lion are among the mammals found here.

Over 1,200 miles of trails extend through this National Forest, easy to strenuous in difficulty. Included is a section of the still-to-be-completed Continental Divide Trail. Motorized vehicles are permitted on many trails outside of wilderness areas. High elevations are under snow at least through June.

SALMON NATIONAL FOREST

SALMON NATIONAL FOREST—P.O. Box 729, Salmon, ID 83467; (208)756-2215. 1,776,994 acres. Located in east-central Idaho, Salmon National Forest borders on the Bitterroot Mountains and includes the Salmon River Mountains, along with some other ranges. Elevations run from under 3,000 feet to more than 11,000 feet. The overall area is rugged with high craggy peaks and magnificent panoramic views. Within the forest boundaries are 427,000 acres of the spectacular 2,361,767-acre Frank Church–River of No Return Wilderness, which extends into five other National Forests—plus a stretch of the Salmon Wild and Scenic River.

The area has many streams and cirque (glacier-carved basin) lakes, alpine meadows and Douglas fir forests—along with spruce, lodgepole and ponderosa pine, plus sagebrush scrublands. Local animals include elk, deer, bighorn sheep, bear, moose, mountain goat, and bobcat.

There are over 1,200 miles of hiking trails, more than half of which are in the Frank Church–River of No Return Wilderness. Difficulty varies from easy to strenuous. A section of the Continental Divide Trail is here. Most trails outside of the wilderness are multi-use. The high country regions are normally snow-free only from July through mid-September.

CLEARWATER NATIONAL FOREST

CLEARWATER NATIONAL FOREST—12730 Highway 12, Orofino, ID 83544; (208)476-4541. 1,831,374 acres. Consisting of several tracts in Idaho's northern panhandle, Clearwater National Forest includes part of the beautiful and rugged Bitterroot Range, and 260,000 acres of the 1,337,910-acre Selway–Bitterroot Wilderness—which extends into nearby National Forests. Terrain ranges from high rocky ridges with sub-alpine areas, deep saddles, and steep canyon gorges, to open buttes and low prairies. There are exceptional panoramic vistas.

The area has hundreds of mountain lakes, creeks with waterfalls, and several major rivers. There are coniferous forests including Douglas fir, ponderosa pine, and larch, along with old-growth cedar. Among the wildlife are elk, black bear, deer, moose, mountain goat, mountain lion, and coyote.

Clearwater has over 1,100 miles of trails, which vary from easy to strenuous. Included is the scenic 35-mile Eagle Mountain Trail. Many trails are not maintained, and most receive light use. High trails may be under snow until July.

BOISE NATIONAL FOREST

BOISE NATIONAL FOREST—1750 Front Street, Boise, ID 83702; (208)364-4100. 2,612,000 acres. Situated in south-central Idaho near Boise, this massive National Forest encloses parts of several significant mountain ranges, with some elevations exceeding 9,000 feet. There are rough, rocky peaks, steep canyons and deep valleys, and many mountain lakes, creeks, and rivers.

Outstanding views are plentiful.

Included are 332,000 acres of the splendid 2,361,767-acre Frank Church–River of No Return Wilderness, which reaches into five other National Forests, along with other substantial roadless areas. There are forests of pine and fir, aspen groves, meadows with wildflowers, and open grasslands. Among the mammals here are elk, mule deer, black bear, bighorn sheep, mountain goat, and lynx.

Boise National Forest has approximately 1,000 miles of trails, which vary in difficulty from easy to strenuous. Some trails are not maintained.

CARIBOU NATIONAL FOREST—Suite 282, Federal Building, 250 South 4th Avenue, Pocatello, ID 83201; (208)236-6700. 1,080,322 acres. Caribou National Forest consists of a number of attractive tracts in the southeast corner of Idaho. There are several chains of mountains running north to south, with elevations from 5,000 feet to over 9,000 feet. Meade Peak (9,953 feet) is the highest point.

The scenery includes high peaks, narrow canyons, ice caves, plus some rivers and a great many streams. There are grasslands and open slopes with sagebrush, meadows with wildflowers, Douglas fir and lodgepole pine forests, along with aspen. Wildlife includes elk, moose, and deer.

This National Forest has about 1,200 miles of hiking trails. Two especially scenic trails are the 55-mile High Line National Recreation Trail and the 35-mile Boundary Trail loop. Difficulty ranges from easy to strenuous. Some trails are open to motorized vehicles.

IDAHO HIKING RESOURCES

HIKING GUIDEBOOKS

Adventures in Idaho's Sawtooth Country— Stone, Lynne. Seattle: The Mountaineers.

Day Hiking Near Sun Valley—Hollingshead, Anne & Moore, Gloria.

50 Eastern Idaho Hiking Trails—Mitchell, Ron. Boulder, CO: Pruett, 1979.

Guide to the Continental Divide Trail: Southern Montana and Idaho—Wolf, James R. Bethesda, MD: Continental Divide Trail Society, 1986.

Hiking Trails of the Bitterroot Mountains— Arkava, Morton L. & Leone K. Boulder, CO: Pruett, 1983.

The Hiker's Guide to Idaho—Maugham, Ralph & Jackie. Helena, MT: Falcon Press, 1984.

Hiking Trails of Southern Idaho—Bluestein, S.R. Caldwell, ID: Caxton Printers, 1981.

North Idaho Hiking Trails—Bluestein, S.R. Boise, ID: Challenge Expedition Co., 1982.

Trails of the Sawtooth and White Cloud Mountains—Fuller, Margaret. Edmonds, WA: Signpost Books, 1979.

Trails of Western Idaho—Fuller, Margaret. Edmonds, WA: Signpost Books, 1982.

INFORMATION ABOUT STATE PARKS

Idaho Department of Parks and Recreation, Statehouse Mall, Boise, ID 83720.

STATE HIGHWAY MAP AND TRAVEL INFORMATION

Idaho Travel Council, 700 West State Street, Boise, ID 83720; (800)635-7820.

IDAHO HIKING CLUBS

Sierra Club, c/o Edwina Allen, 1408 Joyce Street, Boise, ID 83706.

ILLINOIS

Illinois has plenty of small-to-medium-size state parks, fish and wildlife areas, forests, and "conservation areas." Short hiking trails are found in the majority of such tracts, and a few have fair-size trail systems. The one truly large and relatively wild natural area is Shawnee National Forest—and it's amid the attractive scenery here that the best and most extensive hiking in the state is found.

MAJOR TRAILS

ILLINOIS PRAIRIE PATH—55 miles. This multi-use National Recreation Trail in northeastern Illinois is open to horseback riding and cycling as well as hiking. It follows old railroad routes, and has some spurs. The Prairie Path is not a wilderness trail, running through some developed areas as well as pleasant rural countryside, along with some small forest preserves. Trail information: Illinois Prairie Path, P.O. Box 1086, 616 Delles Road, Wheaton, IL 60189.

RIVER TO RIVER TRAIL—47 miles. The River to River Trail in eastern Shawnee National Forest is another multipurpose trail, open to horseback riders and hikers. It's very hilly and crosses several ridges. Difficulty is easy to moderate. Trail information: Shawnee National Forest, 901

South Commercial Street, Harrisburg, IL 62946; (618)253-7114.

BEST HIKING AREAS

SHAWNEE NATIONAL FOREST—901 South Commercial Street, Harrisburg, IL 62946; (618)253-7114. 261,357 acres. Located in southern Illinois, this substantial-size National Forest has scenery which includes high bluffs and sheer sandstone cliffs, rock formations, small canyons and caves, and some natural arches and bridges. There are also many beautiful lakes, rivers, streams, and small waterfalls.

The area has forests of oak and walnut, pine and cedar, with dogwood and wild cherry. The varied wildlife includes white-tailed deer. There are over 135 miles of hiking trails, longest of which is the 47-mile River to River Trail.

OTHER RECOMMENDED LOCATIONS

GIANT CITY STATE PARK—P.O. Box 70, Makanda, IL 62958; (618)457-4836. 3,694 acres. Situated in southern Illinois amid Shawnee National Forest lands, Giant City State Park has huge sandstone cliffs, several attractive streams, small ponds, and forests of oak-hickory. There are over 20 miles of trails, including the 16-mile Red Cedar Hiking Trail.

ILLINOIS HIKING RESOURCES

HIKING GUIDEBOOKS

Illinois Hiking and Backpacking Trails—Zyznieuski, Walter and George. Carbondale, IL: Southern Illinois University Press, 1985.

INFORMATION ABOUT STATE PARKS AND FORESTS

Illinois Department of Conservation, Lincoln Tower Plaza, 524 South Second Street, Springfield, IL 62701.

MAPS

Illinois Atlas & Gazetteer—Freeport, ME: De-Lorme Mapping Co.

STATE HIGHWAY MAP AND TRAVEL INFORMATION

Illinois Office of Tourism, 310 South Michigan Avenue, Suite 108, Chicago, IL 60604; (312)793-2094/ (800)223-0121.

CLUBS AND OTHER ORGANIZATIONS WHICH OFFER HIKES

American Youth Hostels, 3712 North Clark Street, Chicago, IL 60613.

The Prairie Club, 6 East Monroe, Room 1507, Chicago, IL 60603.

Sierra Club, 506 South Wabash, Room 525, Chicago, IL 60605.

INDIANA

The rolling hills of Indiana offer a substantial amount of hiking, and while there's not a lot in the way of real wilderness to be found here, most of the thirty-odd state parks and forests have at least short- to medium-size trails. The best hiking is found in southern Indiana, especially within the confines of Hoosier National Forest, which includes some beautiful forested land abundant with lakes and a number of scenic trails.

MAJOR HIKING TRAILS

KNOBSTONE TRAIL—58 miles. The Knobstone Trail is the longest hiking trail in Indiana, and may eventually be extended to a length of over 200 miles. It passes through some interesting and intermittently rough terrain on public lands in the southern part of the state, leading past some nice lakes and ponds, and over a number of rocky knobs. Trail information: Indiana Division of Outdoor Recreation, 605 State Office Building, Indianapolis, IN 46204; (317)232-4070.

BEST HIKING AREAS

HOOSIER NATIONAL FOREST—811 Constitution Avenue, Bedford, IN 47421; (812)275-5987. 187,812 acres. Consisting of two tracts north of the Ohio River in southern Indiana, this good-size National Forest has major portions of private as well as public lands. The visitor is never far from roads or development, but some attractive southern Indiana scenery is found within the forest boundaries.

The hilly terrain includes hardwood forests of oak and hickory, along with cedar and pine. There are a number of streams and some large lakes, with deer among the wildlife. The one wilderness area (rare for this part of the country) is the 12,935-acre Charles C. Deam Wilderness, which includes a bit of rugged terrain and about 75 miles of trails. Elsewhere in the Forest there are additional hiking trails, most of them easy to moderate in difficulty.

OTHER RECOMMENDED LOCATIONS

CLARK STATE FOREST—P.O. Box 119, Henryville, IN 47126; (812)294-4306. 23,979 acres. This large and beautiful state forest in southern Indiana has seven lakes, forests of oak and hickory, pine and beech—and two significant trails, the 20-mile Clark State Forest Trail and a segment of the 58-mile Knobstone Trail.

HARRISON–CRAWFORD STATE FOREST—7240 Old Forest Road, Corydon, IN 47112; (812)738-8232. 25,619 acres. Harrison–Crawford State Forest stands next to the Ohio River in southern Indiana. It's a hilly region with hardwood forests, large limestone caves, and wildlife including deer. Foremost among the attractive trails here is the circular 35-mile Adventure Trail, which offers some fine views of the Ohio and Blue Rivers.

INDIANA HIKING RESOURCES

INFORMATION ABOUT STATE PARKS
Indiana Division of State Parks, 616 State Office Building, Indianapolis, IN 46204; (317)232-4124.

INFORMATION ABOUT STATE FORESTS
Indiana Division of Forestry, 613 State Office Building, Indianapolis, IN 46204; (317)232-4105.

TRAIL INFORMATION
Division of Outdoor Recreation, 605 State Office Building, Indianapolis, IN 46204; (317)232-4070.

STATE HIGHWAY MAP AND TRAVEL INFORMATION
Indiana Tourism, One North Capitol, Suite 700, Indianapolis, IN 46204; (800)782-3775/ (800)289-6646.

CLUBS AND OTHER ORGANIZATIONS WHICH OFFER HIKES
Central Indiana Wilderness Club, P.O. Box 44351, Indianapolis, IN 46244.

Hoosier Backpackers, 1020 West State Boulevard, Suite 100, Fort Wayne, IN 46808.

The Indianapolis Hiking Club, 5176 Atherton, South Drive, Indianapolis, IN 46219.

Sierra Club, P.O. Box 40275, Indianapolis, IN 46240.

IOWA

Much of Iowa is devoted to agriculture, and there are no National Forests or other large areas of public land here. Limited hiking is available, however, in some small state parks and a couple of medium-size state forests. While most true hiking trails are short, the state does have a large and growing number of multi-use trails which traverse portions of Iowa's nice rural countryside.

MAJOR TRAILS

CEDAR VALLEY NATURE TRAIL—52 miles. This multipurpose National Recreation Trail is open to bicyclists as well as hikers. It runs along an old railroad bed between the towns of Hiawatha and Evansdale in eastern Iowa, paralleling the Cedar River. Scenery includes hilly farmlands and forests, and the trail goes through several towns. A trail pass must be obtained for a nominal fee. Trail information: Iowa Department of Natural Resources, Wallace State Office Building, 900 East Grand, Des Moines, IA 50319; (515)281-5145.

Iowa has no less than 41 multiple-use trails converted from old railroad lines. Several are over 20 miles long. These trails are open to bicycling as well as hiking. For information contact the Iowa Department of Natural Resources (see above address), or the Iowa Trails Council, Cedar Point, IA 52213.

BEST HIKING AREAS

YELLOW RIVER STATE FOREST—Box 115, McGregor, IA 52157; (319)586-2254. 6,550 acres. Yellow River State Forest is in northeastern Iowa. It's a mostly forested area, with streams and some hilly, rugged terrain, which includes precipitous limestone bluffs with fine views. Deer are among the wildlife, and trees include oak and hickory, pine and larch. The major hiking trail here is the 20-mile Backpack Trail. There are some short trails as well.

IOWA HIKING RESOURCES

INFORMATION ABOUT STATE PARKS AND FORESTS
Iowa Department of Natural Resources, Wallace State Office Building, 900 East Grand Avenue, Des Moines, IA 50319; (515)281-5145.

TRAIL INFORMATION
Iowa Trails Council, Cedar Point, IA 52213; (319)849-1844.

STATE HIGHWAY MAP AND TRAVEL INFORMATION
Iowa Division of Tourism, 200 East Grand Avenue, Des Moines, IA 50309; (515)218-3100/ (800)345-IOWA.

IOWA HIKING CLUBS
Sierra Club, c/o The Thoreau Center, 3500 Kingman Boulevard, Des Moines, IA 50311.

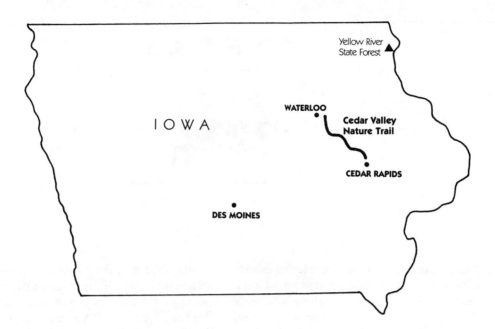

IOWA

KANSAS

Kansas has a landscape which includes gently rolling hills, open plains and prairie grasslands, wooded areas, and a few steep ridges with rock formations. There are also many rivers and creeks, scores of lakes, and thousands of ponds. Agriculture is extensive and natural areas are limited. While most state parks are small and have short trails, some more extensive hiking is available on attractive lands alongside a number of the state's large reservoirs.

BEST HIKING AREAS

CLINTON LAKE—U.S. Army Corps of Engi-neers, Route 1, Box 120G, Lawrence, KS 66044; (913)843-7665. This eight-mile long reservoir west of Kansas City is surrounded by oak and hickory forests, with some high bluffs and rocky hills, open fields, and wildlife including white-tailed deer, coyote, and gray fox. There are over 60 miles of trails here, many of which are open to horseback riding as well as hiking.

PERRY LAKE—U.S. Army Corps of Engineers, Route 1, Box 115, Perry, KS 66073; (913)597-5144. Perry Lake is a large reservoir located northwest of Kansas City. The region includes some hilly rugged terrain with rock outcrop-pings, along with more level areas. There are

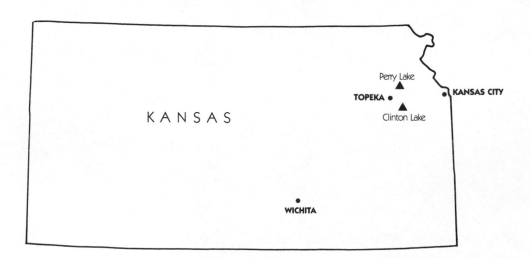

oak-hickory forests with bits of open prairie, many streams and ponds, and fine views. The major hiking trail here is the 30-mile Perry Lake Trail, which forms a large loop. A portion has National Recreation Trail status.

KANSAS HIKING RESOURCES

INFORMATION ABOUT STATE PARKS

Kansas Department of Wildlife and Parks, RR 22, Box 54A, Pratt, KS 67124; (316)672-5911.

STATE HIGHWAY MAP AND TRAVEL INFORMATION

Kansas Division of Travel and Tourism, 400 West 8th, 5th Floor, Topeka, KS 66603; (913)296-2009.

TRAIL INFORMATION

Kansas Trails Council, 1737 Rural Street, Emporia, KS 66801; (316)342-5508.

KANSAS HIKING CLUBS

Sierra Club, c/o Michael Moore, P.O. Box 47319, Wichita, KS 67201.

KENTUCKY

The mountains and hills of Kentucky furnish extremely attractive surroundings for hiking, and while most state parks here have small trail systems, a substantial number of lengthy trails are found on other public and private lands. Included are two important long-distance paths, the Sheltowee Trace Trail and the Jenny Wiley Trail. The most abundant options by far lie within Daniel Boone National Forest, which provides some of the wildest and most striking natural scenery in the state.

MAJOR TRAILS

SHELTOWEE TRACE TRAIL—257 miles. This notable National Recreation Trail, which is the state's longest, runs the length of Daniel Boone National Forest in eastern Kentucky. Fine scenery along the way includes high ridges with great views, rugged cliffs and enormous rock formations, steep gorges and lovely rivers. Difficulty varies from easy to strenuous. Trail information: Daniel Boone National Forest, 100 Vaught Road, Winchester, KY 40391; (606)745-3100.

JENNY WILEY TRAIL—180 miles. The scenic Jenny Wiley Trail begins at South Portsmouth on the Ohio River in the northeastern part of the state, and ends at Jenny Wiley State Park in east-central Kentucky. It follows a long ridge much of the way. Most of the trail is on private lands, although it also passes through the northern end of Daniel Boone National Forest. Difficulty varies from easy to strenuous. Trail information: Kentucky Department of Parks, 12th Floor, Capital Plaza Tower, Frankfort, KY 40601; (502)564-5410.

BEST HIKING AREAS

DANIEL BOONE NATIONAL FOREST—100 Vaught Road, Winchester, KY 40391; (606)745-3100. 661,000 acres. This extremely scenic National Forest in east and southeast Kentucky encompasses some mountainous terrain, with rugged ridges, canyons and sandstone cliffs, rock overhangs, and wonderful views. There are also some lakes and many beautiful rivers, creeks and waterfalls.

Of special interest is the 25,000-acre Red River Gorge Geological Area, which has over 80 natural arches and other outstanding scenery. Elsewhere are hardwood forests of oak and maple along with pine, and wildlife including white-tailed deer and red fox.

All told there are over 500 miles of hiking trails in Daniel Boone National Forest. Among them are the 257-mile Sheltowee Trace Trail, the 66-mile Redbird Crest Trail (a rugged and circular ridge trail), and the 36-mile Red River Gorge National Recreation Trail loop.

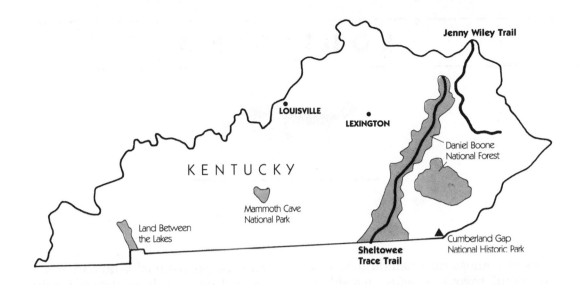

Jenny Wiley Trail

LOUISVILLE

LEXINGTON

Daniel Boone
National Forest

KENTUCKY

Mammoth Cave
National Park

Land Between
the Lakes

Cumberland Gap
National Historic Park

Sheltowee
Trace Trail

OTHER RECOMMENDED LOCATIONS

LAND BETWEEN THE LAKES—Golden Pond, KY 42231; (502)924-5602. 170,000 acres. This large National Recreation Area, managed by the Tennessee Valley Authority, is located in western Kentucky and extends into Tennessee. It consists of a 40-mile long peninsula between two enormous lakes. Included are hilly woodlands with some scenic views. Deer, bison, and coyote are among the wildlife.

There are 200 miles of hiking trails here. Longest is the 60-mile North-South Trail, which follows a winding route the length of the peninsula. Difficulty ranges from easy to strenuous.

CUMBERLAND GAP NATIONAL HISTORIC PARK—P.O. Box 1848, Middlesboro, KY 40965; (606)246-2817. 20,000 acres. Cumberland Gap provided early settlers a passage through the Appalachian Mountains, and it's now protected as a National Historic Park. This scenic area has elevations over 3,000 feet, mountain streams, and more than 50 miles of hiking trails— including a 22-mile trail which extends along Cumberland Mountain for the length of the park. Many trails are open to horses.

MAMMOTH CAVE NATIONAL PARK—Mammoth Cave, KY 42259; (502)758-2251. 52,000 acres. Famous for its vast underground cave system—the longest in the world, with hundreds of miles of passages—Mammoth Cave National Park also has some fine aboveground hiking available. About 70 miles of trails lead through hardwood forests of oak and hickory, and across terrain which is hilly and occasionally rugged, with some nice views of the Green and Nolin Rivers.

KENTUCKY HIKING RESOURCES

INFORMATION ABOUT STATE PARKS, FORESTS, AND HIKING TRAILS
Kentucky Department of Parks, 12th Floor, Capital Plaza Tower, Frankfort, KY 40601; (502)564-5410.

STATE HIGHWAY MAP AND TRAVEL INFORMATION
Kentucky Department of Travel Development, P.O. Box 2011, Frankfort, KY 40602; (502)564-4930/ (800)225-TRIP.

KENTUCKY HIKING CLUBS
Sierra Club, c/o Dave Stawicki, 2004 Writt Court, Lexington, KY 40505.

LOUISIANA

Louisiana's sometimes lush natural scenery includes beautiful bayous, swamps, marshlands, and extensive flatlands. There are also occasional hills and valleys, and the Mississippi is among a number of major rivers here. Some of the fourteen state parks offer trails of limited length, with the state's most extensive hiking found amid the often attractively wild scenery of Kisatchie National Forest.

BEST HIKING AREAS

KISATCHIE NATIONAL FOREST—P.O. Box 5500, 2500 Shreveport Highway, Pineville, LA 71360; (318)473-7160. 600,000 acres. Louisiana's Kisatchie National Forest consists of several parcels of scenic lands in the north-central and northern parts of the state. The region has pine and hardwood forests, natural open areas, and many attractive lake and creeks. Included is one 8,700-acre wilderness area, along with the lovely Saline Bayou National Wild and Scenic River.

Except for a small amount of rough terrain—some steep rocky bluffs, outcroppings, and mesas—most of the land is relatively flat. This National Forest has over a hundred miles of mostly easy hiking trails, among them the 31-mile Wild Azalea National Recreation Trail.

LOUISIANA HIKING RESOURCES

INFORMATION ABOUT STATE PARKS AND FORESTS
Louisiana Office of State Parks, P.O. Box 44426, Baton Rouge, LA 70804; (504)342-8111.

STATE HIGHWAY MAP AND TRAVEL INFORMATION
Louisiana Office of Tourism, P.O. Box 94291, Baton Rouge, LA 70804; (504)342-8119 or (800)33-GUMBO (outside Louisiana).

LOUISIANA HIKING CLUBS
Sierra Club, P.O. Box 19469, Bienville Street, New Orleans, LA 70119.

SHREVEPORT

Kisatchie
National Forest

L O U I S I A N A

BATON ROUGE

NEW ORLEANS

MAINE

A substantial portion of Maine remains relatively wild and undeveloped, although public lands are limited and hiking opportunities are not as extensive as one might expect. However, the 274-mile section of the Appalachian Trail is one of the most beautiful and remote of the entire trail—and the few parks here compensate as well by providing some unusually rewarding hiking, amid some of the most remarkable scenery in the northeastern United States.

MAJOR HIKING TRAILS

APPALACHIAN TRAIL—274 miles in Maine (2,100 total). This is the northernmost portion of the Appalachian Trail, as it proceeds from the New Hampshire line to Baxter State Park in north-central Maine. Near the New Hampshire border the trail crosses the incredibly rugged 30-mile Mahoosuc Range, commonly considered to be the most difficult section of the entire trail, with many steep climbs and extremely rough footing. After passing over some additional mountains in western Maine it becomes a lot easier, leading through the lovely lake country of west-central Maine before reaching the trail's terminus on Mount Katahdin. Trail information: Appalachian Trail Conference, P.O. Box 807, Harpers Ferry, WV 25425.

BEST HIKING AREAS

BAXTER STATE PARK—64 Balsam Drive, Millenocket, ME 04462; (207)723-5140. 201,000 acres. Baxter is an enormous and superb state park, kept in a wilderness condition with no paved roads. It's the home of Mount Katahdin (5,267 feet), Maine's highest mountain and one of the great mountains of the eastern United States. At the higher elevations one is rewarded by the most magnificent views in Maine.

Although Katahdin dominates the park, a number of smaller mountains are found here, along with numerous lakes and ponds. There are forests of spruce, fir, and pine, along with beech and maple-and many wildflowers. Moose, black bear, white-tailed deer, coyote, and bobcat are among the many mammals in the park.

There are nearly 180 miles of hiking trails, including 10 miles of the Appalachian Trail, which begin at the top of rugged Mount Katahdin. One especially exposed trail crosses the Knife Edge, an extremely narrow ridge with dramatic drops on either side. Difficulty ranges from easy to extremely strenuous.

ACADIA NATIONAL PARK—Box 177, Bar Harbor, ME 04609; (207)288-3338. 35,000 acres. Located on Mount Desert Island, along the coast of Maine, Acadia National Park is a splendid place for hiking. Rising up from the ocean is a chain of

17 mountains, including Cadillac Mountain (1,530 feet), the highest point on the Atlantic seaboard.

The unique combination of seashore and mountain scenery makes this area especially attractive—with rugged, precipitous cliffs and ravines, freshwater lakes and sand beaches, steep peaks and roaring surf. The park has forests of spruce and fir along with hardwoods, and wildlife includes white-tailed deer as well as marine animals. There are 120 miles of hiking trails, with an additional 43 miles of carriage roads suitable for walking. Difficulty varies from easy to strenuous.

Acadia is relatively small as National Parks go, and is quite heavily visited. The amount of wilderness is not large, and one is never far from roads or limited development. Some trails are lightly used, however, and the overall beauty of the area—including countless ocean views from barren rock summits—is incomparable for this part of the country.

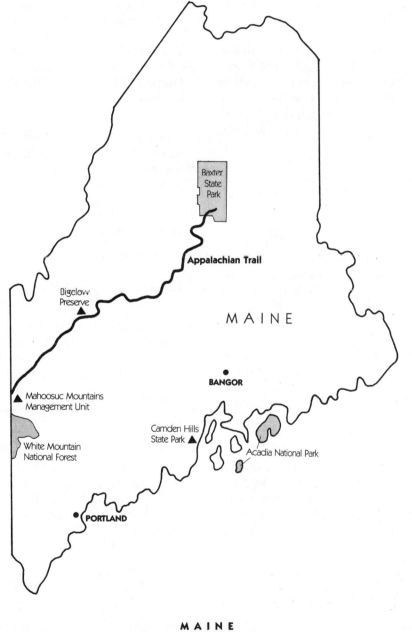

OTHER RECOMMENDED LOCATIONS

BIGELOW PRESERVE—Maine Department of Conservation, Bureau of Public Lands, State House, Station 22, Augusta, ME 04333; (207)289-3061. 34,500 acres. The Bigelow Preserve protects Mount Bigelow (4,150 feet), Maine's second highest mountain. There are several separate peaks, which offer some of the best views in the state. The Appalachian Trail crosses the mountain and preserve, and a few other trails are found here as well. Most of the hiking is moderate to strenuous in difficulty.

CAMDEN HILLS STATE PARK—Belfast Road, Camden, ME 04843; (207)236-3109. 5,474 acres. Located west of Acadia National Park, this state park provides more good hiking along the coast of Maine. A number of small mountains are situated here, including Mount Megunticook (1,380 feet), second highest point along the Atlantic seaboard, with plenty of fine views. There are mixed forests, wildlife including moose and deer, and 25 miles of trails. Difficulty varies from easy to strenuous.

MAHOOSUC MOUNTAINS MANAGEMENT UNIT—Bureau of Public Lands, Maine Department of Conservation, State House, Station 22, Augusta, ME 04333; (207)289-3061. 27,253 acres. This area includes a portion of the extremely rugged and scenic Mahoosuc Range along the Maine–New Hampshire border. There are several trails here, including the Appalachian Trail, providing many hiking options. Some of the hiking is unusually strenuous. Adjacent is Grafton Notch State Park, which offers other short trails.

WHITE MOUNTAIN NATIONAL FOREST—RFD 2, Box 2270, Bethel, ME 04217; (207)824-2134. 49,166 acres in Maine (798,305 in New Hampshire). There's outstanding hiking to be found in this important National Forest, most of which is in New Hampshire. The Maine section includes many mountains—highest of which is Speckled Mountain (2,907 feet)—with a good number of trails.

MAINE HIKING RESOURCES

HIKING GUIDEBOOKS

AMC Guide to Mt. Desert Island and Acadia National Park—Boston: Appalachian Mountain Club.

AMC Maine Mountain Guide—Boston: Appalachian Mountain Club, 1988.

Fifty Hikes in Northern Maine—Caputo, Cloe. Woodstock, VT: The Countryman Press, 1989.

Fifty Hikes in Southern Maine—Gibson, John. Woodstock, VT: The Countryman Press, 1989.

Guide to the Appalachian Trail in Maine—Harpers Ferry, WV: The Appalachian Trail Conference, 1988.

MAPS

Appalachian Mountain Club—5 Joy St., Boston, MA 02108. This major club publishes maps of hiking areas in Maine.

The Maine Atlas and Gazetteer—Freeport, ME: De Lorme Mapping Co.

The Maine Map and Guide—Freeport, ME: De Lorme Mapping Co.

TRAIL INFORMATION

New England Trail Conference, 33 Knollwood Drive, East Longmeadow, MA 01028; (203)342-1425 or (413)732-3719.

INFORMATION ABOUT STATE PARKS

Maine Bureau of Parks and Recreation, State House Station 22, Augusta, ME 04333; (207)289-3821.

STATE HIGHWAY MAP

Maine Department of Transportation, Augusta, ME 04333.

MAINE HIKING CLUBS

Appalachian Mountain Club, 5 Joy Street, Boston, MA 02108; (617)523-0636. This major club has a chapter in Maine.

Maine Appalachian Trail Club, P.O. Box 283, Augusta, ME 04330.

Sierra Club, 3 Joy Street, Boston, MA 02108.

MARYLAND

While it's not a large state, Maryland has over 319,000 acres of public lands, encompassing some mountain wilderness as well as seashore and Chesapeake Bay scenery. A good many small state parks and forests are found throughout Maryland, with the largest wild areas and the best hiking located in the beautiful mountainous northwestern part of the state.

MAJOR TRAILS

CHESAPEAKE AND OHIO (C & O) CANAL TOWPATH TRAIL—185 miles. This trail is contained in the long and narrow C & O National Historical Park, and it's maintained both for hikers and cyclists. The path parallels the scenic Potomac River, running from Washington, DC, to Cumberland, Maryland, and passes through attractive forested lands with some cliffs along the way. The trail is nearly flat and quite easy. Trail information: C & O National Historical park, Box 4, Sharpsburg, MD 21782.

APPALACHIAN TRAIL—41 miles in Maryland (2,100 total). The Appalachian Trail in Maryland traverses a series of low ridges, with a maximum elevation of 2,000 feet. There are many fine views. The trail also crosses and briefly follows the route of the C & O Canal Trail. Trail information: Appalachian Trail Conference, P.O. Box 807, Harpers Ferry, WV 25425.

POTOMAC HERITAGE NATIONAL SCENIC TRAIL—This new National Scenic Trail will eventually run over 700 miles if and when completed, following the route of the Potomac River and leading through some mountain scenery in Maryland, Virginia, and Pennsylvania. It will utilize the C & O Canal Trail and Pennsylvania's Laurel Highlands Hiking Trail, along with other trails. Progress so far has been slow due to lack of funds and other obstacles. Trail information: National Park Service, 1100 Ohio Drive, S.W., Washington, DC 20242.

BEST HIKING AREAS

SAVAGE RIVER STATE FOREST—Route 2, Box 63-A, Grantsville, MD 21536; (301)895-5759. 52,812 acres. This beautiful wilderness area is Maryland's largest state forest, located in the northwestern part of the state. There are small mountains here with elevations up to 3,000 feet, hardwood forests of oak and wild cherry, maple and pine. White-tailed deer, black bear, bobcat, and fox are among the local wildlife. There are 28 miles of trails, including the 17-mile Big Savage Mountain Trail.

GREEN RIDGE STATE FOREST—Star Route, Flintstone, MD 21530; (301)777-2345. 38,811 acres. Situated in the mountainous northwestern part of the state, Green Ridge is Maryland's

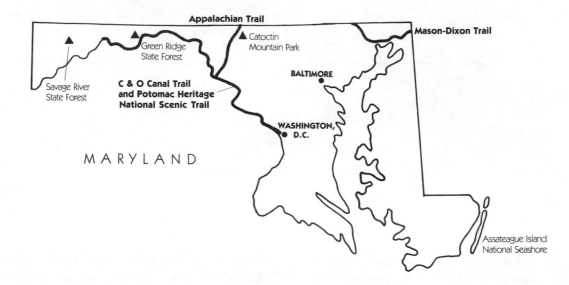

Appalachian Trail

Mason-Dixon Trail

Green Ridge
State Forest

Catoctin
Mountain Park

BALTIMORE

Savage River
State Forest

C & O Canal Trail
and Potomac Heritage
National Scenic Trail

WASHINGTON,
D.C.

MARYLAND

Assateague Island
National Seashore

second largest state forest. There's some nice scenery in this area with mixed forests of oak-hickory and pine, and wildlife including deer, black bear, and fox. The region has a number of hiking trails, including the 26-mile Green Ridge Trail.

CATOCTIN MOUNTAIN PARK—Thurmont, MD 21788; (301)663-9330. 5,768 acres. Located in north-central Maryland and run by the National Park Service, this attractive mountain park includes 1,880-foot Mount Catoctin. It's an area of mixed hardwood forests of oak, hickory, and birch, and wildlife including deer and fox. There are 25 miles of hiking trails, along with the terminus of the 26-mile Catoctin Trail.

OTHER RECOMMENDED LOCATIONS

ASSATEAGUE ISLAND NATIONAL SEA-SHORE—Route 2, Box 294, Berlin, MD 21811; (301)641-1441. 39,200 acres. Thirty-seven-mile-long Assateague Island is one of a string of barrier islands along Maryland's coast. While it's not a marked trail, the 21-mile Backcountry Trail which leads along the ocean shore is of special interest here, offering some wild coastal scenery with beaches, dunes, and marshes, and wildlife including deer and wild horses.

MARYLAND HIKING RESOURCES

HIKING GUIDEBOOKS

Appalachian Trail Guide to Maryland and Northern Virginia—Harpers Ferry, WV: The Appalachian Trail Conference, 1989.

INFORMATION ABOUT STATE PARKS AND FORESTS

Maryland Forest, Park, and Wildlife Service, Tawes State Office Building, C-2, Annapolis, MD 21401; (301)374-3771.

STATE HIGHWAY MAP AND TRAVEL INFORMATION

Maryland Office of Tourism Development, 217 East Redwood Street, Baltimore, MD 21202; 1(800)543-1036.

MARYLAND HIKING CLUBS

Appalachian Mountain Club, 5 Joy Street, Boston, MA 02108; (617)523-0636. This major club has a chapter in Washington, DC.

Center Hiking Club, c/o Marc Anthony Gobleck, 608 Coachway Drive, Rockville, MD 20852.

Mountain Club of Maryland, c/o Thurston Griggs, 5229 Benson Avenue, Baltimore, MD 21227.

Potomac Appalachian Trail Club, 1718 N Street, N.W., Washington, DC 20036.

Sierra Club, 1116 C West Street, Annapolis, MD 21403.

MASSACHUSETTS

Massachusetts is a heavily settled New England state which fortunately has a large number of state parks and forests, with over 300,000 acres of public land. While most wild areas are relatively small, trails are quite abundant here. Some especially fine hiking is found along the mountainous and unspoiled western border of the state, where the views are gratifying and the scenery exceptional.

MAJOR TRAILS

APPALACHIAN TRAIL—85 miles in Massachusetts (2,100 total). The Appalachian Trail runs along the western edge of the state and passes through two of the finest wild areas: the southern Taconic Mountains in the south, and Mount Greylock (highest point in the state) in the north. Terrain is sometimes rugged, and there are many great views. Difficulty varies from easy to strenuous. Trail information: Appalachian Trail Conference, P.O. Box 807, Harpers Ferry, WV 25425.

METACOMET–MONADNOCK TRAIL—98 miles in Massachusetts (117 miles total). This scenic trail runs through the forests of west-central Massachusetts from Connecticut to Mount Monadnock in New Hampshire. It follows the Connecticut River valley and traverses foothills and several small mountain ranges, offering some superb vistas. Difficulty ranges from easy to strenuous. Trail in-

formation: Trails Program, Massachusetts Department of Environmental Management, 225 Friend Street, Boston, MA 02114.

MIDSTATE TRAIL—89 miles. The Midstate Trail runs through Massachusetts from Douglas State Forest on the Rhode Island border to Ashburnham, near the New Hampshire line. It primarily follows old roads and passes through some scenic forested country. Trail information: Trails Program, Massachusetts Department of Environmental Management, 225 Friend Street, Boston, MA 02114.

Massachusetts has several other trails in the 20 to 40 mile range, including the 36-mile Robert Frost Trail, the 29-mile Taconic Crest Trail, and the 24-mile Taconic Skyline Trail. For further information see the *AMC Massachusetts and Rhode Island Trail Guide* or contact New England Cartographics, P.O. Box 369, Amherst, MA 01004.

BEST HIKING AREAS

MOUNT GREYLOCK STATE RESERVATION— Box 138, Lanesboro, MA 01237; (413)499-4262. 11,500 acres. Located in the northwest corner of Massachusetts, Mount Greylock (3,491 feet) is the highest mountain and has the finest views in the state. There are several other mountains nearby, and the area has streams, hardwood and

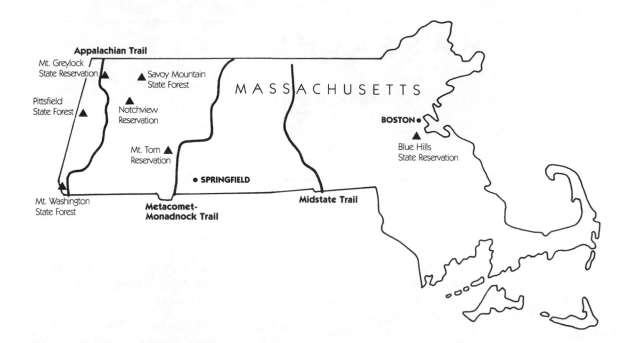

hemlock forests, and wildlife including deer and fox. Some 35 miles of trails extend through the reservation, including a section of the Appalachian Trail. Difficulty varies from easy to strenuous.

MOUNT WASHINGTON STATE FOREST— Mount Washington, MA 01258; (413)528-0330. 3,289 acres. Located in the southwest corner of Massachusetts, this state forest is adjacent to Bashbish Falls State Forest (home of spectacular Bashbish Falls, highest waterfall in Massachusetts) and Taconic State Park in New York. There are some prominent mountains here, including 2,453-foot Mount Frissell.

It's an area of hardwood forest with mountain laurel, and wildlife including white-tailed deer, black bear, and fox. There's a fine trail system and some unusually scenic open ridge walking, with wonderful views. Difficulty varies from easy to strenuous.

OTHER RECOMMENDED LOCATIONS

BLUE HILLS STATE RESERVATION—20 Somerset Street, Boston, MA 02108; (617)727-5114.

6,500 acres. This beautiful preserve just outside of Boston has a number of rocky hills, with granite-topped Great Blue Hill (635 feet) the highest. There are also mixed forests and wetlands, and some streams and glacial ponds. The reservation has an extensive network of marked hiking trails, along with a number of carriage roads and unmarked paths.

MOUNT TOM RESERVATION—Holyoke, MA 01058; (413)527-9858. 1,800 acres. There are several small mountains within this state reservation in western Massachusetts, and some 20 miles of trails, including a section of the Metacomet–Monadnock Trail. The highest elevation here is Mount Tom (1,202 feet), which has great views.

NOTCHVIEW RESERVATION—Windsor, MA 01270; (413)684-0148. 3,000 acres. Located in the hilly Berkshires of western Massachusetts, Notchview Reservation is a beautiful area of hardwood and spruce forest, with wildlife including bear and bobcat. The highest point is 2,297-foot Judges Hill, offering fine views, and there are several brooks. The reservation has over 25 miles of trails.

PITTSFIELD STATE FOREST—Cascade Street, Pittsfield, MA 02101; (413)442-8992. 9,695 acres. This state forest, which is in the Taconic Mountains along the western Massachusetts border, has rocky terrain and encompasses several mountains. Berry Pond (2,070 feet), highest in the state, is located here—along with some waterfalls. Deer and black bear are among the wildlife. There are 30 miles of trails, including half of the 20-mile Taconic Skyline Trail.

SAVOY MOUNTAIN STATE FOREST—RFD 2, North Adams, MA 01247; (413)663-8469. 11,000 acres. There are about 20 miles of trails in this scenic state forest in northwestern Massachusetts. It's a wild area of hemlock and hardwood forest, with some attractive ponds, swamps, and several small mountains as high as 2,500 feet, with rocky outcroppings and views. Wildlife includes black bear and white-tailed deer.

MASSACHUSETTS HIKING RESOURCES

HIKING GUIDEBOOKS

AMC Massachusetts and Rhode Island Trail Guide—Boston: Appalachian Mountain Club, 1989.

Berkshire Trails—Griswold, Whit. East Woods Press, 1983.

Fifty Hikes in Massachusetts—Sadlier, Paul and Ruth. Woodstock, VT: The Countryman Press, 1983.

Guide to the Appalachian Trail in Massachusetts–Connecticut—Harpers Ferry, WV: The Appalachian Trail Conference, 1990.

HIKING MAPS AND GUIDEBOOKS

New England Cartographics, P.O. Box 369, Amherst, MA 01004.

TRAIL INFORMATION

New England Trail Conference, 33 Knollwood Drive, East Longmeadow, MA 01028.

INFORMATION ABOUT STATE PARKS AND FORESTS

Massachusetts Division of Forests and Parks, 100 Cambridge Street, Boston, MA 02202; (617)727-3180.

STATE HIGHWAY MAP AND TRAVEL INFORMATION

Massachusetts Office of Travel and Tourism, 100 Cambridge Street, Boston, MA 02202.

MASSACHUSETTS HIKING CLUBS

Appalachian Mountain Club, 5 Joy Street, Boston, MA 02108; (617)523-0636. This major club has several chapters in Massachusetts.

Sierra Club, 3 Joy Street, Boston, MA 02108.

Williams Outing Club, Williams College, Williamstown, MA 01267.

MICHIGAN

Some of the best hiking in the Midwest is found in Michigan, which has four National Forests and more than four million acres of state lands. There are over 11,000 lakes and 36,000 miles of rivers and streams here, along with the giant freshwater Great Lakes. As in many states, federal lands provide much of the wildest scenery and the most extensive hiking, but many state forests and parks also have excellent trail systems—and here too is an especially long and scenic section of the famous North Country Trail.

MAJOR TRAILS

NORTH COUNTRY TRAIL—When it's finished, the Michigan segment of this 3,200-mile National Scenic Trail will run about 875 miles, traversing the Upper Peninsula and heading down through the Lower Peninsula to Ohio. En route it passes through three beautiful National Forests, state park and forest lands, and a National Seashore. Many of the National Forest portions are completed. Difficulty is easy to moderate. Trail information: North Country Trail Association, P.O. Box 311, White Cloud, MI 49349.

SHORE TO SHORE RIDING–HIKING TRAIL—308 miles. This major trail is designed for horseback riding as well as hiking. It runs from Lake Michigan to Lake Huron, crossing the scenic northern part of Michigan's Lower Peninsula. Much of the trail is on state forest lands or in Huron National Forest. At times it parallels two notable rivers. The main branch of the trail runs 203 miles, with spurs trails providing an additional 105 miles. Difficulty is easy to moderate. Trail information: Michigan Department of Natural Resources, Box 30028, Lansing, MI 48909.

HIGH COUNTRY PATHWAY—50 miles. This is a large loop trail located in Pigeon River Country State Forest and Mackinaw State Forest, in the northern part of Michigan's Lower Peninsula. The terrain ranges from very hilly to flat, and the trail passes a number of lakes. It's open to horseback riding and mountain biking as well as hiking. Trail information: Michigan Department of Natural Resources, Box 30028, Lansing, MI 48909.

BEST HIKING AREAS

ISLE ROYALE NATIONAL PARK—87 N. Ripley Street, Houghton, MI 49931; (906)482-0984. 500,000 acres. Located 50 miles off the coast of Michigan in Lake Superior—largest freshwater lake in the world—Isle Royal National Park is a remote and roadless wilderness island 45 miles long and 9 miles wide. Access is by boat or seaplane.

It's an extremely secluded and beautiful place,

with many inland lakes and rivers, and rather rugged terrain. Wildlife here includes wolves and moose. There's a network of 170 miles of hiking trails, among them the 40-mile Greenstone Ridge Trail and the 26-mile Minong Ridge Trail. Difficulty varies from easy to strenuous.

HIAWATHA NATIONAL FOREST—2727 North Lincoln Road, Escanaba, MI 49829; (906)786-4062. 879,600 acres. Consisting of two tracts in the eastern and central Upper Peninsula, Michigan's Hiawatha National Forest borders on three Great Lakes. Within are several rivers and a large number of lovely lakes and streams.

Among the 150-plus miles of trails here are important segments of the North Country Trail and also the 40-mile Bay De Noc Grand Island Trail, which is open to horseback riders as well as hikers. Most trails are easy to moderate in difficulty.

HURON AND MANISTEE NATIONAL FORESTS—421 South Mitchell Street, Cadillac, MI 49601; (616)775-2421. 912,000 acres. These two jointly-administered National Forests lie in Michigan's Lower Peninsula—Huron in the northeast near Lake Huron and Manistee in the west-central part of the state alongside Lake Michigan.

Over 260 miles of mostly easy trails are located in these hilly and attractive wild lands, home to countless lakes and streams and several outstanding rivers. Included are over 60 miles of the North Country Trail in Manistee National Forest, and 85 miles of the Shore to Shore Riding–Hiking Trail in Huron National Forest.

OTTAWA NATIONAL FOREST—East U.S. 2, Ironwood, MI 49938; (906)932-1330. Located in the western part of Michigan's Upper Peninsula, Ottawa National Forest includes a number of beautiful lakes and two small wilderness areas. Some of the terrain is rough, with ridges and bluffs, river gorges, and many creeks and waterfalls—and fine views.

The area has forests of white pine, hemlock, and hardwoods, with old-growth stands, and the wildlife includes bear and deer. There are nearly 200 miles of hiking trails. Among them is an 118-mile segment of the North Country Trail.

OTHER RECOMMENDED LOCATIONS

PORCUPINE MOUNTAINS WILDERNESS STATE PARK—599 M-107, Ontonagon, MI 49953; (906)885-5275. 63,000 acres. Located on Lake Superior at the western end of the Upper Peninsula, this state park encompasses one of the few large wilderness areas in the Midwest. The terrain is fairly rugged, with elevations to 1,958 feet (Summit Peak).

There are numerous streams, rivers, and falls, several lakes, and outstanding views overlooking Lake Superior. The area has some virgin hemlock and pine forest, wildlife including black bear, and over 90 miles of hiking trails. Difficulty ranges from easy to strenuous.

PICTURED ROCKS NATIONAL LAKESHORE—P.O. Box 40, Minising, MI 49862; (906)387-2607. This narrow park protects over 40 miles of Lake Superior shoreline on Michigan's Upper Peninsula, adjacent to Hiawatha National Forest. It's an area of sandstone cliffs, waterfalls, small lakes, hardwood and evergreen forests, dunes and beautiful white sand beach. There are nearly 100 miles of easy to moderate hiking trails, including the 42-mile Lakeshore Trail, which is now part of the North Country Trail.

SLEEPING BEAR DUNES NATIONAL LAKESHORE—P.O. Box 277, Empire, MI 49630; (616)326-5134. Sleeping Bear Dunes National Lakeshore is located on the shore of Lake Michigan, in the northwestern Lower Peninsula. There are giant sand dunes, small inland lakes, thick deciduous forests, and high bluffs overlooking Lake Michigan. More than 50 miles of trails are found here, plus additional trails on nearby North and South Manitou Islands (accessible by ferry).

TAHQUAMENON FALLS STATE PARK—Star Route 48, Box 225, Paradise, MI 49768; (906)492-

3415. 36,000 acres. Situated by Lake Superior in the northeast Upper Peninsula, Tahquamenon Falls is Michigan's second largest state park. It's mostly wild land with several lakes, pine and hemlock forests, and the Tahquamenon River. The 200-foot wide upper falls here, which drops 15 feet, is said to be one of the largest east of the Mississippi. There are over 25 miles of trails, including a section of the North Country Trail.

LAKE SUPERIOR STATE FOREST—309 West McMillan Avenue, Newberry, MI 49868; (906)293-5131. Located in the Upper Peninsula near Pictured Rocks National Lakeshore, this state forest includes the 28-mile Fox River Pathway, which follows the beautiful Fox River. It's a somewhat isolated area, with pine forests and hardwoods. The Pathway is open to horseback riding and cycling along with hiking. Difficulty is moderate to strenuous.

ALLEGAN STATE GAME AREA—4590 118th Avenue, Allegan, MI 49010. 45,000 acres. Located in southwest Michigan, Allegan State Game Area has several lakes and a beautiful creek. There are wooded areas with oak and pine, marshes, open areas, and 23 miles of trails.

HOLLY RECREATION AREA—8100 Grange Hall Road, Holly, MI 48442; (313)634-8811. 8,000 acres. This state recreation area in southeast Michigan has several attractive lakes. There are over 30 miles of hiking trails.

PINCKNEY RECREATION AREA—8555 Silver Hill Road, Route 1, Pinckney, MI 48169. Located in southeast Michigan, Pinckney Recreation Area has a number of lakes and over 20 miles of hiking trails. Included is a section of the 22-mile Waterloo–Pinckney Trail, which leads to the Waterloo Recreation Area.

WATERLOO RECREATION AREA—16345 McClure Road, Route 1, Chelsea, MI 48118; (313)475-8307. 19,790 acres. Waterloo Recreation Area is situated in the southeastern part of the state. It's an area of glacial hills, forests, marshes, and several lakes. There are more than 20 miles of trails here, including a segment of the 22-mile Waterloo–Pinckney Trail.

LUDINGTON STATE PARK—Box 709, Ludington, MI 49431; (616)843-8671. 5,300 acres. Located north of Ludington on the shore of Lake Michigan, this state park has high dunes along with forests of conifers and hardwoods. The park has about 18 miles of hiking trails, plus a network of cross-country ski trails.

MICHIGAN HIKING RESOURCES

HIKING GUIDEBOOKS

Foot Trails and Water Routes of Isle Royale National Park—DuFresne, Jim. Seattle: The Mountaineers, 1984.

Michigan Hiking Opportunities—Lansing, MI; Michigan Department of Natural Resources, 1983.

Michigan Trail Atlas—Hansen, Dennis R. and Holley, Danforth. Okemos, MI: Hansen Publishing Co., 1988.

MAPS

Michigan Atlas & Gazetteer—Freeport, ME: DeLorme Mapping Co.

INFORMATION ABOUT STATE PARKS AND FORESTS

Michigan Department of Natural Resources, Box 30028, Lansing, MI 48909; (517)373-1220.

STATE HIGHWAY MAP AND TRAVEL INFORMATION

Michigan Travel Bureau, P.O. Box 30226, Lansing, MI 48909; (800)5432-YES.

MICHIGAN HIKING CLUBS

Michigan Trailfinders Club, 2680 Rockhill N.E., Grand Rapids, MI 49505.

Sierra Club, 115 West Allegan, #10B, Cap Hall, Lansing, MI 48933.

MINNESOTA

With a seemingly endless succession of scenic waterways, Minnesota is especially well-known for canoeing. It also happens to offer some of the best hiking in the Midwest, with nearly 800 miles of trails on state parklands alone, and an equal number in two fine National Forests along with numerous state forests. The varied scenery here—especially wild in the northern regions—includes pine forests and prairies, high bluffs and hardwoods, and literally thousands of beautiful lakes, streams, and rivers.

MAJOR TRAILS

NORTH COUNTRY TRAIL—When completed the Minnesota portion of this 3,200-mile trail will run about 375 miles, passing through the relatively level and scenic lake country of north-central Minnesota. The major segment open now is a 68-mile stretch of trail which crosses Chippewa National Forest. Trail information: North Country Trail Association, P.O. Box 311, White Cloud, MI 49349

SUPERIOR HIKING TRAIL—This beautiful new trail will be about 250 miles long when completed. Currently about 150 miles are finished and open. The trail follows ridges above the shoreline of Lake Superior from Duluth, Minnesota, to the Canadian border. It traverses Superior National Forest, several state parks, and some private lands. Parts of the trail are rugged, with outstanding views of Lake Superior along the way. It's open to foot travel only. Trail information: Superior Hiking Trail Association, P.O. Box 4, Two Harbors, MN 55616.

BORDER ROUTE TRAIL—45 miles. Located in the Boundary Waters Canoe Area Wilderness in northeastern Minnesota, and running along the state's border with Canada, the rugged Border Route Trail passes some lovely lakes and offers wonderful views from high cliffs. Trail difficulty varies from easy to strenuous. Trail information: Superior National Forest, P.O. Box 338, Duluth, MN 55801; (218)720-5324.

BEST HIKING AREAS

SUPERIOR NATIONAL FOREST—P.O. Box 338, Duluth, MN 55801; (218)720-5324. This important National Forest in northeastern Minnesota has an enormous number of lakes, and provides some premier canoeing in the famous Boundary Waters Canoe Area Wilderness. It's also a great place to hike, with rolling hills and major expanses of forest wilderness, including a few small mountains amid the countless streams and lakes. There are over 300 miles of hiking trails, among them the 55-mile Pow Wow Trail and the 45-mile Border Route Trail.

CHIPPEWA NATIONAL FOREST—Route 3, Box

244, Cass Lake, MN 56633; (218)335-2226. 660,000 acres. Located in north-central Minnesota and with over 700 lakes, Chippewa National Forest extends over a glaciated landscape with rolling hills, stands of virgin pine, and some nice views. There are a great many streams, along with major areas of wetlands. Wildlife includes white-tailed deer, gray wolf, and bald eagle. Over 200 miles of hiking trails are found here, including a 68-mile segment of the North Country Trail.

OTHER RECOMMENDED LOCATIONS

ST. CROIX STATE PARK—Route 3, Box 450, Hinckley, MN 55037; (612)384-6591. 34,037 acres. Situated in the central part of the state, St. Croix in Minnesota's largest state park. It includes the scenic St. Croix and Kettle Rivers, as well as several creeks. There's an unusually extensive trail network in the rolling hills and forests here, with 127 miles of easy to moderate trails.

RICHARD J. DORAL MEMORIAL HARDWOOD STATE FOREST—Minnesota Department of Natural Resources, Division of Forestry, Box 44, 500 Lafayette Road, St. Paul, MN 55155; (612)296-4491. This large state forest in the southeast corner of Minnesota has over 80 miles of trails. The area is thickly forested with hardwoods, and the terrain is sometimes steep and rugged. Trail difficulty varies from easy to strenuous.

JAY COOKE STATE PARK—500 East Highway 200, Carlton, MN 55718; (218)384-4610. 8,813 acres. This state park in northeastern Minnesota includes a rugged river gorge on the St. Louis River, and there are great views. Hiking options are numerous, with 50 miles of trails. Some of the terrain is rough, and trail difficulty varies from easy to strenuous.

MILLE LACS KATHIO STATE PARK—HC 67, Box 85, Onamia, MN 56359; (612)532-3523. 10,585 acres. There are 35 miles of scenic trails in this hilly and forested state park alongside huge Mille Lacs Lake in central Minnesota. The area includes hardwood forest and the Rum River, with deer among the wildlife. Trail difficulty varies from easy to moderate.

VOYAGEURS NATIONAL PARK—P.O. Box 50, International Falls, MN 56649; (218)283-9821. 217,000 acres. Located in northern Minnesota along the Canadian border, this is a water-based National Park. There are 32 miles of hiking trails, but boats are required to reach all trailheads. Longest is the Cruiser Lake Trail, which has several loops and crosses the massive Kabetogama Peninsula. Scenery here includes lakes, low ridges, and granite outcroppings with nice views.

WILD RIVER STATE PARK—39755 Park Trail, Center City, MN 55012; (612)583-2125. 7,000 acres. Located in east-central Minnesota, Wild River State Park stretches along the lovely and wild St. Croix River, which marks the state's border with Wisconsin. Amid the forests and oak woodlands here are 35 miles of mostly easy trails, some of which are open to horseback riding.

ITASCA STATE PARK—Lake Itasca, MN 56460; (218)266-3654. 32,000 acres. Large and beautiful Itasca State Park in northwestern Minnesota includes rolling hills, numerous lakes, stands of old-growth pine, and the headwaters of the Mississippi. There are 33 miles of easy to moderate trails.

GEORGE COSBY MANITOU STATE PARK—Box 482, Finland, MN 55603; (218)226-3539. 3,400 acres. This hilly and wild park in northeastern Minnesota, situated near the shore of Lake Superior, includes small lakes and the beautiful Manitou River. Wildlife includes deer, black bear, moose, and timber wolf. There's a rugged river gorge with waterfalls, and 23 miles of hiking trails. Difficulty ranges from easy to strenuous.

MAPLEWOOD STATE PARK—Route 3, Box 422, Pelican Rapids, MN 56572; (218)863-8383. 9,250

Map labels:
- Voyageurs National Park
- Border Route Trail
- MINNESOTA
- Superior National Forest
- Chippewa National Forest
- Itasca State Park
- George Cosby Manitou State Park
- Superior Hiking Trail
- Maplewood State Park
- Land O'Lakes State Forest
- Savanna Portage State Park
- DULUTH
- Jay Cooke State Park
- Pillsbury State Forest
- North Country Trail
- Mille Lacs Kathio State Park
- St. Croix State Park
- Wild River State Park
- MINNEAPOLIS
- ST. PAUL
- Minnesota Valley State Park
- Richard J. Dorer Hardwood State Forest

acres. Located in west-central Minnesota, hilly and hardwood-forested Maplewood State Park has 8 good-size lakes, wildlife including white-tailed deer, fine views, and 25 miles of hiking trails, some of which are open to horseback riding. Difficulty varies from easy to strenuous.

MINNESOTA VALLEY STATE PARK—19825 Park Boulevard, Jordan, MN 55352; (612)492-6400. 8,000 acres. This long and narrow park southwest of Minneapolis stretches alongside the Minnesota River. Most notable among the trails here is the 25-mile Minnesota Valley State Trail, a multi-use trail which runs from Belle Plaine to Shakopee (and will soon be extended).

SAVANNA PORTAGE STATE PARK—HCR 3, Box 591, McGregor, MN 55760; (218)426-3271. 15,818 acres. This is a wild forested park in east-central Minnesota. There's some hilly terrain here, with several lakes along with boggy areas. Wildlife includes deer, bear, moose, and coyote. The park has 22 miles of easy to moderate hiking trails, some of which are open to mountain bikes.

PILLSBURY STATE FOREST—1601 Minnesota

Drive, Brainerd, MN 56401; (218)828-2565. 14,756 acres. This state forest in north-central Minnesota has hilly terrain with many lakes and ponds. There are hardwood trees including maple and oak, with some pine and fir, and 27 miles of trails, which are open to horseback riding as well as hiking.

LAND O'LAKES STATE FOREST—Box 34, Backus, MN 56435; (218)947-3232. 49,890 acres. Situated in north-central Minnesota, Land O'Lakes has forests of aspen and birch, with some pine. Of special interest to hikers is the wildernesslike Washburn Lake Solitude Area with 26 miles of hiking trails, also open to horses. The forest has other multi-use trails.

MINNESOTA HIKING RESOURCES

MAPS

Minnesota Atlas & Gazetteer—Freeport, ME: DeLorme Mapping Co.

INFORMATION ABOUT STATE PARKS, FORESTS, AND HIKING TRAILS

Minnesota Department of Natural Resources, 500 Lafayette Road, Box 40, St. Paul, MN 55155; (612)296-6157.

STATE HIGHWAY MAP AND TRAVEL INFORMATION

Minnesota Travel Information Center, 375 Jackson Street, 250 Skyway Level, St. Paul, MN 55101.

CLUBS AND OTHER ORGANIZATIONS WHICH OFFER HIKES

American Youth Hostels, Room 203, 30 South Ninth Street, Minnesota, MN 55402.

Minneapolis Hiking Club, c/o Linda Larson, Minneapolis Park Board, 310 Fourth Avenue South, Minneapolis, MN 55415.

Minnesota Rovers Outing Club, P.O. Box 14133, Minneapolis, MN 55414.

Sierra Club, 1313 Fifth Street S.E., Room 323, Minneapolis, MN 55414.

Superior Hiking Trail Association, P.O. Box 4, Two Harbors, MN 55616.

MISSISSIPPI

Mississippi has not been known for hiking, and trails are less than abundant, yet there are still quite a few good options here. While just a couple of state parks have real trail networks, Mississippi is privileged to have no less than six National Forests. It's on these wild lands—especially within scenic DeSoto National Forest, in the southeast corner of the state—that some truly interesting and attractive hiking can be found.

MAJOR TRAILS

BLACK CREEK NATIONAL RECREATION TRAIL—41 miles. Located in southeastern Mississippi's DeSoto National Forest, this National Recreation Trail follows the route of beautiful Black Creek much of the time. It passes through pine and hardwood forests, and there are sand bluffs along the banks. The trail is easy, with occasionally hilly terrain. Trail information: National Forests in Mississippi, 100 West Capitol Street, Suite 1141, Jackson, MS 39269; (601)965-4391.

BEST HIKING AREAS

DE SOTO NATIONAL FOREST—c/o National Forests in Mississippi, 100 West Capitol Street, Suite 1141, Jackson, MS 39269; (601)965-4391. Situated in southeastern Mississippi, this nota-ble National Forest has low ridges and hills, savannas, bogs, and swamps. In the area are forests of longleaf and slash pine, and oak, plus cypress and magnolia, with wild azalea. Deer and armadillo are among the wildlife, and there are creeks and some small lakes here.

DeSoto National Forest has some 76 miles of hiking trails, far more than any other location in the state. Among the trails are the 41-mile Black Creek National Recreation Trail and the 22-mile long Tuxachanie National Recreation Trail. Most trails are easy to moderate in difficulty.

MISSISSIPPI HIKING RESOURCES

INFORMATION ABOUT STATE PARKS
Department of Wildlife, Fisheries and Parks, P.O. Box 451, Jackson, MS 39205.

INFORMATION ABOUT NATIONAL FORESTS
National Forests in Mississippi, 100 West Capitol Street, Suite 1141, Jackson, MS 39269; (601)965-4391.

STATE HIGHWAY MAP AND TRAVEL INFORMATION
Mississippi Division of Tourism Development, P.O. Box 22825, Jackson, MS 39205; (601)359-3297/(800)647-2290.

MISSISSIPPI HIKING CLUBS
Sierra Club, c/o Bill Kulick, Drawer 6249, Biloxi, MS 39532.

MISSISSIPPI

JACKSON

De Soto
National Forest

**Black Creek
National
Recreation Trail**

MISSOURI

Some good hiking is available in Missouri and it's currently getting even better. Quite a few of the numerous state parks here have fine trail systems, and an especially large and impressive National Forest offers some exceptional trails amid the plateaus and foothills of the Ozarks. Now the up-and-coming Ozark Trail, which crosses scenic southern Missouri, promises to become one of the best long-distance trails in this part of the country.

MAJOR TRAILS

OZARK TRAIL—Currently under construction, this trail will be 500 miles long when completed—leading through the beautiful and sometimes wild scenery of the Ozarks, from St. Louis to the Arkansas border. Located on public and private lands, it will eventually be connected to the Ozark Highlands Trail in Arkansas. Over 200 miles of trail are presently open, primarily within Mark Twain National Forest. Difficulty varies from easy to moderately strenuous. Trail information: Missouri Department of Natural Resources, Ozark Trail Coordinator, P.O. Box 176, Jefferson City, MO 65102; (314)751-2479.

BEST HIKING AREAS

MARK TWAIN NATIONAL FOREST—401 Fairgrounds Road, Rolla, MO 65401; (314)364-4621.

1,500,000 acres. Enormous Mark Twain National Forest consists of several separate tracts in southern Missouri. It includes the St. Francis Mountains as well as the Ozarks—with foothills, rugged mountains and plateaus, rocky bluffs and outcrops, caves, and steep slopes with fine views.

There are seven designated wilderness areas totaling over 63,000 acres, and numerous rivers, streams, and lakes. The area has meadows as well as forests of oak and hickory, red cedar and pine, with wild azalea. Wildlife includes white-tailed deer, coyote, and bobcat. There are several hundred miles of trails, including 200 miles of the Ozark Trail, and the 35-mile Ridge Runner National Recreation Trail.

OTHER RECOMMENDED LOCATIONS

CUIVRE RIVER STATE PARK—Route 1, Box 25, Troy. MO 63379; (314)528-7247. 6,251 acres. Located in the rugged Lincoln Hills of northeastern Missouri, Cuivre River State Park is a wild park with scenery reminiscent of the Ozarks. There are deep valleys, limestone bluffs with great views, oak forests and grasslands, and some beautiful creeks, with white-tailed deer among the wildlife here. The park has over 30 miles of trails.

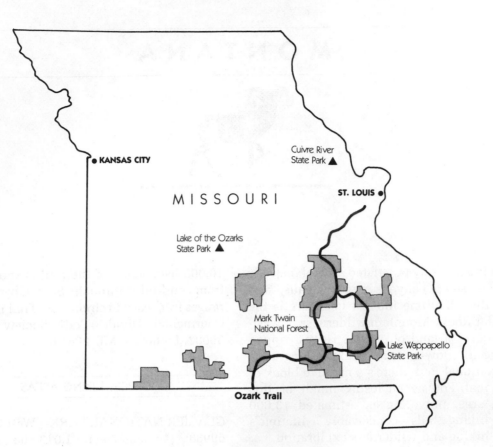

LAKE OF THE OZARKS STATE PARK—P.O. Box C, Kaiser, MO 65047; (314)348-2694. 17,152 acres. Lake of the Ozarks State Park is in south-central Missouri, and it's the largest such park in the state. The scenery here includes many caves, high rocky bluffs and ravines, some creeks, and a large man-made lake. It's an area of oak-hickory forests and the wildlife includes deer. There are 23 miles of trails.

LAKE WAPPAPELLO STATE PARK—Route 2, Box 102, Williamsville, MO 63967; (314)297-3232. 1,854 acres. This scenic park is situated alongside 8,600-acre Lake Wappapello in the Ozarks of southeastern Missouri. There's some rugged terrain here with forests of oak and hick-

ory, wildlife including deer, nice views, and 21 miles of hiking trails.

MISSOURI HIKING RESOURCES

INFORMATION ABOUT STATE PARKS

Missouri Department of Natural Resources, P.O. Box 176, Jefferson City, MO 65102; (314)751-2479/(800)334-6946.

STATE HIGHWAY MAP AND TRAVEL INFORMATION

Missouri Division of Tourism, P.O. Box 1056, Jefferson City, MO 65102; (314)751-4133.

MISSOURI HIKING CLUBS

Sierra Club, 1005 A South Big Bend Boulevard, St. Louis, MO 63117.

MONTANA

Montana is a sparsely populated state of majestic mountains, steep canyons and plateaus, and open plains. Of prime interest to hikers is the spectacular Rocky Mountain wilderness of western Montana—a land of endless ridges capped with rugged, snow-covered peaks. Along with Glacier National Park there's a massive block of ten National Forests enclosing much of this stunning area, providing an estimated 13,000 miles of hiking trails—conceivably a lifetime's worth of hiking and wilderness exploration.

MAJOR TRAILS

CONTINENTAL DIVIDE TRAIL—961 miles (3,100 total). The Montana and Idaho sections of this important National Scenic Trail are the first to be essentially completed, although trail construction is not yet finished. The Montana segment starts just north of the Canadian border (Waterton), runs through Glacier National Park, and continues south through seven National Forests and several wilderness areas before reaching Wyoming and Yellowstone National Park. Along the way is some incredible Northern Rockies scenery, with high peaks and cliffs, glaciated valleys with lovely lakes, alpine tundra and forested slopes, and fantastic vistas. The trail alternates between the actual crest of the Divide and following below, sometimes along jeep roads. Elevations occasionally surpass 10,000 feet. Much of the trail is snow-free only from mid-July through September. Difficulty ranges from easy to strenuous. Trail information: Continental Divide Trail Society, P.O. Box 30002, Bethesda, MD 20814.

BEST HIKING AREAS

GLACIER NATIONAL PARK—West Glacier, MT 59936; (406)888-5441. 1,013,598 acres. This splendid National Park is in northwest Montana along the Canadian border, adjacent to Canada's Waterton National Park. Since 1932 the two parks have been loosely united as the Waterton/ Glacier International Peace Park. This is a truly spectacular wilderness area with unusually striking Rocky Mountain scenery. The glacier-carved mountain features include rugged knife-edged ridges and jagged snow-covered peaks.

The Continental Divide runs the length of Glacier National Park. Highest peak is Mount Cleveland (10,448 feet). There are 50 glaciers and over 200 lakes, scores of waterfalls along countless streams, alpine meadows with wildflowers, cirque basins and glacial valleys, and prairie grasslands, along with forests of Englemann spruce and fir, lodgepole pine, and larch. The wildlife here includes elk, deer, moose, grizzly and black bear, bighorn sheep, mountain goat, gray wolf and mountain lion.

The park receives heavy use in the summer.

There are over 730 miles of hiking trails. Difficulty varies from easy to very strenuous. Lower-elevation trails are open by mid-June, but high mountain passes are often under snow until late July.

FLATHEAD NATIONAL FOREST—1935 Third Avenue East, Kalispell, MT 59901; (406)755-5401. 2,350,508 acres. Located south and west of Glacier National Park in northwest Montana, enormous Flathead National Forest includes some of the state's most magnificent wilderness. It's a glaciated landscape of high snow-capped peaks, precipitous rock walls and deep gorges, open ridges and steep-sloped basins. Elevations range from 4,000 feet to 9,820-foot McDonald Peak. Fantastic panoramas are frequent.

There are three wilderness areas here. Largest and most spectacular—and in fact one of the great mountain wilderness areas of the country—is the 1,009,356-acre Bob Marshall Wilderness, which includes a section of the Continental Divide. This area alone has over a thousand miles of trails. In addition there's the 285,700-acre Great Bear Wilderness and the 73,877-acre Mission Mountain Wilderness. One especially lovely area is the Jewel Basin Hiking Area, which has 25 lakes and 35 miles of trails.

Also in this National Forest is the three-forked Flathead River, an important National Wild and Scenic River. Other scenery includes numerous alpine meadows and lakes, canyons, clear streams and waterfalls, and small glaciers. There are forests of Douglas fir, spruce, larch, plus ponderosa and lodgepole pine, and also some cedar, birch, and aspen. Among the wildlife are grizzly and black bear, elk, deer, mountain goat, gray wolf, and coyote.

All told there are over 2,100 miles of hiking trails in this National Forest. Difficulty varies from easy to strenuous. Most trails are open to horseback riding.

LOLO NATIONAL FOREST—Building 24, Fort Missoula, MT 59801; (406)329-3750. 2,091,944 acres. This National Forest surrounds Missoula, Montana, and consists of several large parcels of land near and alongside the Idaho border in western Montana. It includes the steep eastern slopes of the Bitterroot Mountains, with elevations over 9,000 feet, and the west side of the Continental Divide, with Warren Peak (10,456 feet) the highest point. There are four wilderness areas and vast expanses of absolutely splendid mountain scenery.

The terrain includes steep rocky ridges with narrow valleys, cirque basins, enormous limestone cliffs, and precipitous canyons. There are alpine meadows, high glacial lakes, and many streams with waterfalls. Mountain slopes are forested with Douglas fir, ponderosa and lodgepole pine, and western larch. Among the wildlife are elk, moose, deer, black and grizzly bear, bighorn sheep, and mountain goat.

Within Lolo National Forest are over 1,800 miles of hiking trails, including several National Recreation Trails. Difficulty ranges from easy to strenuous.

GALLATIN NATIONAL FOREST—P.O. Box 130, Bozeman, MT 59715; (406)587-6701. 1,738,138 acres. Located in southwest Montana alongside Wyoming, and bordering on two sides of Yellowstone National Park, Gallatin is a massive National Forest offering spectacular Rocky Mountain scenery. Within the forest are several substantial mountain ranges and a small section of the Continental Divide.

Wilderness areas include the 921,574-acre high mountain Absaroka–Beartooth Wilderness, part of which is in Custer National Forest. This rugged and stunningly beautiful area has 25 peaks over 12,000 feet, including 12,799-foot Granite Peak—Montana's highest.

Of special interest is a 40-square-mile petrified forest with multicolored wood and standing petrified trees. The alpine scenery includes glaciers, mountain meadows, sharp-edged ridges, high plateaus, limestone cliffs and rock outcroppings, and glacial basins. There are also deep canyons, open prairie grasslands, and views too magnificent for words.

The area has some major rivers, hundreds of lakes, and an endless number of creeks and waterfalls. Common trees include pine, spruce,

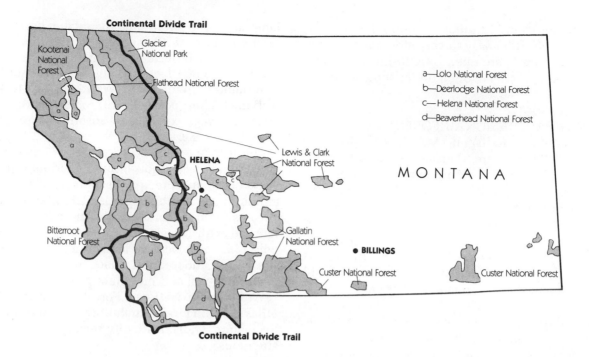

Continental Divide Trail

Kootenai National Forest

Glacier National Park

Flathead National Forest

HELENA

Lewis & Clark National Forest

Bitterroot National Forest

Gallatin National Forest

● BILLINGS

Custer National Forest

Custer National Forest

MONTANA

a—Lolo National Forest
b—Deerlodge National Forest
c—Helena National Forest
d—Beaverhead National Forest

Continental Divide Trail

and fir. Grizzly and black bear, elk, mule deer, moose, bighorn sheep, and mountain goat are among the local wildlife.

Gallatin has over 1,800 miles of hiking trails, including the 42-mile Gallatin Divide Trail. Difficulty ranges from easy to strenuous. Some trails receive heavy use, and horses are permitted on many trails.

LEWIS AND CLARK NATIONAL FOREST—P.O. Box 869, Great Falls, MT 59403; (406)791-7700. 1,843,397 acres. Consisting of several tracts located in northwest and west-central Montana, with one area directly east of the Continental Divide, Lewis and Clark National Forest encompasses part of the magnificent Front Range of the Rockies, plus the rounded Little Belt Mountains and some other ranges.

Elevations run from 4,500 feet to over 9,000 feet. The highest mountain is Rocky Mountain Peak (9,362 feet). Within the National Forest is a portion of the Scapegoat Wilderness, plus part of the vast and spectacular one-million-acre Bob Marshall Wilderness, which extends into Flathead National Forest.

The terrain includes rocky ridges and steep mountain peaks, sheer-walled canyons and grassy prairies. There are many splendid views from open areas. Of interest is the high rock "Chinese Wall," which runs for some distance along the Continental Divide. There are also alpine meadows and slopes forested with ponderosa and lodgepole pine, spruce, and Douglas fir, with stands of aspen. The area has many lakes, rivers, and creeks with high falls and pools. Local wildlife include elk, moose, deer, black and grizzly bear, bighorn sheep, and mountain goat.

Lewis and Clark National Forest has approximately 1,680 miles of hiking trails. Among them is a section of the Continental Divide Trail. Difficulty varies from easy to strenuous.

BEAVERHEAD NATIONAL FOREST—610 North Montana, Dillon, MT 59725; (406)683-3900. 2,148,683 acres. This major National Forest is situated in southwest Montana, northwest of Wyoming's Yellowstone National Park. There are several tracts of land, some of which lie alongside the Continental Divide, with two designated wilderness areas included. The region encompasses a number of spectacular mountain ranges, including the Bitterroot and Beaverhead Mountains, with elevations over 11,000 feet. Striking panoramas are common from many trails.

The Forest contains scores of craggy granite peaks and high ridges, talus slopes and cirque basins, and steep canyons, plus a myriad of lovely mountain lakes, creeks, and some major rivers. Vegetation ranges from grasslands and sagebrush hills to mountain meadows with wildflowers, and hilly spruce and pine forests with lush undergrowth. Among the wildlife are grizzly and black bear, elk, deer, pronghorn, moose, mountain goat, and bighorn sheep.

There are over 1,600 miles of trails in Beaverhead National Forest. Difficulty ranges from easy to quite strenuous. Some trails are not well-marked. Summer arrives late on the highest trails.

BITTERROOT NATIONAL FOREST—316 North Third Street, Hamilton, MT 59840; (406)363-3131. 1,113,838 acres. Located in west-central Montana and extending into Idaho, this huge National Forest encloses portions of two major Rocky Mountain ranges, the incredibly rugged Bitterroot Mountains and the Sapphire Mountains. Nearly half of the Forest consists of three wilderness areas—including 511,547 acres of the gigantic 1,340,681-acre Selway–Bitterroot Wilderness, much of which is in Idaho. There's also a section of the Continental Divide.

Highest mountain is Trapper Peak (10,157 feet), and there are simply stunning views from this and many other mountains and open areas. Along with barren-peaked and often snow-capped mountains, there are alpine meadows with beargrass, high cliffs, deep gulches and glacial canyons with rock outcrops, boulder fields and rock slides.

In the area are scores of lakes and beautiful streams with cascades. Vegetation includes forests of spruce, fir, and western larch, and foothills with sage, paintbrush, and juniper. Among the wildlife are deer, elk, black bear, bighorn sheep, mountain goat, moose, and mountain lion.

Within the Forest boundaries are over 1,600

miles of trails, including about 50 miles of the Continental Divide Trail. Difficulty ranges from easy to very strenuous. Most trails are also open to horseback riding (motorcycles are permitted on some trails outside of wilderness areas). The highest trails are often not free of snow until mid-July.

KOOTENAI NATIONAL FOREST—506 U.S. Highway 2 West, Libby, MT 59923; (406)293-6211. 2,245,000 acres. Kootenai National Forest is located in the northwest corner of Montana, along the Idaho and Canadian borders. It's another of Montana's major National Forests, encompassing several mountain ranges, including the Cabinet and Purcell Mountains. The highest elevation is Snowshoe Peak (8,738 feet), and the terrain is often extremely rough and rocky.

There's one wilderness area, the 94,000-acre Cabinet Mountains Wilderness. Outstanding scenic views are frequent, and some of the terrain consists of high ridges and saddles, prominent peaks, and rock canyons. There are grasslands, forested valley bottoms with creeks and waterfalls, glacial lakes, along with alpine meadows and tundra. Trees include larch and pine, hemlock and fir, and giant cedars. Among the mammals are moose, elk, deer, black and grizzly bear, bighorn sheep, and mountain goat.

There are over 1,300 miles of trails—with five National Recreation Trails. Difficulty ranges from easy to strenuous. Some trails in the Cabinet Mountains Wilderness receive heavy use.

OTHER RECOMMENDED LOCATIONS

HELENA NATIONAL FOREST—301 South Park, Drawer 10014, Helena, MT 59626; (406)449-5201. 976,673 acres. This National Forest consists of several tracts in the west-central part of the state around Helena, Montana. The western portion includes a segment of the Continental Divide. There are several mountain ranges with elevations which occasionally surpass 9,000 feet—and often have fabulous views. Highest point is 9,472-foot Mount Baldy.

There are two wilderness areas, one of which

is the Scapegoat Wilderness (which extends into Lolo and Lewis and Clark National Forests). The scenery here includes some steep peaks, huge limestone cliffs and spires, rugged ridges and rock formations, canyons and creeks. One finds a multitude of meadows, alpine tundra, slopes with Douglas fir, and valleys wooded with lodgepole pine. Among the fauna are elk, deer, grizzly and black bear, moose, antelope, mountain goat, and wolverine.

Helena National Forest has more than 700 miles of hiking trails. Included is a 100-mile section of the Continental Divide Trail. Difficulty ranges from easy to strenuous.

DEERLODGE NATIONAL FOREST—P.O. Box 400, Butte, MT 59703; (406)496-3400. 1,195,771 acres. Deerlodge National Forest consists of several large parcels of land in southwest Montana, and includes a sizable segment of the Continental Divide. The area has a series of mountain ranges, some spectacular scenery, and elevations which sometimes surpass 10,000 feet. The highest point is Mount Evans (10,641 feet), and there's one wilderness area.

The terrain includes snow-covered peaks and massive cirque basins, canyons and rock formations. There are slopes forested with conifers, numerous glacial lakes and streams, and alpine vegetation. Among the animals in the area are elk, moose, grizzly and black bear, deer, and coyote.

Hiking trail mileage totals about 600 miles. The most important trail here is a major stretch of the Continental Divide National Scenic Trail. Difficulty ranges from easy to strenuous.

CUSTER NATIONAL FOREST—2602 First Avenue North, P.O. Box 2556, Billings, MT 59103; (406)657-6361. 1,112,477 acres in Montana. This National Forest is in southern Montana, located directly northeast of Yellowstone National Park, and also has units in South Dakota and North Dakota. Of special interest is the large Absaroka–Beartooth Wilderness, part of which is in Gallatin National Forest. Here are the extremely high,

rugged, and spectacular Beartooth Mountains, with major areas above timberline—and 12,799-foot Granite Peak, Montana's highest mountain, along with 15 other peaks over 12,000 feet in elevation.

There are major areas of alpine tundra, high plateaus and pinnacles, glaciers and canyons. Below timberline are forests of fir, spruce, and pine. Throughout the region are many lakes, streams, and waterfalls. Wildlife include elk, deer, black bear, moose, bighorn sheep, mountain lion, and bobcat.

About 330 miles of hiking trails are found here, more than half of which are in the Absaroka–Beartooth Wilderness. Difficulty varies from easy to very strenuous. Some high trails are snowbound until July and under snow again by late September.

MONTANA HIKING RESOURCES

HIKING GUIDEBOOKS

Bitterroot to Beartooth—Rudner, Ruth. San Francisco: Sierra Club Books.

Guide to the Continental Divide Trail, Northern Montana—Wolf, James R. Bethesda, MD: Continental Divide Trail Society, 1979.

Guide to the Continental Divide Trail, Southern Montana—Wolf, James R. Bethesda, MD: Continental Divide Trail Society, 1979.

Hiker's Guide to Glacier National Park—Nelson, Dick. West Glacier, MT: Glacier Natural History Association, 1978.

The Hiker's Guide to Montana—Henckel, Mark. Helena, MT: Falcon Press.

The Hiker's Guide to Montana's Continental Divide Trail—Brooks, Tad, & Jones, Sherry. Helena, MT: Falcon Press, 1990.

STATE HIGHWAY MAP AND TRAVEL INFORMATION

Travel Montana, Department of Commerce, Helena, MT 59620; (800)541-1447 (out of state); (406)444-2654.

MONTANA HIKING CLUBS

Sierra Club, c/o James Conner, 78 Konley Drive, Kalispell, MT 59901.

NEBRASKA

The natural areas of Nebraska include attractive expanses of prairie grasslands, ponderosa pine forests, broad buttes, and scarred badlands. State landholdings are not large, and hikers have limited choices here, as most parks offer short trails, but a fine National Forest offers some more extensive and enjoyable hiking in the scenic Pine Ridge region of northwest Nebraska.

BEST HIKING AREAS

NEBRASKA NATIONAL FOREST—270 Pine Street, Chadron, NE 69337; (308)432-3367. 140,376 acres. This National Forest consists of several tracts in northwest and north-central Nebraska. There are 34 miles of marked hiking trails here—most of them clustered in the rugged Pine Ridge area, which is in the northwest corner of the Nebraska Panhandle.

The trails lead through forests of ponderosa pine with stands of hardwoods, across grassy prairies and down into wooded canyons, and up over open ridges with panoramic views. Trails are open to horseback riders as well as hikers. Wildlife in the area includes deer, antelope, prairie dog, coyote, and bobcat.

OTHER RECOMMENDED LOCATIONS

INDIAN CAVE STATE PARK—Nebraska Game and Parks Commission, P.O. Box 30370, Lincoln, NE 68503. 3,000 acres. Situated in the southeast

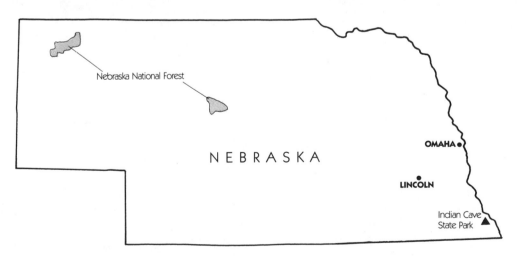

corner of Nebraska, alongside the Missouri River, this scenic state park has fine views and a giant sandstone cave with ancient petroglyphs (Indian picture writings). An entry permit is required and available at the park.

The area consists of oak and walnut woodlands, and grasslands, with wildflowers—and wildlife including deer, coyote, and red fox. There are 20 miles of hiking trails, easy to strenuous in difficulty.

NEBRASKA HIKING RESOURCES

INFORMATION ABOUT STATE PARKS
Nebraska Game and Parks Commission, P.O. Box 30370, Lincoln, NE 68503.

STATE HIGHWAY MAP AND TRAVEL INFORMATION
Nebraska Department of Travel and Tourism, P.O. Box 94666, Lincoln, NE 68509; (800)742-7595 (in state)/(800)228-4307 (out of state).

NEBRASKA HIKING CLUBS
Sierra Club, c/o Clayton Brant, 2036 Randolph, #70, Lincoln, NE 68510.

NEVADA

Sparsely-populated Nevada has truly enormous expanses of publicly-owned wild lands, most of which are administered by the Bureau of Land Management. In addition the state contains two huge National Forests and one new National Park. There are spectacular mountain ranges, deep canyons with rivers or streams, and arid desert basins. Most of Nevada's marked trails are found within the two National Forests, which often provide superb hiking amid some incredibly beautiful and diverse scenery.

BEST HIKING AREAS

TOIYABE NATIONAL FOREST—1200 Franklin Way, Sparks, NV 89431; (702)355-5302. 3,212,545 acres in Nevada (3,855,960 total). This is the largest National Forest in the United States outside of Alaska, consisting of several separate tracts in central and southern Nevada and extending into California. There's quite a range of scenery here, from lofty alpine peaks to deep canyons with precipitous cliffs and desert brushlands. Among the numerous mountain ranges are the eastern Sierras, with elevations over 11,000 feet. Some of the terrain is extremely rugged, portions are remote, and views are often spectacular.

There are now eight wilderness areas. The region has a number of lakes, streams, and rivers, with some waterfalls and hot springs. Vegetation includes mountain meadows with wildflowers, forests of Jeffrey and lodgepole pine and fir,

aspen, sagebrush and juniper flats, plus desert cactus and yucca. Of particular interest are major stands of ancient bristlecone pine, the world's oldest living trees—some of which are believed to be close to 5,000 years old. Among the wildlife are mule deer, black bear, elk, bighorn sheep, wild horse, mountain lion, coyote, and bobcat.

Toiyabe National Forest has 1,165 miles of hiking trails, including the 72-mile Toiyabe Crest National Recreation Trail, and a segment of the new Tahoe Rim Trail. Difficulty ranges from easy to strenuous.

HUMBOLDT NATIONAL FOREST—976 Mountain City Highway, Elko, NV 98901; (702)738-5171. 2,474,985 acres. Humboldt National Forest is made up of a number of separate units in east-central and northern Nevada. It encompasses a good many mountain ranges, with some elevations over 11,000 feet—including 11,350-foot Ruby Dome. There are now eight wilderness areas totaling 466,000 acres. Terrain consists of steep rocky peaks, high-walled glacial canyons and cliffs with interesting rock formations, rolling hills and plateaus, and arid desert.

There are cirque basins with alpine lakes, meadows with wildflowers, some rivers and small streams, stands of mahogany and limber pine, fir and aspen, and bristlecone pine—plus sagebrush-covered expanses of land. Local mammals include mule deer, elk, antelope, bighorn sheep, mountain lion, mountain goat, and cougar.

This National Forest has about 900 miles of

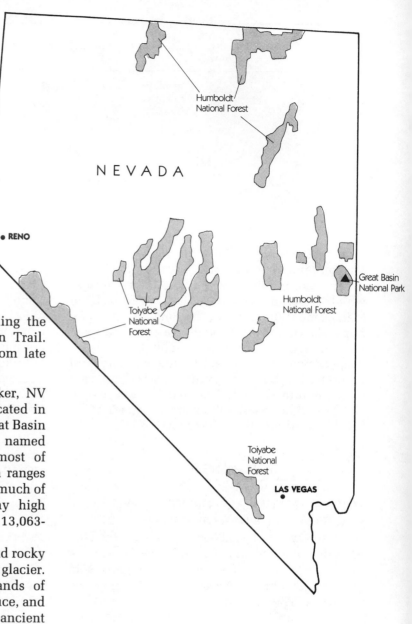

easy to strenuous hiking trails, including the 40-mile Ruby Crest National Recreation Trail. Some high trails are snow-free only from late June through mid-September.

GREAT BASIN NATIONAL PARK—Baker, NV 89311; (702)234-7331. 77,000 acres. Located in eastern Nevada near the Utah border, Great Basin National Park was created in 1986. It's named after the Great Basin which covers most of Nevada, an area of numerous mountain ranges and wide desert basins. The park covers much of the southern Snake Range, with many high peaks. Elevations are from 6,200 feet to 13,063-foot Wheeler Peak.

There are also canyons with streams and rocky outcrops, limestone caves, and a small glacier. Vegetation includes sagebrush, woodlands of piñon-juniper, forests of Douglas fir, spruce, and aspen, with stands of limber pine and ancient bristlecone pine. This new National Park currently has 25-plus miles of hiking trails. Much of the area remains trailless.

NEVADA HIKING RESOURCES

HIKING GUIDEBOOKS
Hiking the Great Basin—Hart, John. San Francisco: Sierra Clubl Books, 1981.

INFORMATION ABOUT STATE PARKS
Nevada Division of State Parks, Capitol Complex, Carson City, NV 89710: (702)687-4370.

STATE HIGHWAY MAP AND TRAVEL INFORMATION
Commission on Tourism, Capitol Complex, Carson City, NV 89710.

NEVADA HIKING CLUBS
Sierra Club, P.O. Box 8096, Reno, NV 89507.

NEW HAMPSHIRE

There's superb hiking to be found in New Hampshire, most notably within White Mountain National Forest in the north-central section of the state. The White Mountains are interlaced by a very large network of trails, and offer some of the most ruggedly spectacular mountain scenery in the eastern United States—with the highest elevations in the Northeast, extensive areas above timberline, and truly magnificent panoramic views.

MAJOR TRAILS

APPALACHIAN TRAIL 157 miles in New Hampshire (2,100 total). The Appalachian Trail winds through the heart of New Hampshire's White Mountain National Forest, traversing the two highest ranges—the Presidential Range and Franconia Range—with the best and most dramatic views in the state and perhaps the Northeast. Much of the trail here is quite rough and strenuous. Trail information: Appalachian Trail Conference, P.O. Box 807, Harpers Ferry, WV 25425.

MONADNOCK–SUNAPEE GREENWAY—51 miles. This trail runs from Mount Monadnock (3,165 feet) to Mount Sunapee (2,743 feet) in southwest New Hampshire, connecting with the Metacomet–Monadnock Trail (which starts in Connecticut). Much of it passes through private land, crossing hills, ridges, and small mountains with occasional stretches of road walking. Trail information: Appalachian Mountain Club, 5 Joy Street, Boston, MA 02108.

BEST HIKING AREAS

WHITE MOUNTAIN NATIONAL FOREST—Box 638, Laconia, NH 03246; (603)528-8721. 750,000 acres. This magnificent National Forest in north-central New Hampshire is a vast evergreen wilderness with numerous mountain ranges and splendid scenery. It includes the famous Presidential Range and the highest mountain in the Northeast, Mount Washington (6,288 feet), known for its notoriously severe weather. Arctic-alpine vegetation is found on this and surrounding mountains. Views are quite spectacular.

On one side of Mount Washington is Tuckerman's Ravine, a dramatic glacier cirque (glacier-scoured bowl) famous for skiing on snow which sometimes lasts into July. The Franconia Range, second highest, is among the other ranges here, and there are two major wilderness areas. In addition, two state parks within the National Forest boundaries (Crawford Notch State Park and Franconia Notch State Park) encompass some especially impressive scenery.

There are also many streams, waterfalls, and small lakes. Between some of the mountains are

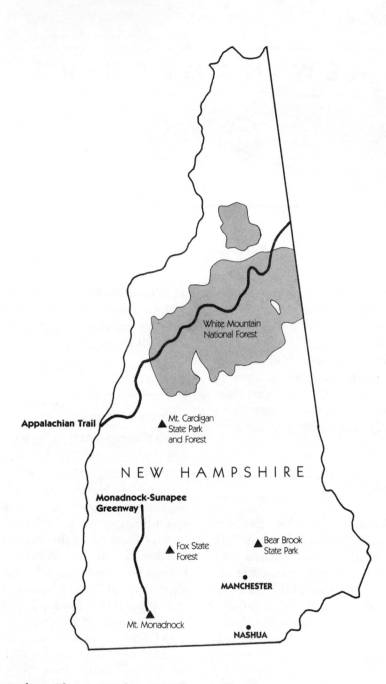

White Mountain
National Forest

Appalachian Trail

Mt. Cardigan
State Park
and Forest

NEW HAMPSHIRE

Monadnock-Sunapee
Greenway

Fox State
Forest

Bear Brook
State Park

MANCHESTER

Mt. Monadnock

NASHUA

steep canyonlike notches. The region has mixed forests of hardwoods as well as fir, spruce, and pine. Animals include white-tailed deer, black bear, moose, bobcat, and fox.

The area attracts a great many hikers, creating crowded conditions on some trails, particularly in the Presidential Range. The sometimes extreme weather requires special precautions, as below-freezing temperatures are possible at any time.

With over 1,100 miles of trails, including an important segment of the Appalachian Trail, this is one of the best and most scenic areas in the East for hiking. Many of the trails are unusually rough and steep. Difficulty varies from easy to very strenuous.

MOUNT MONADNOCK—Monadnock State Park, Jaffrey Center, NH 03454; (603)532-8862. 5,000 acres. This lone mountain in southern New Hampshire is said to be one of the most frequently hiked mountains in the world. It stands at 3,165 feet elevation, with great views from an open, barren rocky top.

The area has mixed forests of pine, spruce, and oak. There are over 30 miles of trails here, including the terminus of the 117-mile Metacomet–Monadnock Trail (which starts in Connecticut) and the 51-mile Monadnock–Sunapee Greenway.

MOUNT CARDIGAN STATE PARK AND FOREST—New Hampshire Division of Parks and Recreation, P.O. Box 856, Concord, NH 03301; (603)271-3254. 5,655 acres. Located in west-central New Hampshire, this park has a fine network of trails and some excellent views from 3,121-foot Mount Cardigan. Adjacent is the 1,000-acre Cardigan Reservation, which includes a lodge for hikers.

BEAR BROOK STATE PARK—Suncook, NH 03275; (603)485-9874. 9,585 acres. This forested state park in southern New Hampshire has a substantial network of hiking trails. Terrain is hilly, and most trails are easy to moderate in difficulty. The scenery includes hills, marshes, bogs, and several attractive small ponds.

FOX STATE FOREST—P.O. Box 1175, Hillsboro, NH 03244; (603)464-3453. 1,445 acres. Located in southern New Hampshire, this small state forest includes hilly terrain with ledges, a hemlock ravine, a small area of virgin forest, and over 20 miles of trails. Difficulty is easy to moderate.

HIKING GUIDEBOOKS

AMC White Mountain Guide—Boston: Appalachian Mountain Club, 1987.

AMC Guide to Mount Washington and the Presidential Range—Boston: Appalachian Mountain Club.

Appalachian Trail Guide to New Hampshire–Vermont—Harpers Ferry, WV: The Appalachian Trail Conference, 1989.

Fifty Hikes in New Hampshire's White Mountains—Doan, Daniel. Woodstock, VT: The Countryman Press, 1983.

Fifty More Hikes in New Hampshire—Doan, Daniel. Woodstock, VT: The Countryman Press, 1986.

MAPS

The Appalachian Mountain Club publishes maps of New Hampshire hiking areas.

The New Hampshire Atlas and Gazetteer—Freeport, ME: DeLorme Mapping Co., 1986.

TRAIL INFORMATION

Appalachian Mountain Club, P.O. Box 298, Gorham, NH 03581; (603)466-2725.

New England Trail Conference, 33 Knollwood Drive, East Longmeadow, MA 01028: (203)342-1425 or (413)732-3719.

INFORMATION ABOUT STATE PARKS AND FORESTS

New Hampshire Division of Parks and Recreation, 105 Loudon Road, Concord, NH 03301; (603)271-3254.

STATE HIGHWAY MAP AND TRAVEL INFORMATION

New Hampshire Office of Vacation Travel, P.O. Box 856, Concord, NH 03301; (603)271-2666.

NEW HAMPSHIRE HIKING CLUBS

Appalachian Mountain Club, 5 Joy Street, Boston, MA 02108; (617)523-0636. This major club has a chapter in New Hampshire.

Sierra Club, 3 Joy Street, Boston, MA 02108.

NEW JERSEY

Although it's a very densely populated state, New Jersey has an impressive number of beautiful parks and forests, and several hundred miles of hiking trails. The majority of trails are in the mountainous and lightly settled northern portion of the state. Elevations are not substantial here, but the terrain is sometimes rugged—and within the larger parks one often finds a surprising sense of isolation.

MAJOR TRAILS

APPALACHIAN TRAIL—72 miles (2,100 total). The Appalachian Trail follows the ridges of the Kittatinny Mountains, which parallel the Delaware River for some 40 miles along the wild northwestern border of New Jersey. Most of the time the trail is on state forest and parklands. There are many fine views from open areas. Difficulty varies from easy to moderately strenuous. Trail information: Appalachian Trail Conference, P.O. Box 807, Harpers Ferry, WV 25425.

BATONA TRAIL—51 miles. The Batona Trail is located in the state's largest wild area, 108,773-acre Wharton State Forest, in the Pine Barrens of south-central New Jersey—a largely flat area of unusual and almost desertlike beauty. This very easy, sandy trail is the only marked hiking trail here. Trail information: Batona Hiking Club, c/o

Robert E. Raine, 514 Inman Terrace, Willow Grove, PA 19090.

BEST HIKING AREAS

DELAWARE WATER GAP NATIONAL RECREATION AREA—Bushkill, PA 18324; (717)588-6637. 66,697 acres. This is a large and beautiful protected area in northwest New Jersey. It includes the Delaware Water Gap (a deep gap in the Kittatinny Mountain ridge), extensive lands along the Delaware River, and some acreage in Pennsylvania.

The region has hardwood forests with oak and hickory, plus cedar and hemlock, rhododendron and mountain laurel. Deer, bear, and coyote are among the wildlife. There are many trails here, including a segment of the Appalachian Trail—with lots of fine views from elevations up to 1,500 feet along the ridges of the Kittatinny Mountains.

WORTHINGTON STATE FOREST—Old Mine Road, Columbia, NJ 07652; (201)841-9575. 5,830 acres. Adjacent to the Delaware Water Gap National Recreation Area at the Delaware Water Gap, Worthington is an especially attractive state forest. Deer and coyote are among the wildlife here. The forest covers a part of the Kittatinny Mountain ridge, with great views overlooking the Delaware River. There are more than 20 miles of trails, including a section of the Appalachian Trail.

NORVIN GREEN STATE FOREST—c/o Ringwood State Park, Box 1304, Ringwood, NJ 07456;
(201)962-7031. 2,331 acres. Norvin Green is an
unusually beautiful and undeveloped state forest in northern New Jersey. The scenery includes
some streams, waterfalls, and nice views from
small rocky mountaintops. There are 36 miles of
trails.

HIGH POINT STATE PARK—RR 4, Box 287,
Sussex, NJ 07461; (201)875-4800. 14,109 acres.
At the northwestern corner of the state and
alongside Stokes State Forest, this park encompasses a portion of the Kittatinny Mountains,
and has the highest elevation in New Jersey at
High Point (1,803 feet). There are forests of oak,
maple, and hickory, and many miles of trails,
including a section of the Appalachian Trail.

STOKES STATE FOREST—RR 2, Box 260,
Branchville, NJ 07826; (201)948-3820. 15,399
acres. This is a large and attractive forest which
covers another portion of the Kittatinny Mountains. The area has mixed forests of oak and
hickory along with cedar and pine, plus some
mountain laurel and rhododendron. Deer are
among the wildlife. A rather large number of
trails are found here, including a section of the
Appalachian Trail.

OTHER RECOMMENDED LOCATIONS

WAWAYANDA STATE PARK—Box 198, Highland Lakes, NJ 07422; (201)853-4462. 11,330
acres. This substantial-size state park in the
Highlands of northern New Jersey includes some
hilly and mountainous terrain, with a large lake,
a couple of beautiful ponds, and other wild
scenery. There are thickets of rhododendron,
cedar and blueberry swamps, and a stand of
virgin hemlock. A section of the Appalachian
Trail is among a number of trails here.

PEQUANNOCK WATERSHED—NWCDC, P.O.
Box 319, Newfoundland, NJ 07435; (201)697-
2850. 35,000 acres. The Pequannock Watershed
is a large expanse of private wild land in north-

ern New Jersey which is open to hikers on a
permit basis. The area includes scenic low
mountain ridges with rock outcroppings, some
lakes and streams, and over 30 miles of hiking
trails.

PALISADES INTERSTATE PARK—Box 155, Alpine, NJ 07620; (201)768-1360. 2,500 acres. This
long and narrow park includes the dramatic
cliffs of the Hudson River Palisades, just north of
New York City. The area has mixed forests
of oak, maple, and birch. There are two trails of
note here, the 13-mile Palisades Shore Trail and
12 miles of New York's 200-mile Long Path,
which runs along the clifftops.

RAMAPO MOUNTAIN STATE FOREST—P.O.
Box 225, Oakland, NJ 07436; (201)337-0960.
2,887 acres. There are 42 miles of trails in this
northern New Jersey state forest. It's an area of
low ridges and small mountains with rocky
terrain, and includes a large lake.

RINGWOOD STATE PARK—Box 1304, Ringwood, NJ 07456; (201)962-7031. 4,317 acres.
Located in the Ramapo Mountains of northern
New Jersey, Ringwood State Park has many
small mountain ridges, lakes, and mixed hardwood forests which include oak and maple, with
some hemlock and pine. Wildlife includes
white-tailed deer, bobcat, and fox. There are over
30 miles of trails.

NEW JERSEY HIKING RESOURCES

HIKING GUIDEBOOKS

Circuit Hikes in Northern New Jersey—Scofield,
    Bruce. New York–New Jersey Trail Confer-
    ence, 1986.
Fifty Hikes in New Jersey—Scofield, Bruce;
    Green, Stella; and Zimmerman, H. Neil. Wood-
    stock, VT: The Countryman Press, 1988.
*Guide to the Appalachian Trail in New York and
    New Jersey*—Harpers Ferry, WV: The Appala-
    chian Trail Conference, 1988.
New York Walk Book—New York–New Jersey

This important trail organization publishes excellent maps of the major hiking areas of northern New Jersey.

Walking News Maps, P.O. Box 352, New York, NY 10013. Another map series which includes northern New Jersey areas.

STATE HIGHWAY MAP
New Jersey Department of Transportation, 1035 Parkway Avenue, Trenton, NJ 08618.

INFORMATION ABOUT STATE PARKS AND FORESTS
New Jersey Division of Parks and Forestry, CN 404, Trenton, NJ 08625.

CLUBS AND OTHER ORGANIZATIONS WHICH OFFER HIKES
Adirondack Mountain Club, P.O. Box 185, Ridgewood, NJ 07451.

Appalachian Mountain Club, 202 East 39 Street, New York, NY 10016. Offers hikes in New Jersey as well as New York.

Basset Valley Single Hikers, c/o Brian McLaughlin, 519 St. Clair Avenue, Spring Lake, NJ.

Cosmopolitan Club of Montclair/Outdoor Group, c/o John Keller, 110 Summit Avenue, Upper Montclair, NJ 07043.

Essex County Trail Walkers, 621 Eagle Rock Avenue, Roseland, NJ 07068.

Hunterdon Hiking Club, P.O. Box 31, Lebanon, NJ 08833.

Interstate Hiking Club, c/o Muriel Morrison, 63 Hillcrest Drive, Wayne, NJ 07470.

Outdoor Club of Southern New Jersey, Box 1508, Delran, NJ 08075.

Sierra Club, 57 Mountain Avenue, Princeton, NJ 08540.

Sierra Club, c/o David Paperman, 44 Gregory Avenue, West Orange, NJ 07052.

Somerset Country Hikers, P.O. Box 5327, North Branch, NJ 08876.

University Outing Club, c/o Ms. Smith, 11 Highwood Road, Somerset, NJ 08873.

West Jersey Hiking Club, c/o George Schelling, 4 Cedar Road, Pompton Plains, NJ 07444.

Woodland Trail Walkers, c/o Mary Crofford, 18 Kensington Avenue, Jersey City, NJ 07304.

Trail Conference. Garden City: Anchor Books, 1984.

TRAIL INFORMATION
New York–New Jersey Trail Conference, 232 Madison Avenue, #908, New York, NY 10016.

HIKING MAPS
New York–New Jersey Trail Conference, 232 Madison Avenue, #908, New York, NY 10016.

NEW MEXICO

Much of New Mexico is mountainous, with strikingly beautiful scenery which includes steep peaks, broad mesas, countless canyons, and other rugged features. There are also open plains and arid desert. Some of the wildest and most impressive areas are found within five major National Forests which blanket central and western New Mexico, providing an enormous variety of trails and terrain, with such a range of elevations that one may enjoy hiking here at practically any time of year.

BEST HIKING AREAS

GILA NATIONAL FOREST—2610 North Silver Street, Silver City, NM 88061; (505)388-8201. 3,320,135 acres. Located in southwestern New Mexico, this truly enormous National Forest is one of the largest in the country. Elevations range from 4,500 feet to over 10,000 feet. The terrain includes several high and beautifully rugged mountain ranges, flat mesas, deep canyons and escarpments, with interesting rock formations and outcrops, and outstanding open vistas.

There are three wilderness areas, including the magnificent 560,000-acre Gila Wilderness on the Mogollon Plateau—and also a section of the Continental Divide. Vegetation ranges from cactus and semidesert grasslands to forests of aspen and spruce, pine and fir, along with high mead-

ows and alpine plants. Some major rivers and a great many mountain streams are here. Among the wildlife are elk, mule deer, antelope, black bear, bighorn sheep, and mountain lion.

Over 1,400 miles of trails lead throughout this National Forest, including a section of the Continental Divide Trail, plus the 33-mile West Fork Trail and the 32-mile Gila River Trail. Difficulty varies from easy to strenuous. Some trails in the Gila Wilderness receive heavy use.

SANTE FE NATIONAL FOREST—1220 St. Francis Drive, P.O. Box 1689, Sante Fe, NM 87504; (505)988-6940. 1,589,184 acres. This large and outstandingly scenic National Forest consists of units on both sides of Sante Fe, in northern New Mexico. There are some major mountain ranges here: the Sangre de Cristo Mountains, the Jemez Mountains, and the San Pedro Mountains. More than half of the land falls within four wilderness areas, which include the 223,000-acre Pecos Wilderness, a small part of which is in Carson National Forest.

It's an area of spectacular high alpine peaks and ridges, glacial lakes and creeks, rugged canyons and mesas, and marshy meadows. Elevations run from 5,300 feet to over 13,000 feet. The highest point is Truchas Peak (13,103 feet), New Mexico's second highest mountain. There are fir and ponderosa pine forests, along with spruce and aspen, piñon-juniper, and open grasslands with semidesert vegetation including cactus. Among the mammals here are elk, black bear,

Carson
National Forest

Carson
National Forest

Sante Fe
National Forest

Bandelier
National
Monument

Sante Fe
National Forest

SANTE FE

ALBUQUERQUE

NEW MEXICO

Cibola
National Forest

Gila
National Forest

Lincoln
National Forest

Carlsbad Caverns
National Park

mule deer, bighorn sheep, and mountain lion.

Sante Fe National Forest has just over 1,000 miles of trails, including the high 50-mile Skyline Trail. Difficulty ranges from easy to strenuous. Some trails are unmarked and not well-maintained. High trails may be under snow until July.

CARSON NATIONAL FOREST—P.O. Box 558, 208 Cruz Alta Road, Taos, NM 87571; (505)758-6200. 1,491,121 acres. Consisting of four large tracts in northern New Mexico, Carson National Forest includes splendid segments of the Sangre de Cristo and San Juan Mountain ranges, which continue north into Colorado. Wheeler Peak

(13,161 feet) is here, highest point in the state, with wonderful views. There are four wilderness areas totaling 86,000 acres.

Along with impressive rocky peaks and lofty ridges with talus slopes, the area has open mesas and steep canyons, and includes the lovely Rio Grande Gorge. There are high lakes, hundreds of miles of creeks, and a number of rivers—and flora which include sagebrush and piñon-juniper, stands of spruce, fir, and aspen, and bristlecone pine, alpine grasses and wildflowers at high elevations. Elk, mule deer, black bear, bighorn sheep, and mountain lion are among the animals here.

Carson has approximately 330 miles of trails, which are also open to horseback riding (some nonwilderness trails are open to motorcycles). Difficulty ranges from easy to strenuous. Trails at high elevations may be under snow until June.

LINCOLN NATIONAL FOREST—Federal Building, 11th and New York, Alamogordo, NM 88310; (505)437-6030. 1,103,495 acres. Lincoln National Forest is made up of three parcels of land in south-central New Mexico, with segments of four mountain ranges. Elevations run from 5,000 to 12,000 feet, and there are two wilderness areas. One tract near the southern border connects Carlsbad Caverns National Park with Guadalupe Mountains National Park in Texas.

It's an extremely scenic and varied environment, with steep ridges, rock outcrops, rugged canyons, and open plains. There are quite a few nice streams and rivers, and some great panoramic vistas available, with desert flora, piñon and juniper, pine and madrone, and high meadows and savannahs. The wildlife includes elk, mule deer, black bear, mountain lion, and bobcat.

More than 250 miles of trails extend through this National Forest, and they're open to horseback riding as well as hiking. Motorcycles are permitted on many trails outside of wilderness areas. Difficulty ranges from easy to strenuous. Some trails are not maintained.

CIBOLA NATIONAL FOREST—2113 Osuna Road N.E., Suite A, Albuquerque, NM 87113; (505)761-4650. 1,653,301 acres. Consisting of a number of separate units in western and central New Mexico, Cibola National Forest covers portions of quite a few mountain ranges, and includes a section of the Continental Divide. Highest point is Mount Taylor (11,301 feet). There are four wilderness areas, and some outstanding scenery, with superb views.

In addition to lofty peaks and steep slopes there are narrow rugged canyons and wide mesas, sheer cliffs and rock formations, high mountain meadows and dry plains. Vegetation includes piñon-juniper plus stands of mixed

conifers and aspen. Among the wildlife are black bear, elk, deer, mountain lion, and bobcat. Very little water is found here.

Inside the National Forest are over 270 miles of trails, which include an attractive section of the Continental Divide Trail. Difficulty varies from easy to strenuous. Except for a few trails near Albuquerque, use is generally light.

OTHER RECOMMENDED LOCATIONS

BANDELIER NATIONAL MONUMENT—Los Alamos, NM 87544; (505)672-3861. 32,737 acres. Located west of Sante Fe, this National Monument is known for its cliff ruins of prehistoric Indian shelters. There are also over 70 miles of hiking trails here, and most of the area is wilderness.

The rugged terrain includes deep canyon gorges and mesas, with vegetation ranging from yucca, cactus, and other desert varieties to piñon-juniper and mixed conifer forests. Among the wildlife are elk, mule deer, and coyote. A free permit is required for hiking into the backcountry.

CARLSBAD CAVERNS NATIONAL PARK—3225 National Parks Highway, Carlsbad, NM 88220; (505)785-2232. 46,755 acres. Situated in southeast New Mexico, Carlsbad Caverns National Park has one of the world's largest systems of caves. Aboveground is an attractive wilderness of steep canyons and rocky ridges, with over 50 miles of trails. Flora range from desert vegetation to stands of juniper and piñon pine, and wildlife includes mule deer, mountain lion, and bobcat.

NEW MEXICO HIKING RESOURCES

HIKING GUIDEBOOKS

50 Hikes in New Mexico—Evans, Harry. Pico Rivera, CA: Gem Guides Book Co., 1984.

Day Hikes in the Sante Fe Area—Sante Fe Group of the Sierra Club. Sante Fe, NM: National Education Association Press, 1981.

Hiking the Southwest—Ganci, Dave. San Francisco: Sierra Club Books, 1983.

STATE HIGHWAY MAP AND TRAVEL INFORMATION

New Mexico Tourism and Travel Division, Joseph Montoya Building, 1100 St. Francis Drive, Sante Fe, NM 87503; (505)827-0291/ (800)545-2040.

NEW MEXICO HIKING CLUBS

New Mexico Mountain Club, 119 40th Street N.W., Albuquerque, NM 87105.

Sierra Club, 207 San Pedro N.E., Albuquerque, NM 87108.

NEW YORK

New York offers outstanding opportunities for hiking, with a wide range of wild scenery and more trails than any eastern state except Pennsylvania. Sizable parks, forests, and preserves are abundant here. Most impressive of all is upstate New York's enormous and magnificent Adirondack Park, which includes the state's highest and most spectacular mountains, an amazing two thousand miles of hiking trails, and the greatest expanse of wilderness east of the Rockies.

MAJOR TRAILS

APPALACHIAN TRAIL—94 miles in New York State (2,100 miles total). The Appalachian Trail traverses several small mountain ranges in the southeastern part of the state. Although elevations rarely exceed 1,300 feet, there are many fine views and quite beautiful scenery. Difficulty varies from easy to strenuous, with some portions very rocky and rugged. Trail information: Appalachian Trail Conference, P.O. Box 807, Harpers Ferry, WV 25425.

FINGER LAKES TRAIL—775 miles. This scenic trail runs over 500 miles across southern New York State, from the Catskills west to the Pennsylvania border. It includes the lovely Finger Lakes area in west-central New York. Several branch trails add additional mileage. When it's

completed, the total distance will be close to 800 miles. Some of the trail is now also part of the North Country Trail. Terrain is hilly. Trail information: Finger Lakes Trail Conference, P.O. Box 18048, Rochester, NY 14618.

LONG PATH—226 miles. The Long Path extends from New York City's George Washington Bridge to the northern Catskills, and will eventually reach another 200 miles to the northern Adirondacks. This trail connects many of the most attractive parks and natural areas west of the Hudson River, and also passes through some developed areas. Difficulty ranges from easy to strenuous. Trail information: New York–New Jersey Trail Conference, 232 Madison Avenue, #908, New York, NY 10016.

NORTH COUNTRY TRAIL—This important National Scenic Trail, currently under construction, will eventually extend 3,200 miles from New York to North Dakota. The New York portion will be about 520 miles long. It begins at Crown Point on Lake Champlain, leads through the wild lake country of the Adirondacks, and for 300 miles follows the scenic and hilly Finger Lakes Trail before entering Pennsylvania. Trail information: North Country Trail Association, P.O. Box 311, White Cloud, MI 49349.

NORTHVILLE–PLACID TRAIL—132 miles. The Northville–Placid Trail runs most of the length of the Adirondack Park, from Northville to Lake

Placid—crossing one of the major wilderness areas of the East. It's a beautiful and unusually easy trail, with only occasional hills and rough spots. Trail information: New York State Department of Environmental Conservation, 50 Wolf Road, Albany, NY 12233.

BEST HIKING AREAS

ADIRONDACK PARK—New York State Department of Environmental Conservation, 50 Wolf Road, Albany, NY 12233; (518)457-2500. 2,400,000 acres (6,000,000 acres including private lands). New York's gigantic Adirondack Forest Preserve is actually the largest single park in the United States outside of Alaska. Like some of our National Forests it's a patchwork of public and private lands, with just 40 percent of the total area publicly owned and fully protected.

The park has several large wilderness areas. Best known by far is the spectacular 180,000-acre High Peaks Wilderness, where most of the major mountains are situated. There are some 46 peaks over 4,000 feet, including 5,344-foot Mount Marcy, highest in the state. Many of the mountains have areas above timberline, alpine vegetation, and splendid panoramic views.

The High Peaks Wilderness attracts a large number of hikers and trails are often crowded. Elsewhere in the park the scenery is less dramatic but still quite beautiful, and often wild and remote. Relatively few visitors see these regions.

Throughout the park are forests of spruce and fir along with hardwoods, marshes and swamps, and an enormous number of lakes and ponds, rivers and streams. Wildlife includes white-tailed deer, black bear, coyote, bobcat, and fox.

A total of over 2,000 miles of hiking trails are found here, providing months or years worth of exploring for the interested hiker—more than any other single location in the East. Major trails include the easy 132-mile Northville–Placid Trail. Overall trail difficulty ranges from very easy to extremely strenuous, with some unusually rugged and steep trails in the High Peaks Wilderness.

CATSKILL PARK—NY State Department of Environmental Conservation, 50 Wolf Road, Albany, NY 12233; (518)457-2500. 250,000 acres. Second largest of New York's parks and located in the southeastern part of the state, the mountainous Catskill Park is another important wilderness preserve. Composed of both public and private lands, this exceptional park has many mountain peaks in the 3,000-4,000-foot range, some with dramatic views.

Highest is Slide Mountain, at 4,180 feet, and a total of 33 peaks are over 3,500 feet. There are several wilderness areas, and mixed forests of conifers and hardwoods. White-tailed deer, black bear, coyote, bobcat, and fox are among the wildlife here.

The park has more than 200 miles of trails. A few are easy, with the majority moderate to strenuous in difficulty. Some receive light use. Especially notable are the scenic 22-mile Escarpment Trail, which has countless views, and the ruggedly challenging 26-mile Devil's Path.

OTHER RECOMMENDED LOCATIONS

BEAR MOUNTAIN AND HARRIMAN STATE PARKS—Palisades Interstate Park Commission, Bear Mountain, NY 10911; (914)786-2701. 54,000 acres. Located only about 40 miles northwest of New York City, in the Ramapo Mountains, these attractive twin parks offer some rugged and rocky scenery, with nice views from elevations over 1,200 feet.

The area is forested with hardwoods, along with hemlock and mountain laurel, and has a number of beautiful lakes—with wildlife including white-tailed deer, bobcat, and fox. There are 40 different trails which have a combined mileage of over 200 miles. Included is the original section of the Appalachian Trail, completed in 1923. Difficulty varies from easy to strenuous. Some trails receive heavy use.

MINNEWASKA STATE PARK—P.O. Box 893, New Paltz, NY 12561; (914)255-0752. 10,248 acres. Located in the Shawangunk Mountains of southeastern New York, Minnewaska is a very wild and beautiful park, with rocky scenery including endless multileveled ledges and cliffs, and outstanding views. Some elevations exceed 2,000 feet. Also here are two lovely lakes (Lake Minnewaska and Lake Awosting), hardwood forests with pine and mountain laurel, and wildlife including deer, black bear, bobcat, and fox. There are many miles of trails and old scenic carriage roads. Difficulty ranges from easy to strenuous.

MOHONK PRESERVE—New Paltz, NY 12561; (914)255-0919. 5,500 acres. This private preserve next to Minnewaska State Park has some more outstanding Shawangunk mountain scenery, including sheer-walled cliffs and ledges with great views. There are hardwood forests along with pine and hemlock, mountain laurel and rhododendron. White-tailed deer, bobcat, and fox are among the wildlife.

The Mohonk Preserve has a large number of hiking trails, along with an extensive network of carriage roads, offering all levels of difficulty. Some challenging routes involve rock scrambling. A trail fee must be paid in order to hike here.

ALLEGANY STATE PARK—RD 1, Salamanca, NY 14779; (716)354-2535. 61,115 acres. Allegany State Park is a hilly, rugged, and very beautiful park on the Allegheny Plateau in western New York. The area has some meadows, streams and ponds, rock outcrops, and forests of hardwoods with beech and maple. Among the wildlife are white-tailed deer, black bear, and fox. There are over 80 miles of trails here, including a section of the North Country Trail. Most trails are moderate in difficulty.

TACONIC STATE PARK—Copake Falls, NY 12517; (518)329-3993. 4,500 acres. Located in the South Taconic Mountains of southeastern New York along the Connecticut and Massachusetts borders, this park offers some lovely scenery. There are steep slopes, small meadows with wildflowers, streams and high waterfalls, and impressive views from elevations as high as 2,300 feet. The area is forested with oak and

pine, and white-tailed deer, bear, bobcat, and fox are among the wildlife. There are over 25 miles of trails. Most are moderate to strenuous in difficulty, and some trails are steep.

FAHNESTOCK STATE PARK—RD 2, Carmel, NY 10512; (914)225-7207. 6,200 acres. Attractive Fahnestock State Park in southeastern New York has terrain which includes small ridges and ravines, hardwood forests and hemlock groves, and a few beautiful lakes and ponds. Among the wildlife are white-tailed deer, bobcat, and fox. There are over 25 miles of trails here, with a segment of the Appalachian Trail. Most trails are easy to moderate in difficulty.

BLACK ROCK FOREST—Continental Road, Cornwall, NY 12518; (914)534-4517. 4,000 acres. This privately-owned mountain forest in southeastern New York includes a number of small rocky mountain summits, with some elevations over 1,400 feet and fine views. There are several scenic lakes and ponds, hardwood forests including oak and hickory, with pine and hemlock, plus mountain laurel. Deer and fox are among the wildlife here, and there's a good-size trail network. Difficulty varies from easy to strenuous.

SCHUNEMUNK MOUNTAIN—Mountainville Conservancy, Mountainville, NY. 2,300 acres. Schunemunk is an eight-mile-long mountain, much of it privately-owned and protected as a preserve. The summit is at 1,664 feet, and there are great views from extensive open rocky ridges and shelves. The mountain has a network of over 20 miles of hiking trails. Difficulty ranges from easy to strenuous.

WARD POUND RIDGE RESERVATION—Box 461, Cross River, NY 10518; (914)763-3993. 4,700 acres. Located in southeastern New York's Westchester County, this park has rolling hills with rocky ledges, attractive mixed hardwood forest with pine and hemlock groves, plus mountain laurel. There are a couple of nice views, and a network of 35 miles of easy to moderate trails. Many of the trails consist of old roads.

NEW YORK HIKING RESOURCES

HIKING GUIDEBOOKS

An Adirondack Sampler—Wadsworth, Bruce. Adirondack Mountain Club, 1988.

Day Walker—New York–New Jersey Trail Conference, 1983.

Discover the Eastern Adirondacks—McMartin, Barbara. Woodstock, VT: Backcountry Publications, 1988.

Discover the Northern Adirondacks—McMartin, Barbara. Woodstock, VT: Backcountry Publications, 1988.

Discover the South-Eastern Adirondacks—McMartin, Barbara. Woodstock, VT: Backcountry Publications, 1986.

Discover the South-Central Adirondacks—McMartin, Barbara. Woodstock, VT: Backcountry Publications, 1986.

Discover the South Western Adirondacks—McMartin, Barbara. Woodstock, VT: Backcountry Publications, 1987.

Discover the Southern Adirondacks—McMartin, Barbara. Woodstock, VT: Backcountry Publications, 1988.

Discover the West-Central Adirondacks—McMartin, Barbara. Woodstock, VT: Backcountry Publications, 1988.

Fifty Hikes in the Adirondacks—McMartin, Barbara. Woodstock, VT: Backcountry Publications, 1988.

Fifty Hikes in Central New York—Ehling, William P. Woodstock, VT: Backcountry Publications, 1984.

Fifty Hikes in the Hudson River Valley—McMartin, Barbara & Kick, Peter. Woodstock, VT: Backcountry Publications, 1985.

Guide to Adirondack Trails: Central Region—Wadsworth, Bruce. Adirondack Mountain Club, 1986.

Guide to Adirondack Trails: Eastern Region—Tisdale, Betsy. Adirondack Mountain Club.

Guide to Adirondack Trails: High Peaks Region—Goodwin, Tony. Adirondack Mountain Club, 1985.

Guide to Adirondack Trails: Northern Region—O'Shea, Peter. Adirondack Mountain Club, 1986.

Guide to Adirondack Trails: Northville–Placid Trail—Wadsworth, Bruce. Adirondack Mountain Club, 1986.

Guide to Adirondack Trails: Southern Region—Laing, Linda. Adirondack Mountain Club.

Guide to Adirondack Trails: West-Central Region—Haberl, Arthur. Adirondack Mountain Club, 1987.

Guide to the Appalachian Trail in New York and New Jersey—Harpers Ferry, WV: Appalachian Trail Conference, 1988.

Guide to the Long Path—New York–New Jersey Trail Conference, 1987.

Guide to Catskill Trails—Wadsworth, Bruce. Adirondack Mountain Club.

Guide to the Catskills—Adams, Arthur, Coco, Roger, Greenman, Harriet & Leon. Walking News Inc., 1975.

Hiking the Catskills—McAllister, Lee & Ochman, Myron S. New York–New Jersey Trail Conference, 1989.

New York Walk Book—New York–New Jersey Trail Conference. Garden City: Anchor Books, 1984.

HIKING MAPS

Adirondack Mountain Club, RR #3, Box 3055, Lake George, NY 12845. This major club publishes maps of the Adirondacks.

New York–New Jersey Trail Conference, 232 Madison Ave., #908, New York, NY 10016. This trail organization publishes maps of the major hiking areas of downstate New York.

Walking News Maps, P.O. Box 352, New York, NY 10013. Another series of maps for hiking areas in southeastern New York.

New York State Atlas & Gazetteer—Freeport, ME: DeLorme Mapping Co., 1988.

TRAIL INFORMATION

New York–New Jersey Trail Conference, 232 Madison Avenue, #908, New York, NY 10016. (212) 685-9699.

INFORMATION ABOUT STATE PARKS

New York State Office of Parks and Recreation,

Empire State Plaza, Albany, NY 12238; (518) 474-0456.

STATE HIGHWAY MAP AND TRAVEL INFORMATION

New York State Division of Tourism, One Commerce Plaza, Albany, NY 12245; (518)474-4116/ (800)CALL NYS.

CLUBS AND OTHER ORGANIZATIONS WHICH OFFER HIKES

Adirondack 46ers, RFD 1, Box 390, Morrisonville, NY 12962.

Adirondack Mountain Club, P.O. Box 2116, Albany, NY 12220.

Adirondack Mountain Club, c/o Robin Geller, 48-05 42 Street, #6F, Sunnyside, NY 11104.

Adirondack Mountain Club, P.O. Box 172, Yaphank, NY 11980.

Adirondack Mountain Club, P.O. Box 604, Billings, NY 12510.

Adirondack Mountain Club, c/o Ruthanne Dhuse, 40 James Street, #10, Ossining, NY, 10562.

Adirondack Mountain Club, c/o Mary Kelly, 70-25 67th Street, Glendale, NY 11385.

Adirondack Mountain Club, c/o Aaron Schoenberg, 15 Mt. View Drive, Warwick, NY 10990.

Adirondack Mountain Club, P.O. Box 733, Schenectady, NY 12301.

Adirondack Mountain Club, P.O. Box 188, Otego, NY 13825.

American Youth Hostels, 891 Amsterdam Avenue, New York, NY 10025.

Appalachian Mountain Club, c/o Don Meltz, RD 3, Box 75A3, Hudson, NY 12534.

Appalachian Mountain Club, 202 East 39 Street, New York, NY 10016.

Catskill 3500 Club, c/o Cy Whitney, 41 Morley Drive, Wyckoff, NJ 07481.

Chinese Mountain Club of New York, c/o George Li, 956 Lincoln Avenue, Piscataway, NJ 08854.

College Alumni Hiking Club, c/o E.E. Weitz, 290 Ninth Avenue, #13D, New York, NY 10001.

Frost Valley YMCA Trailwalkers, c/o Cherryl

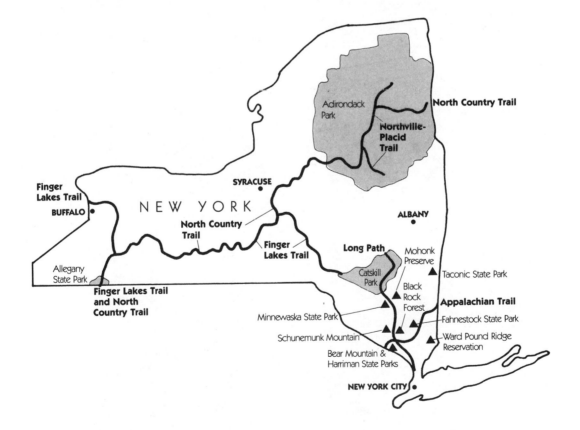

NEW YORK

Short, 102 Passaic Valley Road, Montville, NJ 07045.

Genessee Valley Hiking Club, 94 Sunset Trail West, Fairport, NY 14450.

German–American Hiking Club, c/o Elfi Woschitz, 1577 Third Avenue, New York, NY 10128.

Green Mountain Club, c/o Val Cutajar, 13 Nassau Avenue, Plainview, NY 11803.

Long Island Greenbelt Trail Conference, 23 Deer Path Road, Central Islip, NY 11722.

Nassau Hiking and Outdoor Club, Box 104, Valley Stream, NY 11580.

New York Hiking Club, c/o Leo Tamari, 175 West 73 Street, New York, NY 10023.

New York Ramblers, c/o Don Stevens, 4 Washington Square Village, New York, NY 10012.

Outdoor Bound, 18 Stuyvesant Oval, #1A, New York, NY 10009.

Outdoors Club, P.O. Box 227, New York, NY 10021.

Shorewalkers, P.O. Box 20748, New York, NY 10025.

Sierra Club, Empire State Plaza, Box 2112, Albany, NY 12220.

Sierra Club, P.O. Box 880, New York, NY 10024.

Sierra Club, P.O. Box 1012, Poughkeepsie, NY 12602.

Suffern Historical Hikers, c/o Gardner Watts, 15 Beech Road, Suffern, NY 10901.

Taconic Hiking Club, c/o Willard Hoyt, RD 1, Box 298A, Nassau, NY 12123.

Taconic Hiking Club, 810 Church Street Extension, Troy, NY 12180.

Urban Trail Conference, P.O. Box 264, New York, NY 10274.

Valley Stream Hiking Club, 111 East Euclid Street, Valley Stream, NY 11580.

Westchester Trails Association, c/o Sandra Harrison, 10 Franklin Avenue, #1A, White Plains, NY 10601.

Wilderness Trips with Charlie Cook, P.O. Box 655, Pomona, NY 10970.

NORTH CAROLINA

North Carolina stands out among the eastern states in providing especially rich resources for hiking, with over 2,400 miles of trails. Public lands here include four National Forests, two National Seashores, and a spectacular National Park. Many state parks also have trail systems. The majority of trails and natural tracts lie in the wilder western region, where you find the most awe-inspiring scenery in the state and the highest of all mountains in the eastern United States.

MAJOR TRAILS

APPALACHIAN TRAIL—302 miles in North Carolina (2,100 total). For two-thirds of its distance here the Appalachian Trail follows the lofty mountainous North Carolina–Tennessee border, remaining on National Forest land and passing through Great Smoky Mountains National Park. This is one of the most spectacular sections of the Appalachian Trail, and also one of the most challenging. There are many magnificent views, some from open grassy "balds." The highest elevation of the entire trail is here at Clingman's Dome (6,643 feet). Difficulty is moderate to very strenuous. Trail information: Appalachian Trail Conference, P.O. Box 807, Harpers Ferry, NY 25425.

BARTRAM TRAIL—81 miles in North Carolina. This trail traces the approximate route taken by early naturalist William Bartram. If and when it is completed, the total length could eventually be 2,500 miles. Other sections are open in Georgia and South Carolina. In North Carolina the trail is broken in places by private properties, and includes some road walking. Difficulty varies from moderate to strenuous. There are some superb views along the way. Trail information: North Carolina Bartram Trail Society, 20 Eagle Ridge Drive, Highlands, NC 28741.

MOUNTAINS-TO-SEA TRAIL—This trail is currently under construction and will be over 700 miles long when completed, running the length of North Carolina from Clingman's Dome in Great Smoky Mountains National Park to Cape Hatteras National Seashore. About 250 miles are now finished. Many pre-existing trails are utilized, and some of the scenery is splendid. Difficulty varies from easy to strenuous. Trail information: Division of Parks and Recreation, 512 North Salisbury Street, Raleigh, NC 27611.

BEST HIKING AREAS

GREAT SMOKY MOUNTAINS NATIONAL PARK—Gatlinburg, TN 37738; (615)436-5615. 520,004 acres (275,895 in North Carolina). This is undoubtedly the most magnificent National Park in the East. It's also the most heavily visited in the entire country, and one of the largest. Half of the park is in Tennessee. There are 16 moun-

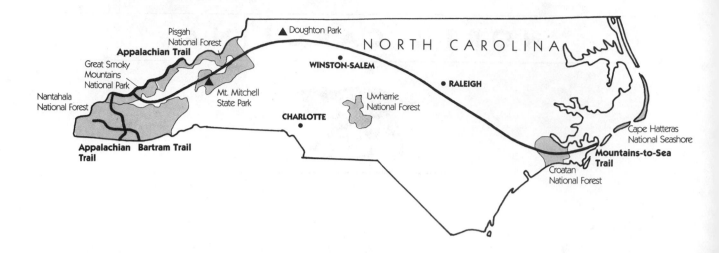

tains over 6,000 feet, including Clingman's Dome (6,643 feet), second highest in the East. There are great expanses of rugged wilderness, and an unmatched variety of flora and fauna.

In the park are mixed hardwood and conifer forests, with major stands of virgin trees, along with rhododendron, mountain laurel and flame azalea. Black bear, deer, wild boar, mountain lions, bobcat, and fox are among the wildlife.

There are over 850 miles of hiking trails, including 68 miles of the Appalachian Trail, which follows the high and rugged ridge crest and offers wonderful views. Numerous other trails run alongside rivers and creeks, with many waterfalls. Trail difficulty varies from very easy to extremely strenuous.

NANTAHALA NATIONAL FOREST—100 Otis Street, P.O. Box 2750, Asheville, NC 28802; (704) 257-4200. 517,436 acres. Situated in the mountainous southwestern corner of the state, this is an extraordinarily beautiful National Forest, and North Carolina's largest. It's a landscape of splendid high mountains (elevations up to 6,000 feet) and deep gorges, with lakes, ponds, and scores of waterfalls, including 411-foot White-water Falls, highest in the East. A number of magnificent rivers are located here, among them the Chattooga National Wild and Scenic River.

Many of the higher mountains, including

some "balds," have spectacular views. Terrain is often rugged. There are three wilderness areas, including the 14,000-acre Joyce Kilmer/Slickrock Wilderness, with some virgin forest. More than 450 miles of hiking trails extend through this National Forest. Among them is the 81-mile Bartram Trail and nearly 90 miles of the Appalachian Trail. Difficulty ranges from easy to very strenuous.

PISGAH NATIONAL FOREST—100 Otis Street, P.O. Box 2750, Asheville, NC 28802; (704)257-4200. 495,979 acres. Located northeast of Nantahala National Forest in western North Carolina, Pisgah is the other outstanding National Forest in the state. It too is a spectacular area, with countless creeks and waterfalls, canyons and cliffs, and grassy bald mountains with superb vistas. The diverse forests here include hardwoods as well as pine and spruce, with thickets of rhododendron and mountain laurel. Among the wildlife are black bear, deer, bobcat, and fox.

There are three wilderness areas. Some of the terrain is especially rugged and remote. Over 550 miles of trails are found here, including the challenging 30-mile Art Loeb Trail and a portion of the Appalachian Trail. Difficulty varies from easy to very strenuous.

UWHARRIE NATIONAL FOREST—100 Otis Street, P.O. Box 2750, Asheville, NC 28802; (704)257-4200. 46,888 acres. Uwharrie National Forest in central North Carolina has low mountains and hills with some nice views, a host of creeks, and one wilderness area. There are pine and hardwood forests, and deer among the wildlife. More than 50 miles of trails are found here, including the 20-mile Uwharrie National Recreation Trail. Difficulty ranges from easy to strenuous.

CROATAN NATIONAL FOREST—100 Otis Street, P.O. Box 2750, Asheville, NC 28802; (704)257-4200. 157,054 acres. Bordered by several rivers along the eastern coast of North Carolina, Croatan National Forest is a relatively flat region of pine and hardwood forests, bogs, and cypress swamps. There are also some streams and several lakes, with wildlife including deer, bear, and bobcat. The forest has 28 miles of trails, foremost of which is the 22-mile Neusiok Trail. Difficulty ranges from easy to moderate.

MOUNT MITCHELL STATE PARK Route 5, Box 700, Burnsville, NC 28714; (704)675-4611. 1,469 acres. This state park is surrounded by Pisgah National Forest in western North Carolina. The centerpiece is 6,684-foot Mount Mitchell, highest mountain in the eastern United States. It's an area of pine, spruce, fir and hardwood forests, with some virgin stands. There are also meadows along with streams and waterfalls.

The park has 18 miles of trails, plus additional paths leading into Pisgah National Forest, with superb views from a mountaintop observation tower. Trail difficulty varies from easy to strenuous.

DOUGHTON PARK—Blue Ridge Parkway, Bluffs District, Route 1, Box 263, Laurel Springs, NC 28644; (919)372-8568. Located on national lands along the Blue Ridge Parkway in northwest North Carolina, Doughton Park includes steep mountain slopes with lovely views, meadows and forests, streams and waterfalls—and over 30 miles of easy to strenuous hiking trails.

CAPE HATTERAS NATIONAL SEASHORE—Route 1, Box 675, Manteo, NC 27954; (919)473-2113. 30,318 acres. This National Seashore is a string of barrier islands along the Atlantic coast, with beautiful beaches and dunes. Vegetation is diverse, with wild palms and beach plants, forested areas, and wildlife including deer. An unmarked 76-mile Beach Trail runs the length of the seashore.

NORTH CAROLINA HIKING RESOURCES

HIKING GUIDEBOOKS

Guide to the Appalachian Trail in North Carolina and Georgia—Harpers Ferry, WV: The Appalachian Trail Conference, 1989.

Guide to the Appalachian Trail in Tennessee and North Carolina—Harpers Ferry, WV: The Appalachian Trail Conference, 1989.

Hiker's Guide to the Smokies—Murlless, Dick, and Stallings, Constance. San Francisco: Sierra Club Books.

Hiking in the Great Smokies—Carson, Brewer. Holston Printing Co.

Hiking Trails of Joyce Kilmer–Slickrock & Citico Creek Wilderness Areas—Homan, Tim. Atlanta: Peachtree Publishers, 1990.

North Carolina Hiking Trails—de Hart, Allen. Boston: Appalachian Mountain Club Books, 1988.

100 Favorite Trails of the Great Smokies and Carolina Blue Ridge—Carolina Mountain Club.

INFORMATION ABOUT STATE PARKS

North Carolina Division of Parks and Recreation, 512 North Salisbury Street, Raleigh, NC 27611; (919)733-4181.

HIGHWAY MAP AND TRAVEL INFORMATION

North Carolina Division of Travel and Tourism, 430 North Salisbury Street, Raleigh, NC 27611; (800)VISIT-NC.

TRAIL INFORMATION

North Carolina Trails Association, P.O. Box 1033, Greensboro, NC 27402; (919)855-9399.

Carolina American Youth Hostels, P.O. Box 10766, Winston-Salem, NC 27108.

Carolina Mountain Club, P.O. Box 68, Asheville, NC 28802.

Nantahala Hiking Club, 31 Carl Slagle Road, Franklin, NC 28734.

Piedmont Appalachian Trail Hikers, P.O. Box 945, Greensboro, NC 27402.

Sierra Club, c/o Bill Thomas, P.O. Box 272, Cedar Mountain, NC 28718.

NORTH DAKOTA

North Dakota's attractive natural scenery ranges from rolling prairies and little forests to high buttes and bluffs, and barren badlands. While state parks and forests are relatively small in size and number here, offering mostly limited hiking on short trails, some abundant and exceptional hiking is available in Theodore Roosevelt National Park. With a major section of the North Country Trail soon to be stretching across much of the state, North Dakota is now becoming an increasingly attractive destination for hikers.

MAJOR TRAILS

NORTH COUNTRY TRAIL—This important new National Scenic Trail is currently under construction. When completed it will run about 435 miles in North Dakota. The western terminus of the 3,200-mile trail is at the Missouri River, in the west-central part of the state. It will follow the Sheyenne River for some distance, and the longest segment now open traverses the 71,000-acre Sheyenne National Grasslands in the southeast corner of the state. Trail information: North Country National Scenic Trail, P.O. Box 5463, Madison, WI 53705.

BEST HIKING AREAS

THEODORE ROOSEVELT NATIONAL PARK—Medora, ND 58645; (701)623-4466. 70,000 acres.

Theodore Roosevelt National Park consists of two separate units located in the western part of the state. Twenty-eight thousand acres of the park have wilderness status. Included is some fine and often colorful badlands scenery—with many buttes and mesas, canyons, a petrified forest, and the scenic Little Missouri River.

The area has extensive grasslands and stands of juniper, along with sage, yucca, and cactus. Bison, wild horse, and prairie dog are among the wildlife here. There are 85 miles of hiking trails, which are also open to horseback riding.

OTHER RECOMMENDED LOCATIONS

LITTLE MISSOURI STATE PARK—c/o Lake Sakakawea State Park, Box 832, Riverdale, ND 58565; (701)487-3315. 5,748 acres. This state park is situated in the badlands of west-central North Dakota, next to Little Missouri Bay on Lake Sakakawea. It's a wild area with vegetation including juniper and cedar, yucca and cactus. Mule deer, coyote, bobcat, and fox are among the wildlife. There are about 75 miles of trails, which are open to horseback riding as well as hiking.

TURTLE MOUNTAIN STATE FOREST—Box 21A, Bottineau, ND 58318; (701)228-3700. 7,494 acres. Located in the Turtle Mountains of northern North Dakota, along the Canadian border, this state forest has a network of several maintained hiking trails. There are a number of small lakes here, and the wildlife includes white-tailed deer, moose, coyote, and fox.

NORTH DAKOTA HIKING RESOURCES

INFORMATION ABOUT STATE PARKS, FORESTS, AND PRESERVES
North Dakota Parks and Recreation Department, 1424 West Century Avenue, Suite 202, Bismarck, ND 58501; (701)224-4887.

STATE HIGHWAY MAP AND TRAVEL INFORMATION
North Dakota Tourism Promotion, Liberty Memorial Building, State Capitol Grounds, Bismarck, ND 58505; 1(800)437-2077 (out of state); 1(800)472-2100 (in state).

NORTH DAKOTA HIKING CLUBS
Sierra Club, P.O. Box 1624, Rapid City, SD 57709.

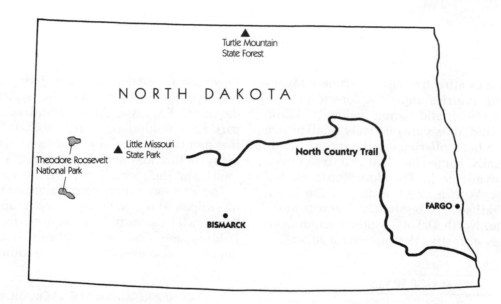

OHIO

Wilderness is rather scarce in Ohio, but there's nevertheless a surprising amount of hiking available in this densely populated state. Many parks and forests have nice trail networks, and Wayne National Forest contains some sizable expanses of attractive natural lands. Most impressive is the ambitious 1,100-mile Buckeye Trail which now encircles Ohio, offering interesting hikes from a host of vantage points throughout the state.

MAJOR TRAILS

THE BUCKEYE TRAIL—1,100 miles. This long and noteworthy trail loops around the entire state of Ohio. It's not a wilderness trail, with some portions following roads and open to bicycling and horseback riding. At other times it's a footpath, leading through scenic state parks, forests, and other natural areas. Substantial sections are on private land. Changes in elevation are minimal, and much of the trail is easy. Trail information: Buckeye Trail Association, P.O. Box 254, Worthington, OH 43085.

NORTH COUNTRY TRAIL—When finished, the Ohio section of this 3,200-mile National Scenic Trail will run about 700 miles. For most of its route here the North Country Trail coincides with the Buckeye Trail, circling through the lower part of the state. The scenery includes some beautiful rivers, rocky bluffs, and the appealing woods of Wayne National Forest. Trail information: North Country Trail Association, P.O. Box 311, White Cloud, MI 49349.

BEST HIKING AREAS

WAYNE NATIONAL FOREST—3527 10th Street, Bedford, IN 47421; (812)275-5987. 178,000 acres. Consisting of four separate tracts, this hilly National Forest is located on the Allegheny Plateau in southeastern Ohio, with some sections bordering on the Ohio River. It's a landscape of sometimes rugged hills and low ridges, with rock shelters, caves, outcrops, and a natural sandstone bridge.

There are lakes and small streams here, and hardwood forests of oak and hickory, with cedar and pine—plus meadows with wildflowers, and wildlife including deer. Over 50 miles of hiking trails are found here, in addition to a segment of the Buckeye/North Country Trail, which will eventually extend 60 miles through the forest. Most trails are easy to moderate in difficulty.

SHAWNEE STATE FOREST—Route 5, Box 151C, Portsmouth, OH 45662; (614)858-6685. 60,000 acres. This is Ohio's largest state forest, situated along the southern border of the state just north of the Ohio River. About 8,000 acres are maintained as wilderness. It's an area of

North Country Trail

CLEVELAND

Buckeye Trail

Buckeye Trail

North Country Trail

North Country Trail

OHIO

COLUMBUS

Hocking Hills State Park

Little Miami Scenic Park

Caesar Creek State Park

Great Seal State Park

Burr Oak State Park

Zaleski State Forest

Wayne National Forest

CINCINNATI

East Fork State Park

Buckeye Trail

Shawnee State Forest

Wayne National Forest

rolling ridges and ravines, with many streams. Some of the terrain is rugged.

In the region one finds forests of oak and hickory, pine and maple, with wildlife including deer. There are 60 miles of hiking trails, including the beautiful 43-mile Shawnee Backpack Trail, which forms a giant loop. Difficulty varies from easy to strenuous.

OTHER RECOMMENDED LOCATIONS

EAST FORK STATE PARK—P.O. Box 119, Bethel, OH 45106; (513)734-4323. 10,580 acres. This state park in southwestern Ohio has rolling hills, steep ravines, small prairies, and a 2,160-acre lake. There are oak-hickory forests, deer, and over 60 miles of hiking trails. A section of

the Buckeye Trail passes through the park. Some trails are open to horseback riding.

CAESAR CREEK STATE PARK—8570 East S.R. 73, Waynesville, OH 45068; (513)897-3055. 10,771 acres. Situated in southwestern Ohio, Caesar Creek State Park is in an area of rolling hills with oak-hickory forests, meadows, and deep ravines. There's also a large lake, nice views, and over 30 miles of trails, including a section of the Buckeye Trail. Difficulty varies from easy to moderate.

BURR OAK STATE PARK—Route 2, Box 286, Glouster, OH 45732; (614)466-0652. 2,592 acres. Located in southeast Ohio, adjacent to Wayne National Forest, this state park has hilly terrain with some rock outcrops and caves, oak-hickory forests and open meadows—plus nice views, and beautiful Burr Oak Lake. Wildlife includes white-tailed deer, fox, and wild turkey. The major trail here is the 29-mile Burr Oak Trail, which loops around the lake. Part of the route is also utilized by the Buckeye Trail.

ZALESKI STATE FOREST—Zaleski, OH 45698; (614)596-5781. 26,313 acres. Located in the southern part of the state, Zaleski is Ohio's second largest state forest. There are streams and a lake here, with hardwoods and mixed conifer forest. The main trail here is the scenic 23-mile Zaleski Backpack Trail. Difficulty varies from easy to strenuous.

GREAT SEAL STATE PARK—825 Rocky Road, Chillicothe, OH 45601; (614)773-2726. 1,864 acres. This southern Ohio state park is in an area of rolling hills, some of them steep, and includes fine views. There are 20 miles of trails, many of which are also open to horseback riding. Difficulty varies from easy to strenuous.

HOCKING HILLS STATE PARK—20160 S.R. 664, Logan, OH 43138; (614)385-6841. 1,943 acres. Located in south-central Ohio, Hocking Hills State Park has forested hills, steep hemlock-filled gorges with sandstone cliffs, and enormous aboveground caves. There are some beautiful waterfalls and over 20 miles of trails, including a section of the Buckeye Trail.

LITTLE MIAMI SCENIC PARK—8570 East S.R. 73, Waynesville, OH 45068; (513)897-3055. 452 acres. This is a narrow corridor along the Little Miami River with a 50-mile multi-use trail, which follows an old railroad bed. The trail is open to horseback riding, with segments open to cycling. It passes through areas of rolling hardwood-forested hills, and past some steep cliffs and gorges.

OHIO HIKING RESOURCES

HIKING GUIDEBOOKS

Backpack Loops and Long Day Trail Hikes in Southern Ohio—Ruchhoft, Robert H. Cincinnati, OH: The Pucelle Press, 1984.
Fifty Hikes in Ohio—Ramey, Ralph. Woodstock, VT: The Countryman Press, 1990.

MAPS

Ohio Atlas & Gazetteer—Freeport, ME: DeLorme Mapping Co.

INFORMATION ABOUT STATE PARKS AND FORESTS

Ohio Department of Natural Resources, Division of Parks and Recreation, Fountain Square, Bldg C-1, Columbus, OH 43224; (614)265-7000.

HIGHWAY MAP AND TRAVEL INFORMATION

Ohio Office of Travel and Tourism, 30 East Broad Street, 25th Floor, Columbus, OH 43215; (800)BUCKEYE.

CLUBS AND OTHER ORGANIZATIONS WHICH OFFER HIKES

Akron Metro Parks Hiking Club, 3415 21st Street, N.W., Canton, OH 44708.
Central Ohio Hiking Club, c/o YMCA, 40 West Long Street, Columbus, OH 42215.
Cleveland Hiking Club, c/o Emily Gregor, 6502 Olde York Road, Cleveland, OH 44130.
Cuyahoga Trails Council, 1607 Delia, Akron, OH 44320.
Sierra Club, 145 North High Street, Columbus, OH 43215.

OKLAHOMA

Oklahoma is much better known for horseback riding than for hiking, but there are nonetheless some fine foot trails to be found throughout the great plains and mountains of this state. The few longer trails and most extensive wild areas are located primarily in the eastern and southeastern parts of the state, where numerous mountain ranges, large lakes, and some dense forests with diverse vegetation offer an appealing landscape for hiking.

MAJOR TRAILS

JEAN-PIERRE CHOUTEAU TRAIL—60 miles. This National Recreation Trail is Oklahoma's longest hiking trail. It runs alongside the McClellan–Kerr Navigation Channel (which consists of rivers and canals) from Catoosa to Fort Gibson, in the northeastern part of the state. The trail is flat and easy, passing through wooded areas as well as grasslands. Some segments of the trail are open to horseback riding. Trail information: Tulsa District, Corps of Engineers, P.O. Box 61, Tulsa, OK 74121.

There are several 15- to 25-mile hiking trails in Oklahoma which connect state, federal, and other lands. Further information about these trails is available from the Oklahoma Tourism and Recreation Department, 500 Will Rogers Building, Oklahoma City, OK 73105.

BEST HIKING AREAS

OUACHITA NATIONAL FOREST—P.O. Box 1270, Hot Springs, AR 71901; (501)321-5202. Most of this major National Forest is situated in Arkansas, but a small yet significant segment is in southeastern Oklahoma. It's a region of mountain ridges and valleys with some rugged terrain, streams and small lakes, beautiful vistas, and forests of oak and pine.

The Oklahoma section of Ouachita National Forest has two wilderness areas, along with the 41,000-acre Indian Nations Wildlife and Scenic Area. There are over 40 miles of hiking trails, including a section of the scenic 225-mile Ouachita National Recreation Trail, which continues into Arkansas and runs the length of the Forest.

U.S. ARMY CORPS OF ENGINEERS—TULSA DISTRICT—Box 61, Tulsa, OK 74121; (918)581-7349. A number of trails are found on U.S. Army Corps of Engineers lands in Oklahoma. Included are parts of the 60-mile Jean-Pierre Chouteau National Recreation Trail, the 18-mile Will Rogers Country Centennial Trail, and the 15-mile Elk River Trail. The area includes many lakes, prairie grasslands, forests of oak and hickory, and wildlife including deer.

BEAVERS BEND STATE PARK—P.O. Box 10, Broken Bow, OK 74728; (405)494-6300. 3,500 acres. This state park and adjacent Hochatown

State Park are situated next to Broken Bow Reservoir in the southeast corner of Oklahoma. It's a wild area with small mountains, some creeks, and wildlife including white-tailed deer and fox. Along with some short trails there's the hilly 24-mile David Boren Trail, which extends the length of the two parks.

U.S. ARMY CORPS OF ENGINEERS—LAKE TEXOMA—Texoma Project office, P.O. Box 60, Cartwright, OK 74731; (903)465-4990. Adjacent to Lake Texoma in southern Oklahoma, these lands include meadows and oak-hickory woodlands, with fine views of the lake from rocky ledges. Wildlife includes deer and coyote. The

24-mile Platter–Lakeside Trail is located here (open to horseback riding as well as hiking) along with the 14-mile Cross Timbers Trail.

OKLAHOMA HIKING RESOURCES

TRAIL INFORMATION, TRAVEL INFORMATION, AND STATE HIGHWAY MAP

Oklahoma Tourism and Recreation Department, 500 Will Rogers Building, Oklahoma City, OK 73105; (405)521-2409 or (800)652-6552.

OKLAHOMA HIKING CLUBS

Sierra Club, c/o Karin Derichsweiler, 312 Keith, Norman, OK 73069.

OREGON

Oregon offers outstanding hiking amid a landscape which includes high mountains, desert, and beautiful Pacific Ocean coastline, much of it in a relatively natural state. Public lands are extremely extensive, with thirteen National Forests, one National Park, and one National Scenic Area. The dominant Cascade Range extends the length of west-central Oregon, with some elevations over ten thousand feet. Here, as well as in the Coast Range and the mountains of the northeast, one finds an enormous variety of trails and a wonderful range of spectacular wilderness scenery.

MAJOR TRAILS

PACIFIC CREST TRAIL—462 miles in Oregon (2,638 total). This unusually beautiful and rugged high-mountain trail enters the state from California and crosses Oregon's Cascades. It traverses several National Forests along with Crater Lake National Park, continuing to the Columbia River at the Washington border. There's some wonderfully remote scenery, with magnificent views. Horseback riding is permitted along with hiking. Parts of the trail are snow-free only during August and September. Difficulty ranges from easy to very strenuous. Trail information: Pacific Crest Trail Conference, 365 West 29th Avenue, Eugene, OR 97405.

OREGON COAST TRAIL—360 miles. This major trail, still under construction, runs the length of Oregon's coast from the Columbia River to the California border. The trail is over three-quarters finished and open. For considerable stretches it's a beach trail, and at other times it travels inland. The trail passes through numerous state parks, and also some towns and developed areas, with stretches of road walking. There's a lot of spectacular coastal scenery along the way. Trail information: Trails Coordinator, Oregon State Parks, 525 Trade Street S.E., Salem, OR 97310.

NORTH UMPQUA TRAIL—This new trail will run about 77 miles when completed. Portions are open. It follows alongside the beautiful North Umpqua River in southwest Oregon for the entire length, mostly on Umpqua National Forest and BLM lands. It also connects with the Pacific Crest Trail. Most of the trail is easy to moderate in difficulty, with a couple of steep stretches. It's open to mountain bikers and horseback riders as well as hikers. Trail information: Umpqua National Forest, P.O. Box 1008, Roseburg, OR 97470.

BEST HIKING AREAS

WALLOWA–WHITMAN NATIONAL FOREST—P.O. Box 907, Baker, OR 97814; (503)523-6391. 2,383,159 acres. Consisting of two enormous tracts in northeast Oregon and extending into Idaho, Wallowa–Whitman National Forest en-

compasses beautifully rugged terrain of the Blue and Wallowa Mountains. Elevations range from under 1,000 feet to 9,845 feet (The Matterhorn). There are four wilderness areas, including the 358,000-acre Eagle Cap Wilderness. Also here is much of the 652,000-acre Hells Canyon National Recreation Area, which is on both sides of the Snake River (a National Wild and Scenic River), and encloses a 7000-foot deep river canyon.

The region has snow-covered peaks of granite and limestone/marble, steep ridges and glaciated valleys, sheer rock walls and deep gorges, talus slopes and glaciers—and wonderful panoramic views. There are many high lakes and streams, some outstanding rivers, lush open meadows with wildflowers, forests of ponderosa pine and Douglas fir, spruce and larch, and alpine vegetation. Wildlife includes elk, mule deer, bighorn sheep, mountain goat, coyote, and cougar.

This National Forest currently has 2,070 miles of hiking trails. Many are open to horses. Difficulty varies from easy to strenuous. Most high trails are snow-free from July through October.

WILLAMETTE NATIONAL FOREST—P.O. Box 10607, 211 East 7th Avenue, Eugene, OR 97440; (503)687-6521. 1,675,407 acres. Willamette National Forest is located in the western Cascades of west-central Oregon. The glaciated landscape here includes major (often snow-covered) mountain peaks and volcanoes, with rock outcroppings and pinnacles, talus slopes and lava fields, craters and cinder cones. Among the many glaciers is Collier Glacier, Oregon's largest.

There are 8 wilderness areas totaling 380,000 acres, including the 283,000-acre Three Sisters Wilderness and the 111,000-acre Mount Jefferson Wilderness—which is dominated by 10,495-foot Mount Jefferson, highest in the forest. The area also has high meadows, river canyons with two Wild and Scenic Rivers, scores of streams, waterfalls, and hundreds of lakes.

Much of the region is forested with Douglas fir (including old-growth stands) and silver fir, lodgepole and ponderosa pine, cedar and hemlock. Among the local wildlife are Roosevelt elk,

black-tailed and mule deer, black bear, coyote, and cougar.

Over 1,400 miles of hiking trails extend through this National Forest, including a 100-mile section of the Pacific Crest Trail, plus the 27-mile McKensie River National Recreation Trail. Difficulty ranges from easy to strenuous.

MOUNT HOOD NATIONAL FOREST—2955 N.W. Division Street, Gresham, OR 97030; (503)666-0771. 1,060,253 acres. Located east of Portland in the Cascades of northern Oregon, this mountainous National Forest includes 11,235-foot Mount Hood, along with other high peaks. The terrain is often rugged, with rock pinnacles and outcrops, precipitous cliffs and rock slides, open ridges and saddles, cinder cones with lava dikes, glaciers and canyons.

There are several wilderness areas totaling over 187,000 acres, and many beautiful views—plus numerous alpine lakes, creeks with waterfalls, and major rivers. Vegetation includes high alpine meadows with flowers, dense conifer forests of Douglas fir, mountain hemlock, and silver fir, as well as hardwoods, with some old-growth stands. Among the wildlife here are black-tailed and mule deer, elk, black bear, mountain lion, mountain goat, and bobcat.

Mount Hood National Forest has over 1,100 miles of hiking trails, easy to strenuous in difficulty. Many trails are open to horses. A section of the Pacific Crest Trail passes through the forest. The highest trails are snow-free only from mid-July through September.

UMATILLA NATIONAL FOREST—2517 S.W. Hailey Avenue, Pendleton, OR 97801; (503)276-3811. 1,088,197 acres in Oregon (1,399,342 total). Umatilla National Forest consists of three tracts of land in the Blue Mountains of northeast Oregon, extending into southeast Washington. Elevations range from 1,600 feet to 8,000 feet. Along with mountains there are plateaus and high cliffs, rock outcrops, deep canyons and steep snow ridges, and outstanding views.

The forest has three wilderness areas totaling over 300,000 acres, including the 121,000-acre North Fork John Day Wilderness, and 66,000 acres of the 177,000-acre Wenaha–Tucannon Wilderness (the balance of which is in Washington). There are three Wild and Scenic Rivers, numerous streams and several rivers flowing through valleys, lovely meadows and grasslands—plus forests of Douglas fir and grand fir, ponderosa and lodgepole pine, and western larch. Rocky Mountain elk, white-tailed and mule deer, bighorn sheep, coyote, and mountain lion are among the wildlife.

This National Forest currently has 735 miles of hiking trails. Many are open to horseback riding, and some to motorized vehicles. Difficulty varies from easy to strenuous.

UMPQUA NATIONAL FOREST—P.O. Box 1008, Roseburg, OR 97470; (503)672-6601. 988,149 acres. Umpqua National Forest is located in the western Cascades of southwest Oregon, west and northwest of Crater Lake National Park. The mountainous scenery includes high peaks and basins, steep canyons, cliffs and bluffs, and interesting volcanic rock formations. The forest has three designated wilderness areas, and many spectacular views. Mount Thielson (9,182 feet) is the highest point.

Along with open alpine meadows with wildflowers there are forests of fir and cedar, pine and hemlock, and some hardwoods—with many old-growth Douglas fir trees. Local mammals include mule and black-tailed deer, Roosevelt elk, black bear, mountain lion, coyote, bobcat, and fox. Some small lakes are found here as well, along with a few rivers, many streams, and numerous waterfalls.

Umpqua has about 600 miles of trails, including a 30-mile section of the Pacific Crest Trail. Most trails are open to horses, and some nonwilderness trails to bikes and motorcycles. Difficulty ranges from easy to strenuous.

DESCHUTES NATIONAL FOREST—1645 Highway 20 East, Bend, OR 97701; (503)388-2715. 1,602,809 acres. Located in the eastern Cascades of west-central Oregon, Deschutes National Forest has lofty peaks, glaciers, craters and volcanoes, and some high desert lands. In the region are many streams and over 150 lakes, with

meadows and some old-growth forest. Common trees are ponderosa and lodgepole pine, Douglas fir and spruce.

There are five wilderness areas, including part of the 283,000-acre Three Sisters Wilderness, and six National Wild and Scenic Rivers. Among the local wildlife are elk, mule deer, black bear, and coyote.

Within the National Forest are over 500 miles of hiking trails. A section of the Pacific Crest Trail crosses the forest. Difficulty ranges from easy to strenuous. High trails may only be snow-free from July through September.

ROGUE RIVER NATIONAL FOREST—P.O. Box 520, Medford, OR 97501; (503)776-3579. 638,259 acres. Rogue River National Forest is made up of two tracts in southwest Oregon—on three sides of Crater Lake National Park, plus along the California border and extending into that state. Elevations range from under 3,000 feet to over 9,000 feet. Highest point is 9,495-foot Mount McLoughlin. Among several wilderness areas is a portion of the 116,000-acre Sky Lakes Wilderness, which continues into Winema National Forest.

Scenery here includes prominent peaks and ridges, high cliffs and deep gorges, cirque basins, granite rock formations and massive lava flows, and great open vistas. There are mountain meadows with wildflowers, beargrass, mixed conifer forests with old-growth Douglas fir and some deciduous trees, ponderosa and white pine, cedar and hemlock. Here too are many lakes and creeks, the beautiful Rogue River, and a number of waterfalls including 600-foot Alkali Falls. Elk, mule deer, black bear, mountain lion, coyote, and bobcat are among the wildlife.

This National Forest has over 400 miles of hiking trails, with a section of the Pacific Crest Trail plus the 48-mile Upper Rogue River Trail. Many are open to horses, some to bikes and motorized vehicles. High country trails may only be snow-free from mid-July through September. Difficulty varies from easy to strenuous.

SISKIYOU NATIONAL FOREST—200 N.E. Greenfield Road, P.O. Box 440, Grants Pass, OR

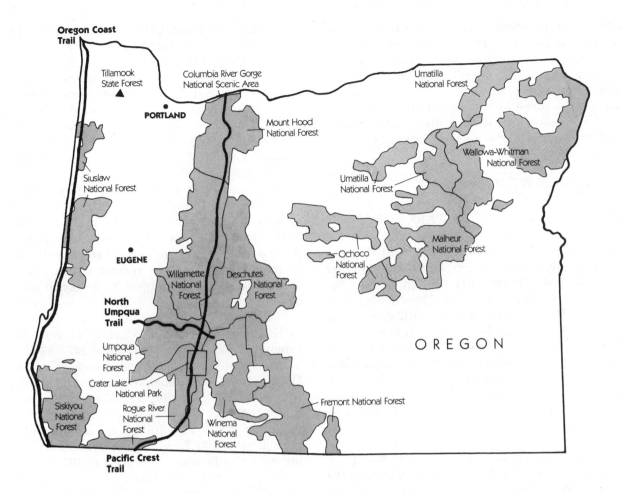

97526; (503)479-5301. 1,093,542 acres. Siskiyou National Forest is situated in the southwest corner of Oregon, encompassing the Siskiyou Mountains, with elevations from 100 feet to 7,055-foot Grayback Mountain. In addition to mountains there are rugged canyons and rocky outcrops, some small lakes, and numerous creeks and rivers, which include the Rogue and Illinois National Wild and Scenic Rivers.

There are five wilderness areas totaling 232,000 acres, and among them is the 178,000-acre Kalmiopsis Wilderness. Vegetation varies from mountain meadows with wildflowers to mixed conifer and hardwood forest, rain forest, and old-growth Douglas fir and redwood. Among the local wildlife are elk, mule deer, black bear, mountain lion, coyote, bobcat, and gray fox.

This National Forest has over 375 miles of hiking trails, including the 40-mile Rogue River Trail and the 27-mile Illinois River Trail. Difficulty varies from easy to strenuous.

MALHEUR NATIONAL FOREST—139 N.E. Dayton Street, John Day, OR 97845; (503)575-1731. 1,458,055 acres. Located in east-central Oregon, Malheur National Forest encloses a portion of the Blue Mountains. The 68,000-acre Strawberry Mountain Wilderness is one of two wilderness areas. The highest point in the forest, 9,038-foot Strawberry Mountain, is located there.

The high country scenery includes alpine

lakes and meadows, many creeks, forests of ponderosa and lodgepole pine along with fir—with some old-growth stands—and grasslands. Among the wildlife are elk, mule deer, bighorn sheep, antelope, mountain lion, and bobcat. Within the forest boundaries are over 200 miles of trails, some of which offer scenic views. Difficulty ranges from easy to strenuous.

OTHER RECOMMENDED LOCATIONS

CRATER LAKE NATIONAL PARK—P.O. Box 7, Crater Lake, OR 97604; (503)594-2211. 183,000 acres. Crater Lake National Park is in the Cascades of southwest Oregon, and centers around six-mile-wide Crater Lake, which lies in the caldera of a collapsed volcano (Mount Mazama). Several mountains are nearby, with most elevations between 6,000 feet and 8,900 feet.

In the park are some old-growth forests of hemlock, pine, and fir. Wildlife includes black bear, elk, coyote, and fox. There are over 100 miles of hiking trails, with a 25-mile section of the Pacific Crest Trail. Most trails are snow-free from July to October.

SIUSLAW NATIONAL FOREST—P.O. Box 1148, Corvallis, OR 97339; (503)750-7000. 630,584 acres. Located along the western coast of Oregon, in the Coast Range, Siuslaw National Forest has elevations from sea level to 4,097 feet (Marys Peak), with some fine views. There are three wilderness areas totaling 22,000 acres. Of special interest in the forest is the Oregon Dunes National Recreation Area, which includes 40 miles of coastline and 14,000 acres of sand dunes, some of which are up to 400 feet high.

The region also has steep slopes and canyons, some lakes and many streams, meadows and dense conifer forests. Elk, deer, bear, and cougar are among the wildlife, with whale, seal, and other marine animals along the coast. There are 100 miles of hiking trails in this National Forest, including a section of the Oregon Coast Trail. Difficulty ranges from easy to strenuous.

WINEMA NATIONAL FOREST—2819 Dahlia Street, Klamath Falls, OR 97601; (503)883-6714. 1,045,003 acres. Located east of Crater Lake National Park in the Cascades of southwest Oregon, and consisting of several tracts of land, Winema National Forest includes some rugged mountainous terrain with a number of peaks and volcanic outcrops, and wonderful vistas. There are two wilderness areas, including part of the 116,000-acre Sky Lakes Wilderness, which continues into Rogue River National Forest.

The region has many small alpine glacial lakes, meadows and streams, and forests of mixed conifers. Among the wildlife are elk, mule deer, black bear, mountain lion, and bobcat. Approximately 100 miles of hiking trails are found here, including a section of the Pacific Crest Trail. Difficulty ranges from easy to strenuous.

OCHOCO NATIONAL FOREST—P.O. Box 490, Prineville, OR 97754; (503)447-6247. 956,877 acres. Situated in the high desert of central Oregon, Ochoco National Forest consists of three tracts of land plus the 111,000-acre Crooked River National Grasslands. It includes rough mountain ridges and rolling hills, with elevations from 2,200 feet to over 7,000 feet. The highest point is Snow Mountain (7,163 feet).

There are three relatively small wilderness areas. Within the region are some steep canyons and cliffs, meadows and streams, ponderosa pine and fir forests with some old-growth trees. Wildlife includes elk, mule deer, wild horse, antelope, and cougar. Currently 86 miles of hiking trails extend through the area, and some offer fine views. Difficulty varies from easy to strenuous.

FREMONT NATIONAL FOREST—524 North G Street, Lakeview, OR 97630; (503)947-2151. 1,196,000 acres. Fremont National Forest is located in the eastern Cascades of south-central Oregon, with some portions along the California border. Elevations range from 4,100 feet to over 8,00 feet, and there's one 22,000-acre wilderness area. Scenery includes mountains and volcanic domes, high cliffs and ridges, rock formations and pinnacles, canyons and desert.

Among the wildlife here are elk, mule deer, antelope, mountain lion, and bobcat. There are forests of ponderosa pine and white fir, and aspen, along with meadows, streams, and some great views. About 77 miles of trails are found here, difficulty ranging from easy to strenuous. Some trails are multi-use.

COLUMBIA RIVER GORGE NATIONAL SCENIC AREA—902 Wasco Avenue, Suite 200, Hood River, OR 97031; (503)386-2333. 285,000 acres. Established in 1986, this National Scenic Area protects the deep canyon of the Columbia River, which runs through the Cascades and forms the Oregon–Washington border. Mount Hood National Forest is adjacent. Not all of it is wild, as it includes some towns and developed areas. Also, the river is dammed and there's an interstate highway close by.

On the edges of the canyon are small mountains and pinnacles with great views, narrow side canyons with steep cliffs, creeks, and high waterfalls. There are many miles of hiking trails in the region, including a section of the Pacific Crest Trail.

TILLAMOOK STATE FOREST—4907 3rd Street, Tillamook, OR 97141. 363,000 acres. Located in northwest Oregon, Tillamook State Forest includes some steep ridges and mountain summits, with panoramic vistas from elevations over 3,000 feet. There are also streams, waterfalls, and forests of Douglas fir, pine, and hemlock. Wild-

life includes mule deer, Roosevelt elk, black bear, and coyote. About 25 miles of trails are found here, easy to strenuous in difficulty. Some trails are open to horses.

OREGON HIKING RESOURCES

HIKING GUIDEBOOKS

50 Hikes in Oregon's Coast Range & Siskiyous—Ostertag, Rhonda & George. Seattle: The Mountaineers, 1989.

Hiking the Bigfoot Country—Hart, John. San Francisco: Sierra Club Books.

Oregon Coast Hikes—Williams, Paul, & Spring, Ira. Seattle: The Mountaineers, 1985.

The Pacific Crest Trail—Volume 2: Oregon & Washington—Schaffer, Jeffrey P., & Selters, Andy. Berkeley: Wilderness Press, 1990.

INFORMATION ABOUT STATE PARKS

Oregon State Parks, 525 Trade Street S.E., Salem, Or 97310; (503)378-5012.

STATE HIGHWAY MAP AND TRAVEL INFORMATION

Oregon Tourism Division, 775 Summer Street N.E., Salem, OR 97310; (800)547-7842 (out of state) / (800)233-3306 (in state).

OREGON HIKING CLUBS

Trails Club of Oregon, P.O. Box 1243, Portland, Or 97207.

Sierra Club, c/o John Albrecht, 3550 Willamette, Eugene, OR 97405.

PENNSYLVANIA

Although it's not widely known for hiking, Pennsylvania actually has the largest trail system in the eastern United States, with an impressive several thousand miles of trails. The terrain is varied and includes high plains and countless mountain ridges. State forest and park lands are unusually extensive here, and many major trails connect these areas. While there are no enormous wilderness areas, some rather remote and ruggedly wild scenery is found in parts of this beautiful state.

MAJOR TRAILS

APPALACHIAN TRAIL—230 miles in Pennsylvania (2,100 total). The Appalachian Trail follows low mountain ridges through southeastern Pennsylvania, crossing from the Alleghenies to the northern Blue Ridge Mountains before reaching Maryland. It passes through some state park and forest lands, and although elevations are rarely over 1,400 feet, there are some nice views along the way. Difficulty varies from easy to strenuous. Trail information: Appalachian Trail Conference, P.O. Box 807, Harpers Ferry, WV 25425.

MASON–DIXON TRAIL—204 miles. This easy but hilly trail runs from southern Pennsylvania through Maryland, into Delaware, and then back into Pennsylvania. It connects with the Horse-Shoe Trail and the Appalachian Trail at each end, and for 65 miles follows the Susquehanna River. The pleasant scenery includes attractive forest and rural countryside. Trail information: Mason–Dixon Trail System, c/o John & Marie Pittenger, 143 Devonshire, Wilmington, DE 19803.

NORTH COUNTRY TRAIL—When completed this major National Scenic Trail will run 3,200 miles, from New York to North Dakota, crossing the northwestern part of Pennsylvania for about 180 miles. The primary portion currently open is the 95-mile segment in Allegheny National Forest. It also follows the Baker Trail. Trail information: North Country Trail Association, P.O. Box 311, White Cloud, MI 49349.

MID STATE TRAIL—168 miles. The Mid State Trail leads through several scenic state forests in central Pennsylvania. Portions are rather wild, but it's rarely far from roads. There are numerous views from narrow rocky ridges, and several side trails which connect with other trails. Difficulty varies from easy to strenuous. Trail information: Mid State Trail Association, P.O. Box 167, Boalsburg, PA 16827.

BAKER TRAIL—140 miles. This scenic trail in western Pennsylvania winds through woodlands, forest, and farm country, and connects with the North Country Trail in Allegheny National Forest. Trail information: Baker Trail

Chairperson, AYH, Pittsburgh Council, 6300 Fifth Avenue, Pittsburgh, PA 15232.

HORSE-SHOE TRAIL—134 miles. This trail in southeastern Pennsylvania is open to hikers as well as horseback riders. It leads from Valley Forge National Historic Park through private and public lands to the Appalachian Trail near Hershey. It also connects with the Mason–Dixon Trail. Trail information: Horse-Shoe Trail Club, c/o Robert L. Chalfant, 509 Cheltena Avenue, Jenkintown, PA 19046.

TUSCARORA TRAIL—105 miles. The Tuscarora Trail in southern Pennsylvania intersects with the Appalachian Trail and leads into Maryland, where it connects with the Big Blue Trail. Some of the terrain is rugged and portions are strenuous. Trail information: Keystone Trails Association, Box 251, Cogan Station, PA 17728.

SUSQUEHANNOCK TRAIL—85 miles. This is a large loop in north-central Pennsylvania's Susquehannock State Forest. Much of the path follows old logging roads and fire trails. It's scenic and relatively easy, and connects with the Black Forest and Donut Hole Trails. Trail information: Susquehannock Trail Club, Box 643, Coudersport, PA 16915.

LAUREL HIGHLANDS HIKING TRAIL—70 miles. Located mostly on public lands in the southwestern part of the state, the Laurel Highlands Trail is one of Pennsylvania's wildest and most scenic trails. Much of the way it follows 2,700-foot Laurel Ridge, with rugged terrain and great views. Difficulty is moderate to strenuous. Trail information: Laurel Ridge State Park, RD 3, Box 246, Rockwood, PA 15557.

WARRIOR TRAIL—67 miles. This is a historic trail, located in the southwest corner of the state. It follows an ancient route used by Indians. Difficulty varies from easy to strenuous. Trail information: Warrior Trail Association, c/o Lucille Phillips, RD 1, Box 35, Spraggs, PA 15362.

LOYALSOCK TRAIL—59 miles. This trail in north-central Pennsylvania leads through some especially scenic and wild country, with numerous streams and waterfalls along the way. The trail travels along mountain ridges and parts are rugged. There are some great views. Difficulty varies from easy to strenuous. Trail information: Alpine Club of Williamsport, P.O. Box 501, Williamsport, PA 17703.

DONUT HOLE TRAIL—56 miles. Located in north-central Pennsylvania, the Donut Hole Trail crosses Sproul State Forest and connects with several other trails. The region is rather wild and remote, and there are some nice views. Trail information: Donut Hole Trail, HCR 62, Box 90, Renovo, PA 07764.

BEST HIKING AREAS

ALLEGHENY NATIONAL FOREST—222 Liberty Street, Box 847, Warren, PA 16365; (814)723-5150. 510,000 acres. Located on the Allegheny Plateau in northwestern Pennsylvania, this sizable National Forest has attractive scenery which includes numerous streams, ponds, and the Allegheny River. The terrain is hilly and occasionally steep.

There are hardwood forests with black cherry and maple, plus pine and hemlock, along with mountain laurel and rhododendron. Wildlife includes white-tailed deer, black bear, and red fox. Within the forest boundaries are over 150 miles of hiking trails, including a 95-mile section of the North Country Trail.

TIADAGHTON STATE FOREST—423 East Central Avenue, South Williamsport, PA 17701; (717)327-3450. 204,600 acres. Located in the north-central part of the state, Tiadaghton State Forest consists of three separate blocks of land on the Allegheny Plateau. This is a region of ridges and valleys, with many streams and waterfalls. There are forests of hardwoods with oak and hemlock, and some wonderful views. Among the wildlife are deer, bobcat, and fox. Over 200 miles of trails are found here, including

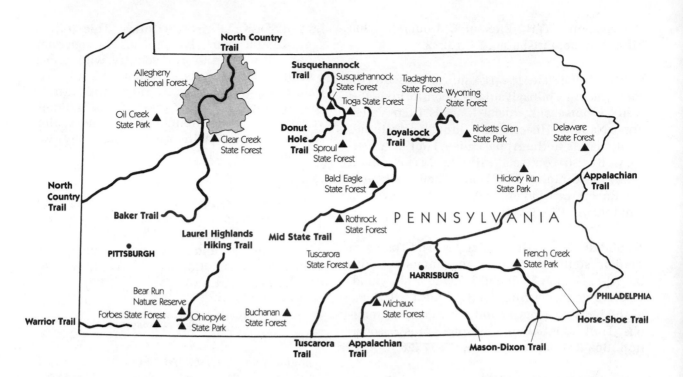

the circular 45-mile Black Forest Trail and 14 miles of the Loyalsock Trail.

TUSCARORA STATE FOREST—RD 1, Box 42A, Blain, PA 17006; (717)536-3191. 90,512 acres. Divided into three tracts in the Tuscarora Mountain area of south-central Pennsylvania, Tuscarora State Forest has oak forests with stands of virgin hemlock, azalea and mountain laurel, and wildlife which includes deer, bear and fox. There are over 200 miles of hiking trails, including a 23-mile section of the Tuscarora Trail.

SPROUL STATE FOREST—HCR 62, Box 90, Renovo, PA 17764; (717)923-1450. 280,000 acres. Sproul is Pennsylvania's largest state forest, located on the Allegheny Plateau in the north-central part of the state. It's a somewhat remote area with major areas of wilderness, elevations to 2,300 feet, and includes rugged terrain along with some more level land.

There are mixed oak forests, and the wildlife includes white-tailed deer, black bear, and bobcat. Among the many trails here are the 56-mile

Donut Hole Trail and the 50-mile Chuck Keiper Trail. Difficulty ranges from easy to strenuous.

SUSQUEHANNOCK STATE FOREST—P.O. Box 673, Coudersport, PA 16915; (814)274-8474. 262,000 acres. This major forest in the north-central part of Pennsylvania is an area of sometimes rugged ridges and valleys, with a great many streams. There are hardwood forests with cherry and ash, and small stands of old-growth hemlock. Deer, bear, coyote, and fox are among the wildlife. There are a number of trails, most of them unmarked. The most prominent marked trail is the circular 85-mile Susquehannock Trail.

BALD EAGLE STATE FOREST—Box 147, Laurelton, PA 17835; (717)922-3344. 196,000 acres. This large state forest in central Pennsylvania has great sandstone ridges, valleys with many streams, and mixed oak forests. Deer, bear, bobcat, and fox are among the wildlife. A number of hiking trails are found here, including more than 60 miles of the Mid-State Trail.

BUCHANAN STATE FOREST—RD 2, Box 3, McConnellsburg, PA 17233; (717)485-3148. 75,000 acres. Consisting of five tracts, this state forest in southern Pennsylvania encompasses some rugged wild land with mountain ridges and valleys. The region is forested with oak, hemlock, and pine, and includes some virgin stands. Among the wildlife are deer, black bear, and bobcat. There are numerous trails, most important of which is a 39-mile segment of the Tuscarora Trail, which follows the crest of Tuscarora Mountain and offers some nice views.

MICHAUX STATE FOREST—10099 Lincoln Way East, Payetteville, PA 17222; (717)352-2211. 85,000 acres. This is an area of low mountain ridges in the south-central part of the state. There are many streams, forests of mixed oak, with pine and hemlock, and wildlife which includes deer and fox. A 40-mile section of the Appalachian Trail is among the many miles of trails here.

ROTHROCK STATE FOREST—P.O. Box 403, Huntingdon, PA 16652; (814)643-2340. 95,000 acres. This forest in central Pennsylvania is comprised of several separate tracts. The scenery is exceptional here, with some rugged terrain including low mountain ridges and sandstone rock formations, and fine views.

There are mountain streams, swamps, and oak forests with hemlock and pine, with some virgin stands—plus rhododendron and mountain laurel. Deer, bear, and fox are among the wildlife. The many miles of trails here include a 40-mile section of the Mid-State Trail.

OTHER RECOMMENDED LOCATIONS

FORBES STATE FOREST—P.O. Box 519, Laughlintown, PA 15655; (412)238-9533. 50,000 acres. Forbes State Forest, located in southwestern Pennsylvania, consists of a number of separate tracts of land. Much of the forest lies along Laurel Ridge, with rock formations, nice views, and many creeks and waterfalls.

The highest point in Pennsylvania, Mount

Davis (3,213 feet), is here. There are mixed oak forests with maple and poplar, plus mountain laurel and rhododendron. Among the wildlife are deer, bear, and bobcat. Forbes has over 40 miles of hiking trails, including a section of the Laurel Highlands Trail.

DELAWARE STATE FOREST—474 Clearview Lane, P.O. Box 150, Stroudsburg, PA 18360; (717)424-3001. 76,000 acres. This state forest is comprised of several parcels of land in the Poconos of eastern Pennsylvania. The terrain is sometimes rocky, with forests of mixed hardwoods—and bear, deer, coyote, and bobcat are among the wildlife. The main area of marked trails is the 45-mile Thunder Swamp Trail System, which includes the 28-mile Thunder Swamp Trail.

CLEAR CREEK STATE FOREST—P.O. Box 705, Clarion, PA 16214; (814)226-1901. 13,000 acres. Clear Creek State Forest is located next to the Clarion and Allegheny Rivers, south of Allegheny National Forest in western Pennsylvania, and consists of three tracts of land. Wildlife includes white-tailed deer and black bear, and there are mixed hardwood forests with mountain laurel and rhododendron. The area has many streams, and over 45 miles of hiking trails.

OHIOPYLE STATE PARK—P.O. Box 105, Ohiopyle, PA 15470; (412)329-8591. 18,719 acres. This rugged park, which is situated in the southwestern part of the state, includes 14 miles of the splendid 1,700-foot-deep Youghiogheny River Gorge. There are also ravines with streams and waterfalls. The southern end of the Laurel Highlands Trail is located here, along with 41 miles of other trails.

OIL CREEK STATE PARK—RD 1, Box 207, Oil City, PA 16301; (814)676-5915. 7,007 acres. Oil Creek State Park in northwestern Pennsylvania has some steep hills and hollows, and includes 12 miles of the scenic Oil Creek Gorge. There are fine views, hardwood and hemlock forests, and some waterfalls. Located here is the circular 36-mile Oil Creek Hiking Trail.

TIOGA STATE FOREST—P.O. Box 94, Route 287 South, Wellsboro, PA 16901; (717)724-2868. 160,000 acres. This large state forest in north-central Pennsylvania is divided into four parcels of land. It features Pennsylvania's "Grand Canyon," the 800-foot-deep Pine Creek Gorge. In the area are forests of mixed oak, wildlife including black bear, deer, and fox—and some fine vistas. The one marked trail here is the 30-mile West Rim Trail.

WYOMING STATE FOREST—Old Berwick Road, Bloomsburg, PA 17815. 40,708 acres. Located in north-central Pennsylvania, this area of ridges and valleys is crossed by beautiful Loyalsock Creek. It has hardwood forests, wildlife including deer and bear, and a portion of the 59-mile Loyalsock Trail.

HICKORY RUN STATE PARK—RD 1, Box 81, White Haven, PA 18661; (717)443-9991. 15,500 acres. There are 30 miles of trails in this state park, which is located in the Poconos of northeastern Pennsylvania. Highlights include the Boulder Field, an area of massive boulders. The park also has streams and waterfalls, and wildlife which includes white-tailed deer and black bear.

FRENCH CREEK STATE PARK—RD 1, Box 448, Elverson, PA 19520; (215)582-1514. 7,339 acres. Located in southeastern Pennsylvania, French Creek State Park has numerous creeks and some lakes, hardwood forests along with mountain laurel and dogwood—and white-tailed deer and fox are among the wildlife. There are over 32 miles of trails, including a few miles of the Horse-Shoe Trail.

RICKETTS GLEN STATE PARK—RD 2, Box 130, Benton, PA 17814; (717)477-5675. 13,050 acres. Ricketts Glen State Park is located in northeastern Pennsylvania. Of special interest here is the Glens Natural Area, which has deep gorges with 22 waterfalls. There are also huge old-growth hemlock, pine, and oak. The park has 20 miles of hiking trails.

BEAR RUN NATURE RESERVE—c/o Western Pennsylvania Conservancy, 316 4th Avenue, Pittsburgh, PA 15222; (412)329-8501. 4,200 acres. This privately-owned nature reserve in southwest Pennsylvania is on the Youghiogheny River, next to Ohiopyle State Park. It includes streams and a beautiful river gorge, oak and hemlock forest, fine views, and over 20 miles of trails. Difficulty varies from easy to strenuous.

PENNSYLVANIA HIKING RESOURCES

HIKING GUIDEBOOKS

Fifty Hikes in Central Pennsylvania—Thwaites, Tom. Woodstock, VT: Backcountry Publications, 1985.

Fifty Hikes in Eastern Pennsylvania—Hoffman, Carolyn. Woodstock, VT: Backcountry Publications, 1982.

Fifty Hikes in Eastern Pennsylvania—Thwaites, Tom. Woodstock, VT: Backcountry Publications, 1983.

Guide to the Appalachian Trail in Pennsylvania—Keystone Trails Association, 1989.

Hiking Guide to Western Pennsylvania—Sundquist, Bruce. American Youth Hostels, 1986.

Pennsylvania Hiking Trails—Keystone Trails Association, 1987.

TRAIL INFORMATION

Keystone Trails Association, P.O. Box 251, Cogan Station, PA 17728.

Trail Coordinator, Pennsylvania Bureau of State Parks, P.O. Box 1467, Harrisburg, PA 17120.

INFORMATION ABOUT STATE PARKS

Pennsylvania Bureau of State Parks, P.O. Box 1467, Harrisburg, PA 17120; (717)787-6640.

INFORMATION ABOUT STATE FORESTS

Pennsylvania Bureau of Forestry, Box 1467, Harrisburg, PA 17120; (717)787-2703.

CLUBS AND OTHER ORGANIZATIONS WHICH OFFER HIKES

Allegheny Outdoor Club, c/o Dorothy Gregerson, 107 North Irvine Street, Warren, PA 16365.

Allentown Hiking Club, c/o Michael F. Wuerstle, 431 Ridge Valley Road, Sellersville, PA 18960.

Alpine Club of Williamsport, P.O. Box 501, Williamsport, PA 17703.

American Youth Hostels, 6300 Fifth Avenue, Pittsburgh, PA 15232.

Appalachian Mountain Club, c/o Alan Kahn, 1601 School House Road, Gwynedd Valley, PA 19437.

Batona Hiking Club, c/o Robert E. Raine, 514 Inman Terrace, Willow Grove, PA 19090.

Blue Mountain Eagle Climbing Club, c/o Sandra Shollenberger, 625 Old Fritztown Road, Reading, PA 19608.

Buck Ridge Ski Club Hikers, P.O. Box 179, Bala Cynwyd, PA 19004.

Chester County Trail Club, c/o Clair Piersol, 16 Lloyd Avenue, Downington, PA 19335.

Flood City 4-H Backpackers, RD 2, Box 71, Johnstown, PA 15904.

Horse-Shoe Trail Club, c/o Robert Chalfant, 509 Cheltena Avenue, Jenkintown, PA 19046.

Kabob Hiking Club, c/o Beula Sheaffer, 2138 North 4th Street, Harrisburg, PA 17110.

Lancaster Hiking Club, P.O. Box 6037, Lancaster, PA 17603.

Lebanon Valley Hiking Club, c/o Nadine Lowry, 116 South Tenth Street, Lebanon, PA 17042.

Northeast Backpacking & Hiking Club, c/o Charles E. Horn III, 401 East Ross Street, Lancaster, PA 17602.

Philadelphia Trail Club, c/o Gerald H. Rusher, 511 Sharpless Road, Springfield, PA 19064.

Pocono Outdoor Club, c/o Wayne Gross, HCR #1, Box 31-5, Swiftwater, PA 18370.

Reading Community Hiking Club, c/o James L. Witman, Orchard Apt. C106, Temple, PA 19560.

Shenango Outing Club, P.O. Box 244, Greenville, PA 16125.

Sierra Club, 600 North Second Street, P.O. Box 663, Harrisburg, PA 17108.

Sierra Club, 619 Catherine Street, 3rd Floor, Philadelphia, PA 19147.

Sierra Club, P.O. Box 8241, Pittsburgh, PA 15217.

Sierra Club, P.O. Box 1311, Scranton, PA 18501.

Springfield Trail Club, c/o Wilma S. Flaig, P.O. Box 441, Media, PA 19063.

Susquehanna Appalachian Trail Club, P.O. Box 215, Harrisburg, PA 17108.

Susquehanna Trailers Hiking Club, c/o Harry West, Box 33-C, Sorber Mountain, Noxen, PA 18636.

Susquehannock Trail Club, P.O. Box 643, Coudersport, PA 16915.

York Hiking Club, c/o Bernard L. Frick, Jr., 168 Springdale Road, York, PA 17403.

RHODE ISLAND

It's no surprise that there's little in the way of real wilderness in Rhode Island, our smallest state. Yet while hiking options are limited here, quite a few state parks, forests, and wildlife management areas do have nice networks of marked trails. Some locations offer quite a range of beautiful natural scenery.

BEST HIKING AREAS

ARCADIA MANAGEMENT AREA—RFD 1, Box 55, Hope Valley, RI 02832. 13,000 acres. The best hiking in Rhode Island is found in this area, which is a group of state parks and "management areas," along with a state forest. Located in southwestern Rhode Island, it's attractive country, with some lovely ponds, streams, waterfalls, and rock ledges with appealing views.

The hilly terrain includes hardwood forests along with pine, hemlock, and some mountain laurel. Deer and fox are among the wildlife. There are more than 65 miles of easy to moderate trails here, offering numerous hiking options.

RHODE ISLAND HIKING RESOURCES

HIKING GUIDEBOOKS

AMC Massachusetts and Rhode Island Trail Guide—Boston: Appalachian Mountain Club, 1989.

Walks and Rambles in Rhode Island—Weber, Ken. Woodstock, VT: The Countryman Press, 1988.

TRAIL INFORMATION

New England Trail Conference, 33 Knollwood Drive, East Longmeadow, MA 01028; (203)342-1425 or (413)732-3719.

INFORMATION ABOUT STATE PARKS AND FORESTS

Rhode Island Department of Environmental Management, 22 Hayes Street, Providence, RI 02908; (401)277-6800.

STATE HIGHWAY MAP

Rhode Island Tourism Division, 7 Jackson Walkway, Providence, RI 02903; (401)277-2601 (in state)/(800)556-2484 (out of state).

RHODE ISLAND HIKING CLUBS

Appalachian Mountain Club, 5 Joy Street, Boston, MA 02108; (617)523-0636. This major club has a chapter in Rhode Island.

Sierra Club, 3 Joy Street, Boston, MA 02108.

SOUTH CAROLINA

South Carolina has fewer trails than its more mountainous neighbors, yet there's no scarcity of appealing and even wild scenery. The majority of state parks offer hiking on limited trail systems, while two National Forests offer the largest expanses of undeveloped lands, with the bulk of the best hiking and longest trails located in these especially attractive natural areas.

MAJOR TRAILS

FOOTHILLS TRAIL—75 miles. This National Recreation Trail is the longest in South Carolina and one of the most beautiful. It's located in the northwest corner of the state, and a segment of the trail is in North Carolina. Scenery is varied and sometimes rugged, with many creeks and waterfalls, stands of virgin hemlock, and fine views. Difficulty ranges from easy to strenuous. Trail information: Foothills Trail Conference, P.O. Box 3041, Greenville, SC 29602.

BEST HIKING AREAS

SUMTER NATIONAL FOREST—P.O. Box 2227, Columbia, SC 29202; (803)765-5222. 360,000 acres. Sumter National Forest stands in three separate segments in the northwestern part of the state, a mixture of public and private lands. A small portion is mountainous, with elevations from 800 feet to 3,400 feet. Other regions are less rugged, with rolling hills, scenic forested areas, wildlife including deer, many beautiful creeks, one wilderness area, and a section of the Chattooga Wild and Scenic River.

There are over 200 miles of trails. Among them are the 28-mile Buncombe Trail, the 26-mile Long Cane Trail, and a section of the 75-mile Foothills Trail. Most are easy to moderate in difficulty. Some trails are open to horses and mountain bikes.

OTHER RECOMMENDED LOCATIONS

FRANCIS MARION NATIONAL FOREST—P.O. Box 2227, Columbia, SC 29202; (803)765-5222. 250,489 acres. This large National Forest is located in southeastern South Carolina on a coastal plain. It includes pine ridges and hardwood forests, with many swamps and bogs. Hiking is limited here, especially considering the Forest's size, but there are two important trails: the 21-mile Swamp Fox Trail, an interesting National Recreation Trail, and the 20-mile Jericho Trail. Both are easy to moderate in difficulty.

SOUTH CAROLINA HIKING RESOURCES

HIKING GUIDEBOOKS
South Carolina Hiking Trails—de Hart, Allen. Charlotte, NC: The East Woods Press,1984.

INFORMATION ABOUT STATE PARKS
South Carolina Division of State Parks, Edgar

Brown Building, 1205 Pendleton Street, Columbia, SC 29201; (803)734-0156.

STATE HIGHWAY MAP AND TRAVEL INFORMATION
South Carolina Division of Tourism, Box 71, Columbia, SC 29202; (803)253-6318.

SOUTH CAROLINA HIKING CLUBS
Sierra Club, P.O. Box 12112, Columbia, SC 29211.

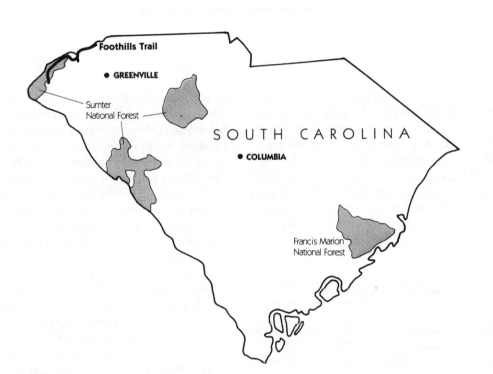

SOUTH DAKOTA

South Dakota's scenery includes large expanses of open prairie, some interesting badlands, and the beautifully mountainous Black Hills. Trails are not abundant throughout much of the state, but a focal point for hikers is found in southwestern South Dakota—especially within Black Hills National Forest and Custer State Park. Here an unusually varied landscape of rugged mountains, steep gorges, and rolling grasslands provides some very rewarding hiking.

MAJOR TRAILS

CENTENNIAL TRAIL—111 miles. This is a new trail which was opened in 1989. It runs from Wind Cave National Park to Bear Butte State Park, traversing much of the finest scenery of the Black Hills. Some of the trail is only open to hikers, but major portions are multi-use, available to horseback riders as well as mountain bikers. Difficulty is easy to moderate. Trail information: South Dakota Department of Game, Fish & Parks, HC 83, Box 70, Custer, SD 57730; (605)255-4515.

BEST HIKING AREAS

BLACK HILLS NATIONAL FOREST—RR 2, Box 200, Custer, SD 57730. Located in southwestern South Dakota, this important National Forest encompasses a substantial portion of the beautiful Black Hills—an area of mountains and forests as well as prairies, lovely streams and lakes, sheer cliffs and open summits with great views. Elevations range from about 3,200 feet to over 7,000 feet. Directly adjacent to the National Forest is the famous Mount Rushmore National Memorial, with the gigantic sculpted figures of four presidents on 5,725- foot Mount Rushmore.

Among the mountains is Harney Peak (7,242 feet), highest elevation in South Dakota and east of the Rockies, and it's located in the 10,700-acre Black Elk Wilderness Area. Also here are canyons and rugged granite formations, wonderful vistas, grassy meadows with wildflowers, and forests of ponderosa pine, limber and lodgepole pine, along with oak, birch, and aspen.

Local wildlife includes white-tailed and mule deer, bighorn sheep, elk, mountain goat, and coyote. There are over 180 miles of hiking trails, longest of which is a 63-mile segment of the Centennial Trail. Difficulty ranges from easy to strenuous. Some trails are also open to horseback riding.

CUSTER STATE PARK—HC 83, Box 70, Custer, SC 57730; (605)255-4515. This large state park in the Black Hills of southwestern South Dakota has ponderosa pine forests and prairie grasslands, steep ridges with fine views, and several lakes. There's also a sheer-walled canyon, giant rock formations, and over 50 miles of hiking trails, including 22 miles of the Centennial Trail. Difficulty varies from easy to strenuous. Bison are among the wildlife found here.

OTHER RECOMMENDED LOCATIONS

WIND CAVE NATIONAL PARK—Hot Springs, SD 57747. 28,232 acres. Adjacent to Black Hills National Forest and Custer State Park, Wind Cave National Park has an enormous underground system of limestone caves, with countless passages and chambers, and interesting formations of crystals. Aboveground is a landscape of open meadows, prairie grasslands, and forests of ponderosa pine, with some fine panoramic views. Among the wildlife are bison, elk, and prairie dog. There are 28 miles of hiking trails, including 6 miles of the Centennial Trail. Difficulty varies from easy to strenuous.

BADLANDS NATIONAL PARK—P.O. Box 6, Interior, SD 57750; (605)433-5361. Famous for its strikingly unusual rock formations, Badlands National Park also contains the most extensive prairie wilderness in the United States. Over 64,000 acres have wilderness status. Although there are only about 10 miles of marked hiking trails, trailless travel is especially easy and enjoyable here on the open prairie. Wildlife includes bison, pronghorn antelope, bighorn sheep, coyote, and bobcat.

SOUTH DAKOTA HIKING RESOURCES

INFORMATION ABOUT STATE PARKS
South Dakota Department of Fish, Game & Parks, 445 East Capitol, Pierre, SD 57501.

STATE HIGHWAY MAP AND TRAVEL INFORMATION
South Dakota Division of Tourism, P.O. Box 6000, Pierre, SD 57501; (800)843-1930 (out of state)/(800)952-2217 (in state).

SOUTH DAKOTA HIKING CLUBS
Sierra Club, P.O. Box 1624, Rapid City, SD 57709.

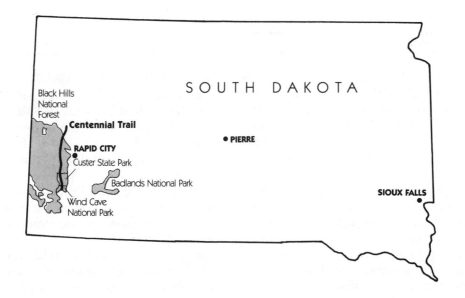

TENNESSEE

Few eastern states can compare with Tennessee when it comes to hiking opportunities. Here it's practically routine for state parks to have extensive and often outstanding trail systems, and there's a proposed (yet-to-be-constructed) series of major State Scenic Trails. Standing above the rest, in the mountainous eastern part of the state, are Great Smoky Mountains National Park and Cherokee National Forest, which encompass some of the wildest and most spectacular scenery east of the Mississippi.

MAJOR TRAILS

APPALACHIAN TRAIL—About 70 miles of the Appalachian Trail fall within Tennessee and for over 200 additional miles the trail straddles the Tennessee–North Carolina border, crossing some of the most spectacular landscape of the southern Appalachians. Highlights include lofty grassy "balds" (treeless mountain tops) with panoramic views in Cherokee National Forest, and the wild scenery of Great Smoky Mountains National Park, which has the highest point of the entire trail at Clingman's Dome (6,643 feet). Much of the trail is moderate to strenuous in difficulty, with some steep climbs. Trail information: Appalachian Trail Conference, P.O. Box 807, Harpers Ferry, WV 25425.

CUMBERLAND TRAIL—This State Scenic Trail, now in the process of being developed, will eventually be 180 miles long. Currently about 85 miles of trail are open. When completed it will run the width of Tennessee—from Kentucky's Cumberland Gap National Historical Park, at the Kentucky and Virginia borders, to Prentice Cooper State Forest near the Georgia border. The trail crosses the Cumberland mountains and parallels the Tennessee River for a distance. Some sections are rugged. Trail information: Tennessee Division of Parks and Recreation, 701 Broadway, Nashville, TN 37243.

BEST HIKING AREAS

GREAT SMOKY MOUNTAINS NATIONAL PARK— Gatlinburg, TN 37738; (615)436-5615. 520,004 acres (244,109 in Tennessee). This is undoubtedly the most magnificent National Park in the East. It's also the most heavily visited in the entire country, and one of the largest. Half of the park is in North Carolina. There are 16 mountains over 6,000 feet, including Clingman's Dome (6,643 feet), second highest in the East. There are great expanses of rugged wilderness, and an unmatched variety of flora and fauna.

In the park are mixed hardwood and conifer forests, with major stands of virgin trees—along with rhododendron, mountain laurel and flame azalea. Black bear, deer, wild boar, mountain lion, bobcat, and fox are among the wildlife.

There are over 850 miles of hiking trails, including 68 miles of the Appalachian Trail, which follows the high and rugged ridge crest and offers wonderful views. Numerous other trails lead alongside rivers and creeks, with many waterfalls. Trail difficulty varies from very easy to extremely strenuous.

CHEROKEE NATIONAL FOREST—2800 North Ocoee Street, P.O. Box 2010, Cleveland, TN 37320; (615)476-9700. 625,000 acres. This important National Forest runs along the eastern border of Tennessee, and it's divided into two tracts north and south of Great Smoky Mountains National Park. There are numerous mountains, including some of the famous "southern balds," with splendid open mountain meadows offering magnificent views.

Many wild streams and several major rivers are found here as well. Among the wildlife are black bear, deer, and wild boar. The forest has over 640 miles of hiking trails, including 138 miles of the Appalachian Trail. Difficulty ranges from easy to very strenuous.

OTHER RECOMMENDED LOCATIONS

BIG SOUTH FORK NATIONAL RIVER AND RECREATION AREA—Route 3, Box 401, Oneida, TN 37841. 120,000 acres. This National River and Recreation Area is located in northeast Tennessee on the border with Kentucky, and extends into that state. It contains the Big South Fork River, and the scenery here includes high bluffs and cliffs, deep canyon gorges, and natural sandstone arches and caves.

The area has diverse forests, fine views, and some beautiful creeks and waterfalls. There are over 100 miles of hiking trails, including a section of Kentucky's Sheltowee Trace Trail. Difficulty varies from easy to strenuous.

SOUTH CUMBERLAND STATE RECREATION AREA—Route 1, Box 2196, Monteagle, TN 37356; (615)924-2980. 12,000 acres. This is a grouping of seven separate natural areas on the Cumberland Plateau of south-central Tennessee. Most notable is the 11,400-acre Savage Gulf Natural Area, which offers some exceptional scenery including deep gorges and waterfalls, giant caves, and great views.

The area has mixed forests of oak and hickory, hemlock and pine, with stands of virgin timber. Deer, bobcat, and fox are among the wildlife. There are over 85 miles of hiking trails in the region, varying in difficulty from easy to strenuous.

PICKETT STATE PARK—Polk Creek Route, Box 174, Jamestown, TN 38556; (615)879-5821. 11,752 acres. Pickett State Park is a wild park in northeastern Tennessee which has varied vegetation and terrain, with interesting rock formations, caves, and some natural bridges. There are steep cliffs, lovely creeks and waterfalls, and many stands of rhododendron. The park has over 50 miles of trails, including a section of Kentucky's Sheltowee Trace Trail. Difficulty ranges from easy to strenuous.

FROZEN HEAD STATE NATURAL AREA—Route 2, Box 1302, Wartburg, TN 37887; (615)346-3318.

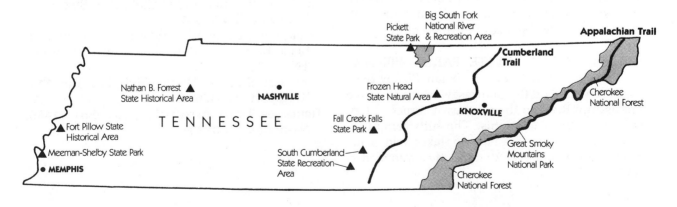

11,562 acres. This outstanding natural area in the Cumberland Mountains of eastern Tennessee has rocky scenery and several impressive peaks, including 3,324-foot Frozen Head Mountain. There's an excellent trail system with 36 miles of trails, most of which are moderate to strenuous in difficulty.

FALL CREEK FALLS STATE RESORT PARK—Route 3, Pikeville, TN 37367; (615)881-3297. 15,800 acres. Located in eastern Tennessee on the western Cumberland Plateau, Fall Creek Falls State Resort Park contains a resort. Among the scenic attractions are several gorges and waterfalls, including 256-foot Fall Creek Falls.

There are forests of oak and hickory, poplar and hemlock (with some virgin stands)—and deer, bobcat, and fox are among the wildlife. The park has over 33 miles of trails, some of which are rocky and rough. Difficulty varies from easy to strenuous.

NATHAN B. FORREST STATE HISTORICAL AREA—Eva, TN 38333; (901)584-6356. Located in the western part of the state, this is a hilly forested park on the west side of the Tennessee River. There are forests of hardwoods with mountain laurel, deer, and over 30 miles of easy to moderate trails here.

FORT PILLOW STATE HISTORICAL AREA—Route 2, Box 108B-1, Henning, TN 38041; (901)738-5581. 1,650 acres. Situated along the Mississippi River on the western border of Tennessee, this park was the site of a Civil War fortification. The terrain is hilly, with hardwood forests, deer, and a lake. There are 21 miles of trails, with difficulty varying from easy to strenuous.

MEEMAN–SHELBY STATE PARK—Millington, TN 38053; (901)876-5215. Meeman–Shelby State Park is situated on the Chickasaw Bluffs along the Mississippi River in the southwest corner of Tennessee, north of Memphis. The hilly terrain includes hardwood forests, two lakes and some streams, deer, and over 20 miles of easy to moderate trails.

TENNESSEE HIKING RESOURCES

HIKING GUIDEBOOKS

Guide to the Appalachian Trail in Tennessee and North Carolina—Harpers Ferry, WV: The Appalachian Trail Conference, 1989.

Hiker's Guide to the Smokies—Muriless, Dick & Stallings, Constance. San Francisco: Sierra Club Books.

Hiking in the Great Smokies—Brewer, Carson. Great Smoky Mountains Natural History Association.

Tennessee Trails—Means, Evan. Chester, CT: The Globe Pequot Press, 1989.

Walks in the Great Smokies—Albright, R. & P. Chester, CT: The Globe Pequot Press.

INFORMATION ABOUT STATE PARKS

Tennessee Division of Parks and Recreation, 701 Broadway, Nashville, TN 37243.

TRAIL INFORMATION

Tennessee Trails Association, P.O. Box 41446, Nashville, TN 37204.

MAPS

Tennessee Atlas & Gazetteer—Freeport, ME: DeLorme Mapping Co.

STATE HIGHWAY MAP AND TRAVEL INFORMATION

Tennessee Tourist Development, P.O. Box 23170, Nashville, TN 37202; (615)741-2158.

CLUBS AND OTHER ORGANIZATIONS WHICH OFFER HIKES

Greenville Hiking Club, Route 3, Box 274, Chuckey, TN 37641.

Sierra Club, c/o Richard Mochow, 871 Kensington Place, Memphis, TN 38107.

Smoky Mountains Hiking Club, P.O. Box 1454, Knoxville, TN 37901.

Tennessee Citizens for Wilderness Planning, c/o Liane B. Russell, 130 Tabor Road, Oak Ridge, TN 37830.

Tennessee Eastman Hiking Club, P.O. Box 511, Kingsport, TN 37662.

Tennessee Trails Association, P.O. Box 41446, Nashville, TN 37204.

TEXAS

Our largest state outside of Alaska, Texas has an amazing diversity of scenery and terrain—from magnificent high mountains and multicolored canyons, with major expanses of desert, to lush lowlands and beautiful mixed forests. The hiker has plenty of choices here, since many state parks and recreation areas have small to medium-size trail systems—and two superb National Parks with ruggedly wild and spectacular scenery offer memorable hiking.

MAJOR TRAILS

LONE STAR TRAIL—140 miles. The Lone Star is the longest hiking trail in Texas. It follows a meandering and attractive forested route through Sam Houston National Forest in East Texas, and includes a number of small loops. A segment of the trail has been given National Recreation Trail status. Most of the hiking is easy. Fall through spring are the best seasons to hike here. Trail information: National Forests in Texas, Homer Garrison Federal Building, 701 North First Street, Lufkin, TX 75901.

BEST HIKING AREAS

BIG BEND NATIONAL PARK—Big Bend National Park, Texas 79834; (915)477-2251. 740,118 acres. Big Bend is located in southwest Texas alongside the Rio Grande (River), which defines the U.S.–Mexican border. It contains the largest areas of wilderness in the state.

There's quite a variety of terrain here, from the Rio Grande floodplain at 1,800-foot elevation to 7,825-foot Emory Peak in the Chisos Mountains. Winter is a lovely time to visit lower-elevation areas. Along with expanses of desert there are steep canyons with colored limestone cliffs, giant boulders and interesting rock formations—and also beautiful meadows and wooded areas with maple, oak, and ponderosa pine. Some of the mountain views are magnificent. Water is generally scarce. Wildlife includes mountain lion, bobcat, and mule deer.

The park has over 150 miles of trails. Difficulty varies from easy to very strenuous. Only about 30 miles of trails are completely developed and frequently used. Some trails leading into the more remote areas are not well-marked or easy to follow.

GUADALUPE MOUNTAINS NATIONAL PARK—HC 60, Box 400, Salt Flat, TX 79847; (915)828-3251. 76,923 acres. Situated in west Texas along the state's border, this splendid National Park encloses a segment of the Guadalupe Mountains, which extend into neighboring New Mexico. Among the summits here is Guadalupe Peak (8,749 feet), highest in Texas, with spectacular views from the top.

In addition to a small area of Chihuahuan

Guadalupe Mountains
National Park

DALLAS

TEXAS

Davy Crockett
National Forest

Sam Houston
National Forest

Lone Star Trail

Pedernales Falls
State Park ▲ **AUSTIN**

▲ Lake
Somerville
State Park

Big Thicket ▲
National Preserve

Big Bend
National Park

HOUSTON ●
▲
Brazos Bend
State Park

Desert, the park has high-walled canyons—among them McKittrick Canyon, an especially attractive and popular destination—and a wide mix of flora and fauna. Yucca and prickly pear cacti are common in the lower desert regions, with a coniferous forest (pine and fir) and aspen in the mountains. Wildlife of the upper regions include elk, black bear, mountain lion, and mule deer. Water is scarce.

There are over 80 miles of hiking trails, many of which are also open to horseback riding. Some are not in good condition or easy to follow. Difficulty ranges from easy to very strenuous.

OTHER RECOMMENDED LOCATIONS

SAM HOUSTON NATIONAL FOREST—Homer Garrison Federal Building, 701 North First Street, Lufkin, TX 75901; (713)592-6462 or (409)344-6205. 158,647 acres. This scenic National Forest, located in East Texas, includes the

140-mile Lone Star Trail with its many loops—along with a number of short hiking and nature trails. The terrain is nearly flat, with extensive pine and hardwood forest and many lovely streams. Among the wildlife are bobcat, gray fox, and armadillo.

DAVY CROCKETT NATIONAL FOREST—Homer Garrison Federal Building, 701 North First Street, Lufkin, TX 75901; (409)544-2046 or (409)831-2246. 161,478 acres. Situated not far north of Sam Houston National Forest, Davy Crockett National Forest is another area of hardwood and pine forest, with numerous streams and boggy areas, and some small man-made ponds. Along with shorter trails, the 20-mile 4-C National Recreation Trail passes through a portion of this scenic National Forest, and includes a fine view.

BIG THICKET NATIONAL PRESERVE—P.O. Box 7408, Beaumont, TX 77706; (409)839-2689. 84,550 acres. The Big Thicket National Preserve consists of 8 separate tracts of land in southeast Texas. It's an area of unusual biological diversity, with several ecosystems in very close proximity—including desert, subtropical, mountain, mixed forest, and prairie species. There are some large streams, and about 20 miles of hiking trails.

PEDERNALES FALLS STATE PARK—Route 1, Box 450, Johnson City, TX 78636; (512)868-7304. 4,800 acres. Situated in south-central Texas, this state park includes a six-mile stretch of the Pedernales River, along with three miles of the ruggedly beautiful Pedernales Falls Gorge. There are several canyons and creeks, oak woodlands, and wildlife include deer and bald eagle. The park has about 20 miles of trails.

BRAZOS BEND STATE PARK—21901 FM 762, Needville, TX 77461; (409)553-3243. 4,897 acres. This state park borders on the Brazos River, south of Houston in East Texas. The area has hardwood forest and prairie, with a large creek and several lakes. Wildlife includes armadillo and alligator. There are over 20 miles of trails.

LAKE SOMERVILLE STATE PARK—Route 1, Box 499, Somerville, TX 77879; (409)535-7763. This state park consists of two units located along the western shore of Somerville Reservoir, in east-central Texas. It's an area of low rolling hills, oak and hickory forests with yaupon, and white-tailed deer, coyote, fox, and armadillo are among the wildlife. There's a 21-mile trail system called the Lake Somerville Trailway, which runs the length of the park. Horseback riding and cycling are permitted along with hiking.

TEXAS HIKING RESOURCES

HIKING GUIDEBOOKS
Hiking and Backpacking Trails of Texas—Little, Mickey. Houston: Gulf Publishing Co., 1990.

INFORMATION ABOUT STATE PARKS AND TRAILS
Texas Parks and Wildlife Department, 4200 Smith School Road, Austin, TX 78744; (512)389-4800.

INFORMATION ABOUT NATIONAL FORESTS
National Forests in Texas, Homer Garrison Federal Building, 701 North First Street, Lufkin, TX 75901.

STATE HIGHWAY MAP AND TRAVEL INFORMATION
Texas Division of Tourism, P.O. Box 12728, Austin, TX 78711; (512)462-9191/(800)888-8839.

TEXAS HIKING CLUBS
Sierra Club, Box 1931, Austin, TX 78767.
Sierra Club, 1 Main Street, 5106A, Houston, TX 77002.
West Texas Trail Walkers, 1100 Wayland Drive, Arlington, TX 76012.

UTAH

Utah is an uncommonly beautiful state with lofty mountain ranges and plateaus, deep and often spectacular multicolored canyons, and areas of desert. Some regions have unusual rock formations, including pinnacles and spires, arches and natural bridges. Except for the high country, much of Utah is arid. Over 60 percent of the state is public land, with no less than five National Parks and six major National Forests, providing thousands of miles of trails and almost endless resources for the avid hiker.

MAJOR TRAILS

GREAT WESTERN TRAIL—This ambitious new national trail will eventually run some 2,400 miles in a north-south direction from Canada to Mexico. It's a multi-use trail, with some sections open to horses, mountain bikes, and motorized vehicles—and others just to hikers (parallel routes designed for different purposes are being built in some regions). About 90 percent of the Utah section is now complete. It utilizes other trails and roads and passes through 5 National Forests, crossing some of the state's most scenic lands. Trail information: Great Western Trail Association, P.O. Box 1428, Provo, UT 84602.

BEST HIKING AREAS

WASATCH–CACHE NATIONAL FOREST—8234 Federal Building, 125 S. State Street, Salt Lake City, UT 84138; (801)524-5030. 1,302,523 acres. This large National Forest consists of a number of tracts in northern Utah, some of them close to Salt Lake City. It's rugged and often spectacular country which includes the Wasatch and Uinta Mountains—with sheer-faced, snow-covered peaks, red-rock ridges and outcroppings, deep canyons, and hundreds of lakes and streams. There are several substantial wilderness areas, including part of the 460,000-acre High Uintas Wilderness—and many mountains over 10,000 feet, with 13,442-foot Gilbert Peak the highest.

Vegetation ranges from alpine varieties, and meadows with wildflowers, to forests of spruce, fir, and pine, and stands of aspen. There's quite an array of wildlife including mule deer, moose, elk, black bear, pronghorn antelope, bighorn sheep, mountain goat, and bobcat.

Wasatch–Cache National Forest has about 1,050 miles of hiking trails, many of which are open to horseback riding. This is a very popular National Forest, with some trails crowded in season. High trails are typically under snow until July, and open only through September.

FISHLAKE NATIONAL FOREST—115 East 900 North, Richfield, UT 84701; (801)896-9233. 1,425,126 acres. Fishlake National Forest is made up of four separate units in south-central Utah. The region contains a number of high mountain ranges and plateaus, with beautiful craggy snow-capped peaks and barren slopes, narrow red-rock canyons, open meadows, and superb vistas.

Vegetation varies from desert varieties to sub-alpine plants and wildflowers, with forests of fir and spruce, pine and aspen, along with piñon-juniper. Deer, elk, antelope, black bear, mountain goat, fox, mountain lion, and bobcat are among the mammals found here. There are a good many streams, lakes, and ponds—and several mountains over 12,000 feet, including 12,173-foot Delano Peak, the highest.

Approximately 1,040 miles of trails extend through this National Forest. Most are also open to horses, and some to all-terrain vehicles. A portion of the trails is not maintained. Snow generally remains on high trails until July. A section of the Great Western Trail is here.

ASHLEY NATIONAL FOREST—355 North Vernal Avenue, Vernal, UT 84078; (801)789-1181. 1,288,422 acres in Utah. Located in northeast Utah and reaching into Wyoming, Ashley National Forest encompasses a portion of the Uinta Mountains, the state's highest range—and includes part of the outstanding 460,000-acre High Uintas Wilderness, which is also in Wasatch–Cache National Forest. There are many high rugged peaks, and Utah's highest point is here, 13,528-foot Kings Peak.

The area has lofty ridges and red-rock mountains, alpine basins with high lakes and meadows, glacial canyons containing rivers or creeks, conifer forests of fir, spruce, and pine. Elk, bear, antelope, moose, deer, bighorn sheep, mountain lion, and lynx roam throughout the area.

This National Forest has more than 750 miles of trails, including the 53-mile Highline Trail. Difficulty ranges from easy to strenuous. Horseback riding is allowed on most trails. High routes may not be snow-free until July.

DIXIE NATIONAL FOREST—82 North 100 East, P.O. Box 580, Cedar City, UT 84720: (801)586-2421. 1,883,745 acres. This is the state's largest National Forest, with four tracts in south-central and southwest Utah. Sections are adjacent to Bryce Canyon National Park and Zion National Park. Some outstanding scenery is found here,

with elevations from under 4,000 feet to over 11,000 feet. Highest point is 11,322-foot Bluebell Knoll. There are three wilderness areas.

Some of the terrain is quite rugged, with steep slopes and precipitous cliffs, canyons, mesas and plateaus, pinnacles and colorful rock formations, and great views. Included are many lakes and streams, alpine meadows, pine and fir forests, piñon and juniper, and sagebrush. Among the wildlife are elk, mule deer, pronghorn, black bear, and mountain lion.

Dixie National Forest has 640 miles of hiking trails, including a section of the new Great Western Trail. Most trails are open to horses and are lightly used. Mountain bikes and motorized vehicles are permitted on some trails.

UINTA NATIONAL FOREST—P.O. Box 1428, Provo, UT 84603; (801)377-5780. 812,787 acres. Popular because of its proximity to developed areas, this National Forest in north-central Utah offers a mixture of high desert, rugged peaks and rocky slopes, valleys and foothills, steep canyons and cliffs. There are three wilderness areas, and many spectacular views. Some of the lofty mountains include 11,750-foot Mount Timpanogos and 11,877-foot Mount Nebo.

The region also has high basins with lakes, many streams and waterfalls, and vegetation ranging from alpine meadows and tundra to sagebrush, with forests of fir and spruce—plus some aspen, willow, maple and oak. Among the animals present are elk, moose, mule deer, black bear, mountain goat, and cougar.

Uinta National Forest contains over 500 miles of easy to strenuous trails, including a 65-mile section of the Great Western Trail. Horses are generally permitted. Some trails receive very heavy use.

ZION NATIONAL PARK—situated in southwest Utah, Zion National Park is a spectacular area of steep-walled, multicolored canyons, some of red rock, with massive high cliffs (up to 3,000 feet) and incredible slickrock sandstone formations. There are also elevated plateaus and mesas, with wonderful open views.

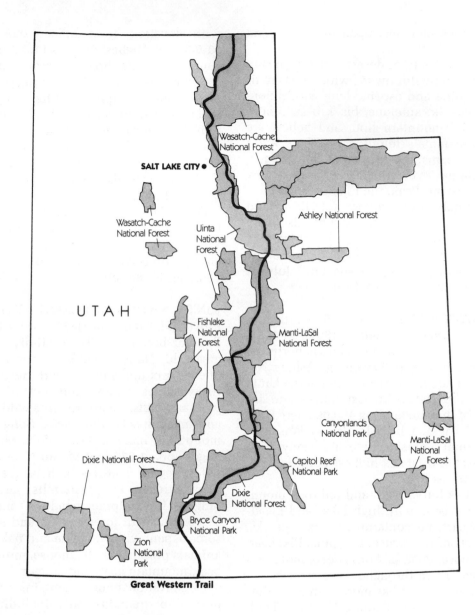

Wasatch-Cache
National Forest

SALT LAKE CITY ●

Wasatch-Cache
National Forest

Uinta
National
Forest

Ashley National Forest

UTAH

Fishlake
National
Forest

Manti-LaSal
National Forest

Canyonlands
National Park

Manti-LaSal
National
Forest

Dixie National Forest

Capitol Reef
National Park

Dixie
National Forest

Bryce Canyon
National Park

Zion
National
Park

Great Western Trail

A highway runs through enormous Zion Canyon, so the area attracts crowds of sightseers, especially in the summer. The beautiful Virgin River also flows through the canyon. Elsewhere in the park is a petrified forest, and 310-foot Kolob Arch, said to be the largest natural arch in the world. Vegetation varies from willow and cottonwood trees at lowest elevations, and desert flora, to piñon and juniper forests, along with fir and ponderosa pine. The wildlife includes mule deer, mountain lion, bobcat, and fox.

Zion National Park has over 140 miles of hiking trails. Some are unmaintained. Horseback riding is permitted on many trails. Difficulty ranges from easy to strenuous. Spring and fall are the best hiking seasons, as summer temperatures can be extreme.

CANYONLANDS NATIONAL PARK—125 West

200 South, Moab, UT 84532; (801)259-7164. 337,570 acres. Located on the Colorado Plateau in southeast Utah, Canyonlands National Park is beautifully wild and undeveloped, with many canyons and high mesas. Elevations range from 3,600 feet to nearly 7,000 feet. There are outstanding views.

This arid area has a myriad of eroded, multi-colored rock formations, including needles, high spires, arches, and balanced rocks. Of interest is the Maze, an intricate complex of canyons. The Colorado and Green Rivers are also here, flowing through deep canyons. Desert vegetation and piñon-juniper are found in the region, along with deer, bighorn sheep, coyote, fox, and other wildlife.

There are over 80 miles of trails, some minimally marked. Difficulty varies from easy to strenuous. Summer is hot, so spring and fall are the best hiking seasons in the park.

CAPITOL REEF NATIONAL PARK—Torrey, UT 84775; (801)425-3791. 241,865 acres. This long and narrow National Park is located in southern Utah, northeast of Bryce Canyon and Zion National Parks. It's a desert-canyon wilderness, enclosing the Waterpocket Fold, a giant eroded uplift of land. There are open mesas, dramatic views, and deep, sheer-walled canyons and gulches with red-orange or brown and white slick-rock sandstone—sometimes smooth-surfaced—plus pinnacles and sculpted rock arches and bridges, overhangs and caves.

Wildlife in the area includes black bear, mule deer, mountain lion, coyote, and fox. Much of the vegetation consists of desert varieties, with some piñon-juniper woodlands. There are about 26 miles of marked trails and another 50-plus miles of trails which are unmarked except for occasional rock cairns. Difficulty ranges from easy to strenuous, with rock scrambling required on a couple of trails. Summer heat can be extreme, so spring and fall are the best seasons for hiking.

BRYCE CANYON NATIONAL PARK—Bryce Canyon, UT 84717; (801)834-5322. 37,102 acres. Bryce Canyon National Park is located in south-

west Utah, surrounded by the lands of Dixie National Forest. It's on an eroded plateau, with elevations from under 7,000 feet to over 9,000 feet—and includes a series of canyons with an astonishing array of sculpted spires, pinnacles, and unusually shaped limestone forms of many colors and shadings.

There are also fantastic views, with evergreen forests of ponderosa pine and fir, plus aspen, and assorted wildflowers. Local mammals include mule deer, coyote, and prairie dog. This National Park has more than 65 miles of trails. Difficulty varies from easy to strenuous. The hiking season here is spring through fall (summer temperatures are moderate).

MANTI–LASAL NATIONAL FOREST—599 West Price River Drive, Price, UT 84501; (801)637-2817. 1,265,423 acres. Consisting of a block of land in central Utah and two distant units in southeast Utah, Manti–Lasal National Forest includes the high Wasatch Plateau, with elevations over 11,000 feet, and the Abajo and Lasal Mountains—the latter with peaks over 12,000 feet.

There are numerous narrow canyons, cirque basins, red rock cliffs and mesas, grassy hills and ridges, high mountain meadows and creeks. Some parts are forested with spruce-fir, ponderosa pine, and aspen, and there's also piñon-juniper, plus sagebrush and cactus. Elk, mule deer, moose, black bear, mountain lion, and coyote inhabit the area.

Over 200 miles of hiking trails extend through Manti–Lasal. Some are unmaintained and difficult to follow.

UTAH HIKING RESOURCES

HIKING GUIDEBOOKS

Cache Trails—Schimpf, Ann, & Davis, Mel. Salt Lake City: Wasatch Publishing, 1978.

High Uinta Trails—Davis, Mel. Salt Lake City: Wasatch Publishing, 1974.

The Hiker's Guide to Utah—Hall, Dave. Billings, MT: Falcon Press, 1982.

Hiking the Southwest's Canyon Country—

Hinchman, Sandra. Seattle, WA: The Mountaineers.

Hiking in Zion National Park, The Trails—Lineback, Bob. Zion Natural History Association.

Wasatch Trails, Volume I—Bottcher, Betty, and Davis, Mel. Salt Lake City: Wasatch Publishing, 1973.

Wasatch Trails, Volume II—Geery, Daniel. Salt Lake City: Wasatch Publishing, 1976.

Utah Valley Trails—Paxman, Shirley & Monroe; Taylor, Gayle & Weldon. Salt Lake City: Wasatch Publishing, 1978.

INFORMATION ABOUT STATE PARKS

Utah Division of Parks and Recreation, 1636 West North Temple, Suite 116, Salt Lake City, UT 84116; (801)538-7220.

STATE HIGHWAY MAP AND TRAVEL INFORMATION

Utah Travel Council, Council Hall/Capitol Hill, Salt Lake City, UT 84114; (801)538-1030.

UTAH HIKING CLUBS

Sierra Club, 177 East 900 South, Suite 102, Salt Lake City, UT 84111.

Wasatch Mountain Club, 888 South 200 East, Salt Lake City, UT 84111.

VERMONT

Vermont's lovely Green Mountains provide an exceptional setting for hiking on a well-developed trail system. Most notable and famous is the 265-mile Long Trail, which runs along the mountain spine of this heavily forested state. Several hundred miles of other trails wind through scenic river valleys and over scores of rounded and occasionally rocky-topped mountains. The range of choices and consistently appealing scenery help make this one of New England's best hiking states.

MAJOR TRAILS

THE LONG TRAIL—270 miles. One of the oldest marked hiking trails in the country, the Long Trail runs the length of Vermont from Massachusetts to Canada. This important trail takes in most of the highest mountains and the wildest scenery in the state. Although there are some easy sections, portions are rough and the trail is typically moderate to strenuous in difficulty. With an additional 175 miles of side trails, The Long Trail is the focal point of the best hiking in Vermont. Trail information: The Green Mountain Club, P.O. Box 889, Montpelier, VT 05602; (802)223-3463.

APPALACHIAN TRAIL—137 miles in Vermont (2,100 total). The Appalachian Trail coincides with the Long Trail for 98 miles from the Massachusetts border to Sherburne Pass, where it turns east toward New Hampshire. On route the trail climbs a number of mountains in the 3,000-4,000-foot range, with some great views, and passes several lovely mountain ponds. Difficulty varies from easy to strenuous. Trail information: Appalachian Trail Conference, P.O. Box 807 Harpers Ferry, WV 25425.

BEST HIKING AREAS

MOUNT MANSFIELD STATE FOREST—RFD, Stowe, VT 05672; (802)253-4014. 27,499 acres. Located in northern Vermont, Mount Mansfield is Vermont's highest and most massive mountain. At 4,393 feet, it has an incredibly rugged, rocky top somewhat the shape of a human face in profile—and the finest views in the state. There are areas of arctic-alpine tundra around the summit.

It's a region of hardwood and conifer forests with spruce, fir, and pine. White-tailed deer, black bear, bobcat, and fox are among the wildlife. The area also has some streams and ponds. In part because of an auto road which leads almost to the top, Mount Mansfield receives a great many visitors. The number of actual hikers is not as high.

There are over 30 different trails on or around

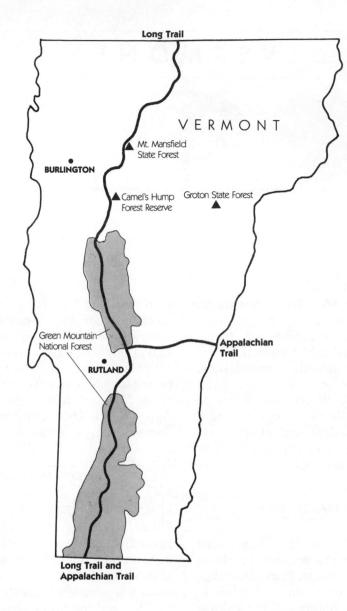

VERMONT

Mt. Mansfield
State Forest

BURLINGTON

Camel's Hump
Forest Reserve

Groton State Forest

Green Mountain
National Forest

Appalachian
Trail

RUTLAND

Long Trail and
Appalachian Trail

the mountain, including a section of the Long Trail, offering some superb hiking which ranges from easy to very difficult. A few trails lead through caves, crevices, and involve rock scrambling.

GREEN MOUNTAIN NATIONAL FOREST—P.O. Box 519, Rutland, VT 05701; (802)773-0300. 325,534 acres. Green Mountain National Forest is by far the largest area of public land in the state, and includes some of Vermont's most beautiful forested scenery. Divided into two parcels in central and southern Vermont, the forest has six wilderness areas. Two of these, the Bread Loaf Wilderness and Lye Brook Wilderness, are of substantial size.

This mountainous region has some rugged terrain, including steep peaks along with plateaus, and many lakes, ponds, streams, and waterfalls. There are spruce and fir forests with hemlock and mixed hardwoods. White-tailed deer, black bear, coyote, bobcat, and fox are among the wildlife. There's plenty of fine hiking here, including 130 miles of the Long Trail plus numerous other trails. Difficulty varies from easy to strenuous.

OTHER RECOMMENDED LOCATIONS

CAMEL'S HUMP FOREST RESERVE—Department of Forests, Parks, and Recreation, 103 South Main Street, Waterbury, VT 05676; (802)828-3375. 19,500 acres. Located in north-central Vermont and second highest in the state, Camel's Hump (4,083 feet) is an especially wild and scenic mountain, with rock formation, arctic-alpine tundra, and wonderful open views.

The area has fir and hardwood forests, and wildlife including white-tailed deer, bear, coyote, and bobcat. The mountain attracts many hikers. There are several trails here, including a segment of the Long Trail. Much of the terrain is rugged. Trail difficulty ranges from easy to strenuous.

GROTON STATE FOREST—Marshfield, VT 05658; (802)584-3820. 26,000 acres. Situated in the north-central part of the state, attractive Groton State forest is the largest area of state land in Vermont. The scenery here includes some lakes, ponds, and small mountains with fine views. There are mixed forests of hardwoods along with fir and spruce, and wildlife including deer and bear. A network of over 40 miles of trails extends through the region. Terrain varies but most trails are not difficult.

VERMONT HIKING RESOURCES

HIKING GUIDEBOOKS

Appalachian Trail Guide to New Hampshire–Vermont—Harpers Ferry, WV: The Appalachian Trail Conference, 1989.

Day Hiker's Guide to Vermont—Montpelier, VT: The Green Mountain Club, 1989.

Fifty Hikes in Vermont—Sadlier, Heather & Hugh. Woodstock, VT: The Countryman Press, 1985.

Guidebook of the Long Trail—Montpelier, VT: The Green Mountain Club, 1990.

MAPS

The Green Mountain Club, P.O. Box 889, Montpelier, VT 05602. This club publishes maps of hiking areas in Vermont.

The Vermont Atlas and Gazeteer—Freeport, ME: De Lorme Publishing Co., 1986.

TRAIL INFORMATION

The Green Mountain Club, P.O. Box 889, Montpelier, VT 05602; (802)223-3463.

INFORMATION ABOUT STATE PARKS AND FORESTS

Vermont Department of Forests, Parks, and Recreation, 103 South Main Street, Waterbury, VT 05676; (802)244-8711.

STATE HIGHWAY MAP AND TRAVEL INFORMATION

Vermont Travel Division, 134 State Street, Montpelier, VT 05602; (802)828-3236.

CLUBS AND OTHER ORGANIZATIONS WHICH OFFER HIKES

Ascutney Trail Association, 32 Elm Street, Windsor, VT 05089.

The Green Mountain Club, P.O. Box 889, Montpelier, VT 05602.

Sierra Club, 3 Joy Street, Boston, MA 02108.

VIRGINIA

One of the loveliest of the mid-Appalachian states, Virginia has rather vast federal landholdings, located primarily in the mountainous western portion of the state. An exceptionally beautiful National Park and two major National Forests provide some appealingly wild environs for hiking, along with a number of fine state parks which offer more limited opportunities. All told there are over 3,000 miles of trails winding through this scenic state.

MAJOR TRAILS

APPALACHIAN TRAIL—550 miles in Virginia (2,100 total). Fully one-fourth of the Appalachian Trail is in Virginia, more than any other state. It follows the ridges of the Blue Ridge Mountains down through the western part of the state, remaining most of the time in the two National Forests after traversing Shenandoah National Park. Along the way there's some great hiking and an incredible wealth of scenery. Difficulty varies from easy to strenuous. Trail information: Appalachian Trail Conference, P.O. Box 807, Harpers Ferry, WV 25425.

BIG BLUE TRAIL—112 miles in Virginia (143 miles total). This scenic trail runs from Shenandoah National Park to Maryland, passing through part of West Virginia. It includes some rugged mountain scenery and fine views. Diffi-

culty varies from easy to strenuous. Trail information: Potomac Appalachian Trail Club, 1718 N Street. N.W., Washington, DC 20036.

BEST HIKING AREAS

SHENANDOAH NATIONAL PARK—Luray, VA 22835; (703)999-2243. 195,363 acres. Located in northern Virginia, 80-mile long and narrow Shenandoah National Park encompasses the northernmost portion of the Blue Ridge Mountains. There's a wonderful range of scenery here, with seemingly endless views from ridge tops and rocky overlooks, plus steep cliffs and small canyons, and many streams and major waterfalls.

The highest point is 4,409-foot Hawksbill Mountain. Major portions of the park are maintained as wilderness. There are beautiful mixed forests of oak, maple, and hemlock, meadows with wildflowers, and wildlife including black bear, deer, bobcat, and gray fox.

In the park are 300 miles of hiking trails, plus 200 additional miles of marked trails which are open to horseback riding as well as hiking. Longest is the Appalachian Trail, which runs through the park for some 95 miles. Difficulty varies from easy to strenuous.

JEFFERSON NATIONAL FOREST—210 Franklin Road S.W., Roanoke, VA 24001; (703)982-6270. 690,000 acres. This large and splendid

National Forest in the Blue Ridge Mountains of western Virginia has some of the finest scenery in the state. Elevations range from 600 feet to over 5,000 feet. There are many high mountains, rocky ridges, and open "balds" with magnificent views, countless streams and roaring waterfalls.

Within the National Forest is the 154,000-acre Mount Rogers National Recreation Area. Here is Virginia's highest mountain, spruce and fir-covered Mount Rogers (5,729 feet). The area has alpine meadows, and elsewhere there's mixed hardwood and conifer forest, with rhododendron, azalea, and dogwood.

Wildlife in the forest consists of white-tailed deer, bear, bobcat, fox, and other mammals. Over 550 miles of trails are found here, including more than 300 miles of the Appalachian Trail. Difficulty ranges from easy to strenuous.

GEORGE WASHINGTON NATIONAL FOREST—Harrison Plaza, 101 North Main Street, P.O. Box 233, Harrisonburg, VA 22801; (703)433-2491. 1,330,000 acres. Located in northwestern Virginia, this is a vast natural area, the largest National Forest in Virginia or east of the Mississippi. The rugged mountainous terrain includes rocky cliffs and outcroppings with countless views, along with a seemingly endless array of creeks and rivers, waterfalls and cascades.

Elevations range from 600 feet to 4,472-foot Elliott Knob. There are forests of hardwoods with oak and hickory, pine and hemlock, plus rhododendron and mountain laurel, with some stands of virgin timber. Also in the region are open meadows, and the beautiful Shenandoah Valley.

Among the wildlife are white-tailed deer, black bear, mountain lion, bobcat, and gray fox. The forest is home to over 500 miles of hiking trails, including a 70-mile section of the Appalachian Trail. Difficulty ranges from easy to strenuous.

OTHER RECOMMENDED LOCATIONS

CUMBERLAND GAP NATIONAL HISTORICAL PARK—Box 840, Middleboro, KY 40965; (606)248-2817. 20,270 acres (7,526 in Virginia). A portion of Kentucky's beautiful Cumberland Gap National Historical Park extends into the southwestern corner of Virginia. It's an area of rugged and lovely Allegheny mountain scenery. There are oak-hickory forests with pine and hemlock, and wildlife including deer and bobcat. About 25 miles of easy to strenuous trails are found in this section of the park.

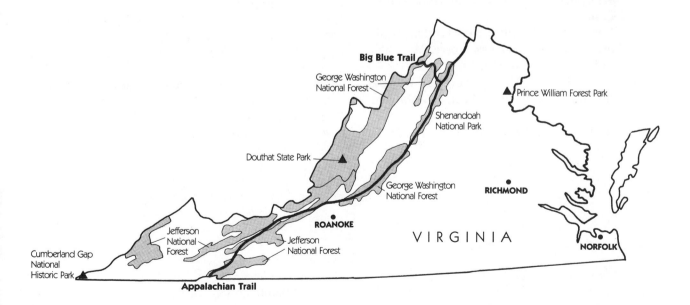

DOUTHAT STATE PARK—Route 1, Box 212, Millboro, VA 24460; (703)862-7200. 4,493 acres. Located in west-central Virginia, Douthat State Park is surrounded by George Washington National Forest lands. It's an attractive forested and mountainous area with streams, a lake, and over 40 miles of scenic hiking trails. Difficulty varies from easy to strenuous.

PRINCE WILLIAM FOREST PARK—P.O. Box 209, Triangle, VA 22172; (703)221-7181. 18,570 acres. Located just west of the Potomac River in northeast Virginia, Prince William Forest Park is administered by the National Park Service. It's an area of mixed forest of oak, hickory, and beech, with dogwood and mountain laurel. Wildlife includes white-tailed deer and fox. There are several scenic creeks here and 35 miles of easy to moderate hiking trails.

VIRGINIA HIKING RESOURCES

HIKING GUIDEBOOKS

Appalachian Trail Guide: Central and Southern Virginia—Harpers Ferry, WV: The Appalachian Trail Conference, 1988.

Appalachian Trail Guide: Shenandoah National Park—Harpers Ferry, WV: The Appalachian Trail Conference, 1986.

Appalachian Trail Guide to Maryland and Northern Virginia—Harpers Ferry, WV: The Appalachian Trail Conference, 1989.

Hiking Virginia's National Forests—Wuertz-Schaefer, Karin. Charlotte: Fast & McMillan, 1978.

Hiking the Old Dominion: The Trails of Virginia—de Hart, Allen. San Francisco: Sierra Club Books, 1984.

MAPS

Virginia Atlas & Gazetteer—Freeport, ME: DeLorme Mapping Co.

INFORMATION ABOUT STATE PARKS

Virginia State Parks, 203 Governor Street, Suite 306, Richmond, VA 23219; (804)786-1712.

STATE HIGHWAY MAP AND TRAVEL INFORMATION

Virginia Division of Tourism, 1021 East Cary Street, Richmond, VA 23206; (804)786-4484.

TRAIL INFORMATION

Virginia Trails Association, 13 West Maple Street, Alexandria, VA 22301; (703)548-7490.

VIRGINIA HIKING CLUBS

Appalachian Mountain Club, 5 Joy Street, Boston, MA 02108; (617)523-0636. This major club has a chapter in Washington DC.

Capitol Hiking Club, 3324 Glenmore Drive, Falls Church, VA 22041.

Mount Rogers Appalachian Trail Club, Route 7, Box 345, Abingdon, VA 24210.

Natural Bridge Appalachian Trail Club, P.O. Box 3012, Lynchburg, VA 24503.

Old Dominion Appalachian Trail Club, P.O. Box 25283, Richmond, VA 23260

Potomac Appalachian Trail Club, 1718 N Street, N.W., Washington, DC 20036.

Roanoke Appalachian Trail Club, P.O. Box 12282, Roanoke, VA 24024.

Sierra Club, P.O. Box 14648, Richmond, VA 23221.

Tidewater Appalachian Trail Club, P.O. Box 8246, Norfolk, VA 23503.

Wanderbirds Hiking Club, 2001 Columbia Pike, #125, Arlington, VA 22204.

WASHINGTON

Washington offers wonderfully diverse and often spectacular environs, from rugged high mountains to lush rain forests. The most massive blocks of wilderness by far are found in the Cascades, which run the length of west-central Washington. This region is blanketed by an almost continuous belt of National Forests, and also includes two National Parks. Along with the extremely scenic Olympic Peninsula, these wild lands provide thousands of miles of trails and a rich range of possibilities for hikers.

MAJOR TRAILS

PACIFIC CREST TRAIL—500 miles in Washington (2,638 total). This magnificent National Scenic Trail, which runs from Mexico to Canada, enters Washington at the Columbia River. From this point near sea level it heads high into the Cascades, proceeding through the state to a point just north of the Canadian border. Along the way it passes through Mount Rainier National Park, North Cascades National Park, and eight wilderness areas within several National Forests. There's some incredibly wild and remote scenery, with splendid views. It's only completely snow-free during August and September, and passable (with some snow) from about July 15 to October 15. Horses are permitted. Difficulty varies from easy to very strenuous. Trail information: Pacific Crest Trail Conference, 365 West 29th Avenue, Eugene, OR 97405.

WONDERLAND TRAIL—93 miles. This enormous loop-trail encircles 14,410-foot Mount Rainier, in Mount Rainier National Park. There are considerable elevation changes and a great diversity of scenery and terrain—including glaciers, alpine meadows, old-growth forests, and many spectacular views of the mountain. Portions of the trail are strenuous. Trail information: Mount Rainier National Park, Tahoma Woods, Star Route, Ashford, WA 98304.

BEST HIKING AREAS

WENATCHEE NATIONAL FOREST—301 Yakima Street, P.O. Box 811, Wenatchee, WA 98807; (509)662-4335. 1,618,287 acres. Situated in central Washington, Wenatchee National Forest encompasses a huge and often rugged area of high peaks and scenic ridges, glaciers and snowfields, steep slopes and river valleys. Elevations range from under 1,000 feet to over 9,000 feet, with a wide range of climates. The western part of the forest is in the Cascades, with substantial areas above timberline and spectacular views.

There are several wilderness areas, including a major portion of the 464,000-acre Glacier Peak Wilderness, which extends into Mount Baker–Snoqualmie National Forest. Glacier Peak is here, at 10,541 feet the highest in the forest, along with other steep peaks, ice fields, and glaciers.

The scenery also includes some rivers, numerous small lakes, countless creeks, and gorges with waterfalls. One lake—Lake Chelan—is over 50 miles long. There are many mountain meadows and wildflowers, boggy areas, forests of pine and Douglas fir, along with spruce and hemlock. Among the wildlife are elk, deer, moose, black bear, bighorn sheep, mountain goat, coyote, fox, and mountain lion.

Wenatchee National Forest has over 2,500 miles of hiking trails, easy to strenuous in difficulty. Among them is a section of the Pacific Crest Trail. Most trails are open to horses and some to mountain bikes. A free permit is required for day hiking into parts of some wilderness areas. Hiking season in the high country is short: July to September.

MOUNT BAKER–SNOQUALMIE NATIONAL FOREST—21905 64th Avenue West, Mountlake Terrace, WA 98043; (206)744-3409. 1,700,000 acres. This enormous National Forest is located in the western Cascades of west-central and north-central Washington, surrounding Mount Rainier National Park and on both sides of North Cascades National Park. It's wonderfully wild and scenic country, with volcanic Mount Baker (10,778 feet) the highest point. There are 8 wilderness areas, including part of the 464,000-acre Glacier Peak Wilderness, which is also in Wenatchee National Forest—and some substantial areas of old-growth forest.

The terrain includes steep glacier-covered mountains, alpine meadows and valleys, open areas with magnificent views, scores of glaciers and snowfields, and hundreds of lakes and streams, plus the Skagit Wild and Scenic River. There are dense forests of spruce and fir, cedar, and hemlock. Among the local mammals are black bear, deer, elk, mountain goat, mountain lion, coyote, and bobcat.

Mount Baker–Snoqualmie National Forest has over 1,400 miles of trails, including a section of the Pacific Crest Trail. Difficulty ranges from easy to strenuous. Some high trails are under snow until August and covered again by the end of September.

OKANOGAN NATIONAL FOREST—1240 South Second, P.O. Box 950, Okanogan, WA 98840; (509)422-2704. 1,706,000 acres. Okanogan National Forest is in the eastern Cascades of northern Washington, near North Cascades National Park, and includes some separate tracts further east. It's a very rugged region with jagged peaks over 7,000 feet, high walls and deep gorges, scenic lakes and creeks with waterfalls. The highest point is 8,974-foot North Gardner Mountain.

Among two wilderness areas is the impressive 505,000-acre Pasayten Wilderness, which extends into Mount Baker–Snoqualmie National Forest. Wildlife includes mule deer, black bear, moose, coyote, mountain lion, and bobcat. Vegetation ranges from alpine varieties with wildflowers to grasslands and slopes of Douglas fir and ponderosa pine. Some of the forests are old-growth.

Over 1,500 miles of trails are found in this National Forest. There's a 63-mile section of the Pacific Crest Trail, which passes through the Pasayten Wilderness, along with six National Recreation Trails. Some are open to horseback riding. Difficulty ranges from easy to strenuous.

GIFFORD PINCHOT NATIONAL FOREST—6926 East 4th Plain Boulevard, P.O. Box 8944, Vancouver, WA 98668; (206)696-7500. 1,251,160 acres. Located in the Cascades of southwest Washington, Gifford Pinchot National Forest includes the Mount Saint Helens National Volcanic Monument, centering around the crater and dome of now-famous 8,365-foot Mount Saint Helens (previously 9,677 feet), which erupted in 1980. There are still many signs of devastation, and access to the area around the volcano remains restricted.

Also here is 12,307-foot Mount Adams, Washington's second highest mountain—located in one of several wilderness areas—along with rugged ridges and peaks, high snowfields, buttes, and outstanding scenic views. There are old lava flows and volcanoes, open subalpine meadows, lakes, creeks, waterfalls, wildflowers—plus dense conifer forests, with old-growth Douglas fir, ancient hemlock and cedar. Animals in the region include elk, bear, deer, mountain goat, coyote, mountain lion, fox, and bobcat.

This National Forest has 1,165 miles of easy to strenuous hiking trails. Among them is a major section of the Pacific Crest Trail, and the 32-mile Boundary National Recreation Trail. High elevation hiking trails may only be snow-free from late July through mid-September.

OLYMPIC NATIONAL PARK—600 East Park Avenue, Port Angeles, WA 98362; (206)452-4501. 908,720 acres. Located on the Olympic Peninsula in northwest Washington, west of Seattle, this extremely beautiful National Park includes the Olympic Mountains—a rugged region of steep peaks and cliffs, rocky ridges and walls, canyons and talus slopes, and 60 glaciers. Highest point is 7,965-foot Mount Olympus. Some of the views are outstanding. There are also lush rain forests, natural hot springs, and 57 miles of wilderness beaches.

The park contains old-growth virgin forests with some enormous trees. Douglas fir, pacific silver fir, Sitka spruce, western hemlock, and cedar are common here—along with alpine areas and wildflowers. The area also has lakes, many streams and rivers, and some high waterfalls. Elk, deer, bear, mountain goat, coyote, and cougar are among the area's mammals, with whale, sea lion, and seal found along the coast.

Olympic National Park has about 600 miles of scenic hiking trails. Difficulty varies from easy to strenuous.

MOUNT RAINIER NATIONAL PARK—Tahoma Woods, Star Route, Ashford, WA 98304; (206)569-2211. 235,404 acres. Located in west-central Washington, this National Park is centered around massive Mount Rainier (14,410 feet), of volcanic origin and highest peak in the Cascades. It's a spectacular mountain with 26 glaciers, which extend down to about 6,500 foot elevation. One of them, Emmons Glacier, is said to be the largest in the lower forty-eight states.

The scenery here includes high ridges with alpine meadows, lakes and ice caves, rivers and streams with waterfalls, wildflowers in season, plus hot springs and a rain forest. There's some

ample old-growth forest in valley areas, with high hemlocks and Douglas fir, Sitka spruce and western red cedar. Deer, elk, bear, mountain goat, coyote, mountain lion, and cougar are among the larger animals here.

Mount Rainier National Park has over 300 miles of hiking trails. Difficulty ranges from easy to strenuous. Horses are permitted on some trails. Hiking season is generally mid-July through mid-October (at other times the higher trails are under snow). Especially notable is the 93-mile Wonderland Trail, which circles around Mount Rainier and passes through a range of scenery beneath the glaciers, offering frequent views of the mountain. There's also a section of the Pacific Crest Trail along the eastern border of the park.

NORTH CASCADES NATIONAL PARK—2105 Highway 20, Sedro Woolley, WA 98284; (206)856-5700. 504,780 acres. Consisting of two large tracts of wilderness located in the spectacular Cascades of northern Washington, and established in 1968, North Cascades National Park is part of a park complex which also includes 107,000-acre Ross Lake National Recreation Area and 62,000-acre Lake Chelan National Recreation Area.

Aside from the recreation areas it's an isolated region of ruggedly wild alpine scenery, almost surrounded by National Forest lands—with countless sharp and snow-capped granite peaks, crags, and spires, many over 7,000 feet—and 318 glaciers.

There are cirque basins with alpine lakes, precipitous cliffs, dramatic mountain passes with superb panoramas, talus slopes, and flower-filled meadows. Some valleys have old-growth forests of Douglas fir and western red cedar, along with hemlock and lodgepole pine— plus streams and waterfalls. Wildlife includes grizzly and black bear, blacktail and mule deer, mountain goat, fox, bobcat, lynx, and wolverine.

The park has over 360 miles of hiking trails, which vary in difficulty from easy to strenuous. Included is a 14-mile stretch of the Pacific Crest Trail. Lower trails are snow-free by April, with higher trails generally open by July.

COLVILLE NATIONAL FOREST—695 South Main, Federal Building, Colville, WA 99114; (509)684-3711. 1,095,368 acres. Consisting of several tracts in the northeast corner of Washington, on both sides of the Columbia River, Colville National Forest encompasses some medium-size mountains with elevations over 6,000 feet, and includes the 41,000-acre Salmo–Priest Wilderness. There are steep rocky peaks, slopes and outcrops, glacier-sculpted valleys and canyons, and great open views. Highest point is 7,309-foot Gypsy Peak.

The area has a number of lakes, streams, grassy meadows with wildflowers, mixed conifer forests of Douglas fir and lodgepole pine—plus some old-growth ponderosa pine, along with cedar and hemlock. Local wildlife includes moose, white-tailed and mule deer, black bear, mountain lion, and lynx.

Colville has some 310 miles of hiking trails, among them the 29-mile Kettle Crest Trail and the 22-mile Shed Roof Divide National Recre-

ation Trail. Many trails are open to horses. Difficulty varies from easy to strenuous.

OLYMPIC NATIONAL FOREST—801 South Capitol Way, P.O. Box 2288, Olympia, WA 98507; (206)753-9534. 631,514 acres. This National Forest consists of several parcels of land surrounding Olympic National Park, on the Olympic Peninsula in northwest Washington. Elevations range from just above sea level to over 7,000 feet, and there's much variety in the scenery here—from the huge trees and lush vegetation of rain forests to steep rugged mountains and high ridges, with superb views.

The region has a number of lakes and rivers, streams and falls, and some hot springs. There are deep canyon gorges, meadows and cedar swamps, forests of Douglas fir, hemlock, and western red cedar. Wildlife in the area includes elk, black bear, black-tailed deer, mountain goat, cougar, and coyote. There are five wilderness areas adding up to 88,000 acres.

Olympic National Forest has just over 200 miles of hiking trails. Difficulty varies from easy to strenuous. Some of the trails continue into Olympic National Park.

OTHER RECOMMENDED LOCATIONS

CAPITOL STATE FOREST—Washington Department of Natural Resources, 1405 Rush Road, Chehalis, WA 98532; (206)748-8616. 84,000 acres. Located west of Olympia in Washington's Black Hills, this state forest has numerous streams and some small mountains with fine views. Wildlife includes deer, black bear, and coyote. The area has Douglas fir and hemlock forests, with cedar and maple. There are 100 miles of trails, which are open to horseback riding as well as hiking.

MORAN STATE PARK—Star Route Box 22, Eastsound, WA 98245; (206)376-2326. 4,064 acres. Located on Orcas Island off the northwest coast of Washington, Moran State Park has some small mountains and several beautiful lakes. Much of the area is forested with hemlock and cedar, and there's a scenic creek with waterfalls. More than 30 miles of trails wind through the park. Difficulty ranges from easy to strenuous.

WASHINGTON HIKING RESOURCES

HIKING GUIDEBOOKS

55 Hikes in Central Washington—Spring, Ira, & Manning, Harvey. Seattle: The Mountaineers, 1990.

50 Hikes in Mt. Rainier National Park—Spring, Ira, & Manning, Harvey. Seattle: The Mountaineers, 1988.

The Hiker's Guide to Washington—Adkinson, Ron. Helena, MT: Falcon Press.

Hiking the North Cascades—Darvill, Fred T. San Francisco: Sierra Club Books.

Olympic Mountains Trail Guide—Wood, Robert L. Seattle: The Mountaineers, 1988.

100 Hikes in the Alpine Lakes—Spring, Vicky & Ira, & Manning, Harvey. Seattle: The Mountaineers, 1985

100 Hikes in the Glacier Peak Region—Spring, Ira. Seattle: The Mountaineers, 1988.

100 Hikes in the Inland Northwest—Landers, Rich, & Dolphin, Ida Rowe. Seattle: The Mountaineers.

100 Hikes in the North Cascades—Spring, Ira, & Manning, Harvey. Seattle: The Mountaineers, 1988.

100 Hikes in the South Cascades and Olympics—Spring, Ira, & Manning, Harvey. Seattle: The Mountaineers, 1985.

The Pacific Crest Trail—Volume 2: Oregon & Washington—Schaffer, Jeffrey P., & Selters, Andy. Berkeley: Wilderness Press, 1990

TRAIL INFORMATION

Washington Trails Association, 1305 Fourth Avenue, Suite 512, Seattle, WA 98101; (206)625-1367.

CLUBS AND OTHER ORGANIZATIONS WHICH OFFER HIKES

The Mountaineers, 300 Third Avenue West, Seattle, WA 98119.

Recreational Equipment Inc., 1525 11th Avenue, Seattle, WA 98122.

Seattle Audubon, 8028 55th Avenue. N.E., Seattle, WA 98115

Sierra Club, 1516 Melrose, Seattle, WA 98119.

Volunteers for Outdoor Washington, 4516 University Way N.E., Seattle, WA 98105.

Washington Trails Association, 1305 Fourth Avenue, Suite 512, Seattle, WA 98101.

WEST VIRGINIA

West Virginia is a beautiful and mostly forested state of rugged mountains and other wild scenery. The hiking is exceptionally good here, with over 1,700 miles of trails to choose from. There are many medium-size state parks and forests, but fully half of all the trails are in magnificent Monongahela National Forest—one of the outstanding natural areas of the eastern United States.

MAJOR TRAILS

ALLEGHENY TRAIL—270 miles. This scenic trail will eventually be 300 miles long when completed. Passing through varied and often wild terrain, it runs from the Pennsylvania border to the Appalachian Trail near the West Virginia–Virginia line. Much of the trail is on National Forest and other public lands. Trail information: West Virginia Scenic Trails Association, P.O. Box 4042, Charleston, WV 25304.

BIG BLUE TRAIL—66 miles in West Virginia. With a total length of 144 miles, this scenic blue-blazed trail begins in Virginia's Shenandoah National Park and ends in Maryland. It also connects with Pennsylvania's Tuscarora Trail and Maryland's C & O Canal Towpath Trail. Trail information: Potomac Appalachian Trail Club, 1718 N Street., N.W., Washington, DC 20036.

GREENBRIER RIVER TRAIL—76 miles. This is an easy trail which follows a former railroad bed alongside the Greenbrier River, passing through some rural countryside in south-central West Virginia. The trail is also open to cyclists and horseback riders. Trail information: Greenbrier River Trail, Star Route, Box 125, Caldwell, WV 24925.

BEST HIKING AREAS

MONONGAHELA NATIONAL FOREST—200 Sycamore Street, Elkins, WV 26241; (304)636-1800. 849,783 acres. By far the largest wild area in West Virginia and situated along the eastern border of the state, Monongahela National Forest is a superbly scenic place for hiking—with roaring rivers and streams, steep rocky ridges, plateaus, and ledges with rock outcrops. There are also heath meadows and bogs, small canyons and waterfalls, and an endless array of mountains.

The region has forests of eastern hardwoods with oak and hickory, maple and birch—along with rhododendron and dogwood, and many wildflowers. The varied wildlife here includes deer, black bear, bobcat, and fox. There are four designated wilderness areas. Among the many mountains is Spruce Knob (4,863 feet), highest in the state. There are about 850 miles of hiking trails, with 124 miles of the Allegheny Trail. Some easy trails are available, but the majority are moderate to strenuous in difficulty.

GEORGE WASHINGTON NATIONAL FOREST—
Room 210, Federal Building, Harrisonburg, VA
22801; (703)433-2491. 101,056 acres in West Virginia (1,054,922 total). This is the largest National
Forest in the East, and most of it is located in
Virginia. The West Virginia portion includes some
rugged terrain, attractive mountain scenery, with
hardwood forests of oak and hickory, along with
hemlock and pine. Among the wildlife are white-
tailed deer, black bear, and bobcat. There are over
90 miles of hiking trails, most of which are moderate to strenuous in difficulty.

OTHER RECOMMENDED LOCATIONS

COOPERS ROCK STATE FOREST—Route 1, Box
270, Bruceton Mills, WV 26525; (304)594-1561.
12,713 acres. Located in the Alleghenies, in the
northern part of the state, Coopers Rock is West
Virginia's largest state forest. The area includes
rock formations and fine views, with forests of
oak and hickory, some virgin hemlock, and
mountain laurel—along with wildlife including
deer. There are some 30 miles of easy to moderate hiking trails here.

HOLLY RIVER STATE PARK—Box 70, Hacker Valley, WV 26222; (304)493-6353. 8,292 acres. This beautiful mountain park is located in central West Virginia. It's thickly forested with hardwoods, and wildlife includes bear and bobcat. Terrain is rugged. There are several waterfalls, a nice view from Potato Knob, and 33 miles of trails.

PIPESTEM RESORT STATE PARK—Pipestem, WV 25979; (304)466-2780. 4,023 acres. This exceptionally beautiful and rugged mountain park in southern West Virginia is partially developed as a resort. It's an area of oak-hickory forests, wildlife including bear and bobcat, some streams, and the Bluestone River gorge. There are 29 miles of trails, some of which offer fine views. Most trails are at least moderate in difficulty.

WATOGA STATE PARK—Star Route 1, Box 252, Marlinton, WV 24954; (304)799-4087. 10,100 acres. Watoga State Park is West Virginia's largest state park, located in the southeastern part of the state next to Monongahela National Forest. Like some other state parks it's partially developed with recreational facilities.

The mountain scenery is lovely, and some great views are available. Deer, black bear, and fox are among the wildlife—along with hardwood forests, stands of pine, and also rhododendron and flame azalea. There are 32 miles of trails in this park.

LOST RIVER STATE PARK—Route 2, Box 24, Mathias, WV 26812; (304)897-5372. 3,712 acres. Located in northeast West Virginia, this mountainous and scenic park has some great views, with forests of pine and oak, plus azalea and mountain laurel—and a variety of wild animals including deer, bear, and bobcat. There are 22 miles of hiking trails. Difficulty varies from easy to strenuous.

KANAWHA STATE FOREST—Route 2, Box 285, Charleston, WV 25314; (304)346-5654. 9,052 acres. An attractive forest near Charleston, Kanawha State Forest has some interesting terrain, including cliffs and rock formations. There are 21 miles of easy to moderate trails.

WEST VIRGINIA HIKING RESOURCES

HIKING GUIDEBOOKS
Hiking Guide to the Allegheny Trail—West Virginia Scenic Trails Association.
Hiking Guide to Monongahela National Forest and Vicinity—West Virginia Highlands Conservancy.
Hiking the Mountain State—de Hart, Allen. Boston: Appalachian Mountain Club, 1986.

TRAIL INFORMATION
West Virginia Scenic Trails Association, P.O. Box 4042, Charleston, WV 25304; (304)744-6157.

INFORMATION ABOUT STATE PARKS AND FORESTS
Travel West Virginia, Department of Commerce, State Capitol, Charleston, WV 25305; (800) CALL-WVA.

STATE HIGHWAY MAP AND TRAVEL INFORMATION
Travel West Virginia, Department of Commerce, State Capitol, Charleston, WV 25305; (800) CALL-WVA.

CLUBS AND OTHER ORGANIZATIONS WHICH OFFER HIKES
Kanawha Trail Club, P.O. Box 4474, Charleston, WV 25364.
Potomac Appalachian Trail Club, 1718 N Street, N.W., Washington, DC 20036.
Sierra Club, P.O. Box 4142, Morgantown, WV 26505.
West Virginia Highlands Conservancy, P.O. Box 306, Charleston, WV 25321.
West Virginia Scenic Trails Association, P.O. Box 4042, Charleston, WV 25304.

WISCONSIN

There's a considerable amount of beautiful North Country scenery in Wisconsin, and the hilly forests here are home to some fine hiking. Most state parks and forests have trails, as do Wisconsin's two National Forests. Opportunities are now expanding much further with the construction of two new outstanding National Scenic Trails within the state, the 1000-mile Ice Age Trail and a segment of the 3,200-mile North Country Trail.

MAJOR TRAILS

ICE AGE TRAIL—Currently under construction, this National Scenic Trail will be approximately 1000 miles long. About 340 miles of the trail are presently open. The winding route lies entirely within the State of Wisconsin, following along glacial moraines (ridges formed by glacial deposits) from the last ice age. Located on public and private lands, it takes in a wide range of Wisconsin's natural scenery, from Lake Michigan's shore to the St. Croix River at the Minnesota border. Trail information: Ice Age National Scenic Trail, National Park Service, 1709 Jackson Street, Omaha, NE 68102.

NORTH COUNTRY TRAIL—When completed this National Scenic Trail will be a total of 3,200 miles long, with 155 miles in Wisconsin. The largest segment currently open in the state is 60 miles of trail in Chequamegon National Forest. Crossing the northwestern corner of Wisconsin, the trail offers scenery which includes waterfalls and a stretch of the St. Croix River. Trail information: North Country Trail Association, P.O. Box 311, White Cloud, MI 49349.

Wisconsin also has an extensive system of multi-use State Trails which follow old railroad beds. There are 13 trails adding up to almost 400 miles, open to bicycling and sometimes horseback riding in addition to hiking. Longest are the 76-mile Tuscobia–Park Falls State Trail and the 47-mile Glacial Drumlin Trail. Four have National Recreation Trail status. The majority are surfaced with crushed limestone, and most pass through towns and other developed areas, along with attractive countryside. Nominal fees are charged to use some trails. For more information contact the Wisconsin Bureau of Parks and Recreation, P.O. Box 7921, Madison, WI 53707.

BEST HIKING AREAS

CHEQUAMEGON NATIONAL FOREST—1170 4th Avenue South, Park Falls, WI 54552; (715)762-2461. 850,000 acres. Consisting of three separate tracts, Chequamegon National Forest preserves some of the beautiful natural landscape of northern Wisconsin. The hilly terrain includes many glacial lakes and rivers,

North Country Trail

Governor Knowles
State Forest

Chequamegon
National Forest

Ice Age
Trail

Nicolet National
Forest

Newport
State Park

WISCONSIN

Kettle Moraine
State Forest-
North Unit

Kettle Moraine
State Forest-
South Unit

MADISON

MILWAUKEE

streams, meadows with wildflowers, rocky out-croppings and bluffs with views.

There are two wilderness areas. The region is covered by pine and hardwood forests, with wildlife which includes white-tailed deer, black bear, coyote, and fox. The forest has 200 miles of hiking trails, including a 60-mile section of the North Country Trail and 41 miles of the Ice Age Trail. Most trails are easy to moderate in difficulty.

NICOLET NATIONAL FOREST—68 South Stevens Street, Rhinelander, WI 54501; (715)362-3415. 657,520 acres. Located in northeastern Wisconsin, Nicolet National Forest has several rivers, countless streams, and over 1,200 lakes. There are three wilderness areas, regions of rugged terrain with rock formations and boulders, and some fine views.

It's an area of diverse forests which include hardwoods, hemlock, and 300-year-old white pine. Deer and bear are among the wildlife. About 100 miles of hiking trails are found here, most of them relatively short. Difficulty ranges from easy to moderate.

OTHER RECOMMENDED LOCATIONS

KETTLE MORAINE STATE FOREST/SOUTHERN UNIT—Highway 59, Eagle, WI 53119; (414)594-2135. 19,000 acres. Located on a 100-mile long glacial moraine, this hilly state forest in southeastern Wisconsin has many lakes and ponds, oak forests, steep ravines, meadows and prairies. White-tailed deer are among the wildlife. There are 75 miles of hiking trails, including a 36-mile section of the Ice Age Trail, which runs the length of the forest.

KETTLE MORAINE STATE FOREST/NORTHERN UNIT—Box 410, Campbellsport, WI 53010;

(414)626-2116. 27,700 acres. The northern unit of this large state forest in southeastern Wisconsin has hilly terrain and a number of lakes. Included are woodlands, hardwood forests with stands of pine, and over 70 miles of hiking trails.

GOVERNOR KNOWLES STATE FOREST—P.O. Box 367, Grantsburg, WI 54840; (715)463-2898. 32,000 acres. Located in northwestern Wisconsin, 55-mile long (and narrow) Governor Knowles State Forest protects the St. Croix National Scenic Riverway. Local wildlife includes white-tailed deer and black bear. There are two 22-mile hiking trails which follow the river.

NEWPORT STATE PARK—475 South Newport Lane, Ellison Bay, WI 54210; (414)854-2500. 2,300 acres. This wild forested park in eastern Wisconsin has 11 miles of Lake Michigan shoreline. Local wildlife includes deer, coyote, and fox, and there are 28 miles of hiking trails.

WISCONSIN HIKING RESOURCES

INFORMATION ABOUT STATE PARKS AND FORESTS

Wisconsin Department of Natural Resources, Bureau of Parks and Recreation, P.O. Box 7921, Madison, WI 53707.

MAPS

Wisconsin Atlas & Gazetteer—Freeport, ME: DeLorme Mapping Co.

STATE HIGHWAY MAP AND TRAVEL INFORMATION

Wisconsin Tourist Information Center, 123 West Washington Avenue, Box 7606, Madison, WI 53707; (608)266-2161/(800)432-TRIP.

WISCONSIN HIKING CLUBS

Sierra Club, 111 King Street, Madison, WI 53703.
Wisconsin Go-Hiking Club, 5556 North 103 Street, Milwaukee, WI 53225.

WYOMING

Wyoming's stunning scenery includes jagged, snow-covered Rocky Mountain peaks, glaciers and grasslands, sheer-walled canyons, hilly plains and plateaus, badlands and desert. This is truly a state for hiking, with 6000 miles of trails on 18 million acres of public land. Most trail-hiking takes place in two absolutely splendid National Parks and four enormous National Forests—and here within the Rockies of northwest Wyoming you find some of America's most magnificent wilderness.

BEST HIKING AREAS

YELLOWSTONE NATIONAL PARK—P.O. Box 168, Yellowstone National Park, WY 82190; (307)344-7381. 2,219,736 acres (2,020,625 in Wyoming). Founded in 1872 as this country's first National Park, Yellowstone is also the largest outside of Alaska—and undoubtedly one of the greatest. There's a fantastic amount of wilderness here, much of it infrequently visited due to the park's size and the remoteness of some areas.

Located in the northwest corner of Wyoming and spilling over into Montana and Idaho, Yellowstone consists of a series of high plateaus and mountain ranges. Elevations vary from 5,300 feet to 11,358 feet, with Eagle Peak the highest point. There are numerous mountains over 10,000 feet. The Continental Divide crosses the southern region. Coniferous forests cover most of the park, and there are also meadows and areas of sagebrush desert.

Yellowstone is especially famous, of course, for its thousands of geysers and hot springs—more than anywhere else in the world—among them Old Faithful and Mammoth Hot Springs. Also of special scenic interest is the multicolored, 1,500-foot Grand Canyon of the Yellowstone River, with its 308-foot Lower Falls, plus enormous (139-square-mile) Yellowstone Lake. Wildlife includes elk, pronghorn antelope, bighorn sheep, moose, mule deer, and grizzly as well as black bear.

More than 1,100 miles of hiking trails extend throughout the park, and most do not receive heavy use. Difficulty ranges from easy to strenuous. Off-trail travel is not recommended due to the thick forest and thermal hazards. Snow is present both in spring and fall, with summer the primary hiking season.

GRAND TETON NATIONAL PARK—Drawer 170, Moose, WY 83012; (307)733-2880. 310,520 acres. Situated directly south of Yellowstone National Park in northwest Wyoming and nearly surrounded by National Forest lands, this splendid National Park encompasses the Teton Mountain Range—some of the most spectacular mountains in the country. High jagged peaks and crags tower dramatically over a number of beautiful lakes and the level Jackson Hole plain, with forests of pine, spruce, and fir along with aspen

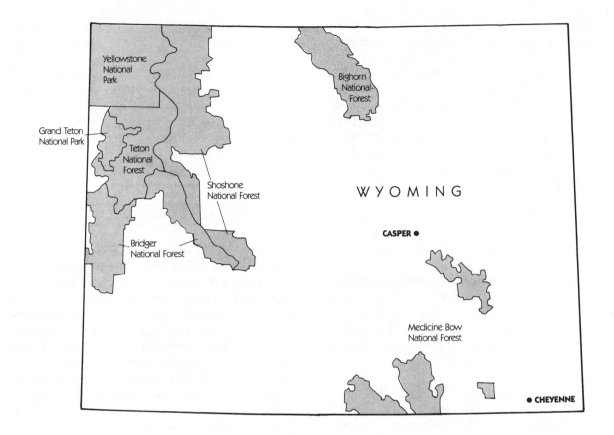

in between. There are 55 peaks over 10,000 feet, 8 over 12,000 feet, and highest is the Grand Teton (13,770 feet).

Seven percent of the park is above treeline, and there are high alpine meadows. Between some of the more striking mountains are steep canyons. Also in the park is the scenic Snake River. Wildlife includes bighorn sheep, grizzly and black bear, elk, pronghorn, moose, and mule deer.

There are more than 200 miles of trails, with connections to trails in nearby National Forests. Difficulty ranges from easy to very strenuous. Most trails begin at 6,800-foot elevation or above. Views are often wonderful. Horses are permitted on many of the trails. The hiking season is essentially summer (July and August), with snow and ice typically remaining on high mountain passes through late July and returning again in September.

BRIDGER–TETON NATIONAL FOREST—P.O. Box 1888, Jackson, WY 83001; (307)733-2752. 3,400,309 acres. This giant and magnificent National Forest is our second largest outside of Alaska. It includes three massive wilderness areas, plus vast additional undeveloped expanses. Most popular is the 428,169-acre Bridger Wilderness in the Wind River Range of the Rockies. There are more than 1,300 lakes here, along with Wyoming's highest mountain, Gannett Peak (13,804 feet).

At the northern end of the National Forest and alongside Grand Teton and Yellowstone National Parks is the 585,468-acre Teton Wilderness, which is bisected by the Continental Divide and includes elevations to 12,165 feet (Yount's Peak) as well as forested ridges, high plateaus, and mountain meadows.

Finally, there's the 287,000-acre Gros Ventre Wilderness, which encompasses the Gros Ventre Mountains, with 8 peaks over 11,000 feet and many others over 10,000 feet. The highest here is Doubletop Peak (11,682 feet). Many of the rocky peaks are massive, with striking rock formations above timberline.

Vegetation varies from sagebrush at the lowest elevations to aspen, spruce, fir, and pine. There are legions of lovely streams and alpine lakes, glaciated canyons, and the Gros Ventre River. Among the wildlife here are moose, elk, deer, antelope, bighorn sheep, bison, black bear, and grizzly bear.

All told there are over 2,800 miles of trails in Bridger–Teton National Forest, including the 70-mile Wyoming Range National Recreation Trail and over 200 miles of the Continental Divide Trail. Fantastic panoramic views are common. Difficulty varies from easy to strenuous. Many trails are also open to horseback riding. Only a handful receive substantial use. The highest trails may be under snow till mid-July, and snow usually returns by early fall.

SHOSHONE NATIONAL FOREST—225 West Yellowstone Avenue, P.O. Box 2140, Cody, WY 82414; (307)527-6241. 2,433,029 acres. Located directly east and southeast of Yellowstone National Park, Shoshone is another enormous National Forest which has spectacularly wild mountain scenery. It includes portions of the Absaroka, Wind River, and Beartooth Ranges, with a section of the Continental Divide. There are five different wilderness areas, adding up to nearly 1.4 million acres. Most frequently visited and especially attractive are the 198,838-acre Fitzpatrick Wilderness and the 101,991-acre Popo Agie Wilderness.

Terrain includes sagebrush flats and high plateaus, volcanic mountains and rugged rocky peaks, steep canyons and low valleys—with hundreds of lakes and streams, waterfalls, and several major rivers. There are alpine meadows, extensive coniferous forests, and 156 glaciers—more than anywhere outside of Alaska. Two hundred thirty-six peaks are over 12,000 feet, and 20 over 13,000 feet, including Gannett Peak (13,804 feet)—Wyoming's loftiest, which stands on the Bridger–Teton National Forest border.

Among the wildlife are elk, bighorn sheep, moose, mountain goat, deer, black and grizzly bear.

More than 1,500 miles of trails extend through this National Forest. Most of them receive light use, and the hiker can find plenty of isolation. Difficulty varies from easy to strenuous. Some trails are open to horseback riding. Hiking season is mainly July and August, with snow remaining on high trails till mid-July.

OTHER RECOMMENDED LOCATIONS

BIGHORN NATIONAL FOREST—1969 South Sheridan Avenue, Sheridan, WY 82801; (307)672-0751. 1,107,670 acres. Located in north-central Wyoming, this large National Forest includes the Bighorn Mountain Range. There's one wilderness area, the 195,000-acre Cloud Peak Wilderness—which is centered around 13,167-foot Cloud Peak, highest elevation in the National Forest.

It's an area of barren peaks, glaciers, alpine meadows, precipitous canyons, forests of spruce, pine, and fir, aspen, and some sagebrush. There are major rivers and hundreds of lakes and streams. Among the wildlife are black bear, elk, moose, deer, bighorn sheep, coyote, and fox.

The region has over 600 miles of easy to strenuous hiking trails, many of which are in the Cloud Peak Wilderness Area. Hiking season is essentially July through mid-September, with the highest trails under snow the rest of the year.

MEDICINE BOW NATIONAL FOREST—605 Skyline Drive, Laramie, WY 82070; (307)745-8971. Situated in southeast Wyoming, Medicine Bow National Forest is divided into four separate tracts, and includes the Medicine Bow Range and other mountain ranges. The highest elevation is Medicine Bow Peak (12,013 feet).

One finds no extensive remote areas here, with four relatively small wilderness areas totaling 79,323 acres. There's nevertheless some superb scenery, with steep-walled canyons and rocky peaks, open meadows and pine forests, and rolling high plateaus. The area also has numerous lakes and streams, and several rivers. Wildlife includes black bear, bighorn sheep, mountain lion, pronghorn, elk, deer, and coyote.

There are just under 300 miles of trails, most of them relatively short. Difficulty ranges from easy to strenuous. Snow often remains on trails over 10,000 feet till mid-July. Hiking season is normally limited to summer and early fall.

WYOMING HIKING RESOURCES

HIKING GUIDEBOOKS

Climbing and Hiking in the Wind River Range—Kelsey, Joe. San Francisco: Sierra Club Books.

Guide to the Continental Divide Trail: Wyoming—Wolf, James R. Bethesda, MD: Continental Trail Society, 1986.

Hiking the Teton Backcountry—Lawrence, Paul. San Francisco: Sierra Club Books.

Hiking the Yellowstone Backcountry—Bach, Orville E., Jr. San Francisco: Sierra Club Books.

Wind River Trails—Mitchell, Finis. Salt Lake City: Wasatch Publishing Co.

Wyoming Hiking Trails—Sudduth, Tom and Sanse. Boulder, CO: Pruett.

Yellowstone Trails, A Hiking Guide—Marschall, Mark. Yellowstone Library and Museum Association, 1984.

STATE HIGHWAY MAP AND TRAVEL INFORMATION

Wyoming Travel Commission, I-25 at College Dr., Cheyenne, WY 82002; (307)777-7777.

WYOMING HIKING CLUBS

Sierra Club, c/o Meredith Taylor, RR 31, Box 807, Dubois, WY 82513.

READER RESPONSE

Your assistance can help to make the next edition of this book even more complete. Do you know of a trail or hiking area which belongs in this book? If so, please write. Any information you're able to offer will be gratefully received. Also, please submit the name and address of any club, trail association, or other hiking-related organization you're aware of which isn't listed in the book. Finally, any corrections or suggestions you could provide will be welcomed. Write to the following address:

Charles Cook
Michael Kesend Publishing, Ltd.
c/o 1025 Fifth Avenue,
New York, N.Y. 10028

TRIP INFORMATION

From March through November each year Charles Cook leads hikes and wilderness trips throughout the northeastern United States. Day trips are offered to natural areas within three hours of New York City, and overnight trips (three to ten days) to wilderness areas in the New England states and New York's Adirondacks. Write to the address below for further information.

INDEX

MP4X